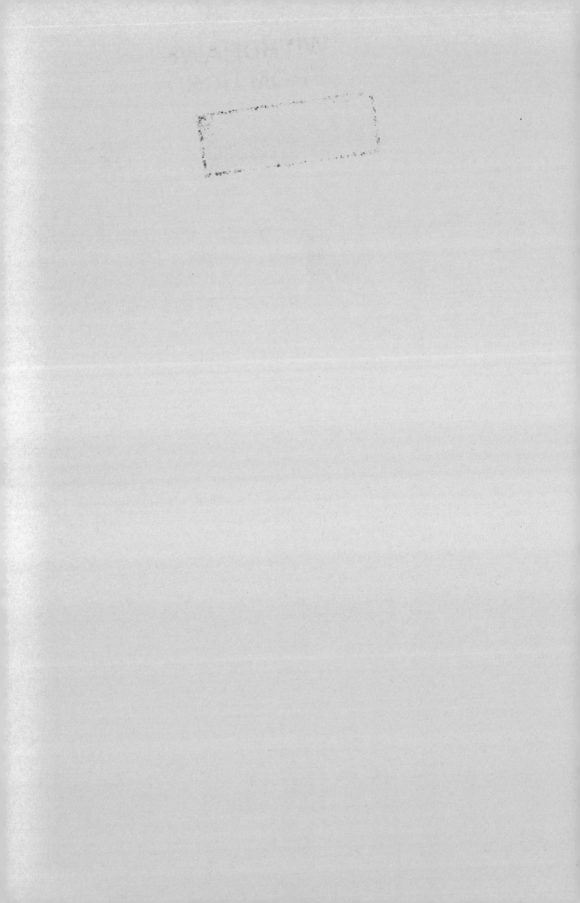

PERSPECTIVES IN ARTIFICIAL INTELLIGENCE
Volume II: Machine Translation, NLP, Databases and Computer-aided Instruction

ELLIS HORWOOD SERIES IN ARTIFICIAL INTELLIGENCE

Joint Series Editors: Professor JOHN CAMPBELL, Department of Computer Science, University College London, and
Dr JEAN HAYES MICHIE, Knowledgelink Limited, Edinburgh

Andrew, A.M.	**Continuous Heuristics***
Bläsius, K.H. and Bürckert, H.-J.	**Deduction Systems in AI***
Bramer, M.A. (editor)	**Computer Game Playing: Theory and Practice**
Campbell, J.A. (editor)	**Implementations of PROLOG**
Campbell, J.A. and Cuena, J. (editors)	**Perspectives in Artifical Intelligence, Vols. 1 & 2**
Campbell, J. A. & Cox, P.	**Implementations of PROLOG, Vol. 2***
Carter, D.	**Interpreting Anaphors in Natural Language Texts**
Davies, R. (editor)	**Intelligent Information Systems: Progress and Prospects**
Evans, J.B.	**Structures of Discrete Event Simulation**
Farreny, H.	**AI and Expertise**
Forsyth, R. & Rada, R.	**Machine Learning: Applications in Expert Systems and Information Retrieval**
Gabbay, D.M.	**Programming in Pure Logic***
Gergely, T. & Futó, I.	**Artificial Intelligence in Simulation***
Hawley, R. (editor)	**Artificial Intelligence Programming Environments**
Hayes, J.E. & Michie, D. (editors)	**Intelligent Systems: The Unprecedented Opportunity**
Lopez de Mantaras, R.	**Approximate Reasoning and Knowledge Acquisition***
Łukaszewicz, W.	**Nonmonotonic Reasoning***
Mellish, C.	**Computer Interpretation of Natural Language Descriptions**
Michie, D.	**On Machine Intelligence, Second Edition**
Mortimer, H.	**The Logic of Induction**
Mozetic, I.	**Machine Learning of Qualitative Models***
Partridge, D.	**Artificial Intelligence: Applications in the Future of Software Engineering**
Ramsay, A. & Barrett, R.	**AI in Practice: Examples in POP-11**
Savory, S.E.	**Artificial Intelligence and Expert Systems**
Spacek, L.	**Advanced Programming in PROLOG***
Sparck Jones, K. & Wilks, Y. (editors)	**Automatic Natural Language Parsing**
Steels, L. & Campbell, J.A. (editors)	**Progress in Artificial Intelligence**
Smith, B. & Kelleher, G. (editors)	**Reason Maintenance Systems and their Applications**
Torrance, S. (editor)	**The Mind and the Machine**
Turner, R.	**Logics for Artificial Intelligence**
Wallace, M.	**Communicating with Databases in Natural Language**
Wertz, H.	**Automatic Correction and Improvement of Programs**
Yazdani, M. (editor)	**New Horizons in Educational Computing**
Yazdani, M. & Narayanan, A. (editors)	**Artificial Intelligence: Human Effects**

* *In preparation*

PERSPECTIVES IN ARTIFICIAL INTELLIGENCE

Volume II: Machine Translation, NLP, Databases and Computer-aided Instruction

Editors:

J. A. CAMPBELL
Department of Computer Science, University College London

J. CUENA
Laboratorio de Sistemas Inteligentes
Universidad Politécnica, Madrid, Spain

ELLIS HORWOOD LIMITED
Publishers · Chichester

Halsted Press: a division of
JOHN WILEY & SONS
New York · Chichester · Brisbane · Toronto

First published in 1989 by
ELLIS HORWOOD LIMITED
Market Cross House, Cooper Street,
Chichester, West Sussex, PO19 1EB, England
The publisher's colophon is reproduced from James Gillison's drawing of the ancient Market Cross, Chichester.

Distributors:
Australia and New Zealand:
JACARANDA WILEY LIMITED
GPO Box 859, Brisbane, Queensland 4001, Australia
Canada:
JOHN WILEY & SONS CANADA LIMITED
22 Worcester Road, Rexdale, Ontario, Canada
Europe and Africa:
JOHN WILEY & SONS LIMITED
Baffins Lane, Chichester, West Sussex, England
North and South America and the rest of the world:
Halsted Press: a division of
JOHN WILEY & SONS
605 Third Avenue, New York, NY 10158, USA
South-East Asia
JOHN WILEY & SONS (SEA) PTE LIMITED
37 Jalan Pemimpin # 05–04
Block B, Union Industrial Building, Singapore 2057
Indian Subcontinent
WILEY EASTERN LIMITED
4835/24 Ansari Road
Daryaganj, New Delhi 110002, India

British Library Cataloguing in Publication Data
Perspectives in artificial intelligence. —
(Ellis Horwood series in artificial intelligence).
Vol. 2, Machine translation, NLP, databases and computer-aided instruction.
1. Artificial intelligence
I. Campbell, J. (John) II. Cuena, J. (Jose) III. Series
006.3

Library of Congress Card No. 89–1819

ISBN 0–7458–0660–0 (Ellis Horwood Limited)
ISBN 0–470–21435–X (Halsted Press)

Printed in Great Britain by Hartnolls, Bodmin

Table of contents

Introduction

As the preface to the first volume states, the origin of the collection of articles that makes up this two-volume set was the conference on artificial intelligence (AI) within the Second World Basque Congress in September 1987. The purpose of the conference was to survey developments in AI that were of particular value for those people already teaching in advanced computer science or concerned with the development of industrial enterprises using advanced computer science, in the Basque country. The organizers had this audience in mind when they outlined their programme and issued invitations to speakers. As a consequence, the collection is of potential value to similar audiences elsewhere: the scientific contents of the articles are obviously not tied to particular national surroundings.

Collections that cover relatively large areas within AI usually belong in one of two classes: proceedings of general conferences like IJCAI or AAAI, or surveys that start from the work of a single laboratory (e.g. Winston and Brown, 1979) or that approximate the ideal of a single-author textbook (Yazdani, 1986). The present volumes do not fit neatly into any of these classifications. The differences are not accidental. The primary reason is that the AI conference of the Basque World Congress was intended to include both invited survey papers, setting out points of view on some basic issues, and research-level contributions which could give an audience (containing university faculty members in computer science, graduate students and interested technical staff from appropriate companies) an exposure to research issues without demanding any extensive experience in carrying out that research. The present volumes have been compiled with exactly this type of audience in mind: they give a post-introductory view of AI which should also be an effective bridge between the levels of basic AI texts and proceedings of IJCAI, AAAI and single-topic AI research conferences. This type of bridge is not yet as common as it deserves to be, in the published AI literature.

These volumes do not attempt to take up all the topic-headings that appear in indexes to basic AI textbooks. Instead, there is a conscious bias in the choice of subjects towards issues that have not got the past attention that they deserve or are likely to occupy more of the central stage in AI in the future. These predictions do not come from some infallible oracle; they are expressions of various opinions from the people who planned the programme of the conference and some of the invited speakers. One of the benefits of taking part in a conference in such capacities is that one can express subjective prejudices about the lessons of the past and bets on the future. In AI, there is still room both for subjective opinions and for formulae drawn up by committees of trainee elder statesmen.

The invited material that begins the first volume covers topics that fit the description just given. 'Expert systems' takes the first place here, because expert systems were responsible for the initial commercial successes of AI and are still by far the most heavily exploited products of AI technology. Despite their successes, however, or perhaps *because* of the limits to their successes throughout the 1980s, most present expert systems are perceived as failing to be enough like real experts in their behaviour to please the most demanding or experienced customers. There are several manifestations of this failing: for example, a lack of flexibility or human-oriented facilities for *automated explanation* of the outputs of the systems, and (possibly one reason why the level of explanation is most often less than satisfactory) limited or no mechanisms to connect standard rule-based surface knowledge of a subject with typical human experts' deeper knowledge of that subject, based on concepts like models that can justify or at least give some support to the surface rules. One phrase used to describe the research field whose objective is to correct those defects is 'second-generation expert systems'. This is the subject of the first invited articles. Another way to look at the same subject in this book is simply as an update on what has been happening in research to improve the quality of AI's most mature or exportable current technology.

Learning is a long-lived issue in AI. It will be with us as long as AI exists as a scientific activity. The obvious reason for this interest is that non-artificial intelligence and learning are inseparable. In fact, there are schools of thought which say that the latter is the best specific evidence for the former. Inside AI, there are similar schools of thought — visible if not necessarily heavily populated — which prefer to regard nothing as *real* AI unless some component of machine learning is involved. Fortunately there is no shortage of sources on machine learning in the AI literature (Michalski *et al.*, 1983, 1986). The relevant contribution to the present volumes therefore takes the chance to make a point that deserves more attention than it has received in the past: that analogical methods are likely to be significant in future AI. This prediction is a good one because 'analogy' has prospects of being useful in two rather different sub-fields of AI: reasoning and learning. In the language of horse racing, 'analogy' is a good bet for AI because it is an each-way bet. The coverage of the subject in the present collection is good source material for readers who want to be informed, or to calculate the odds.

The survey articles in the first volume conclude with a subjective view of computer architectures that are likely to be helpful for work in AI. This is a topic which will have an increasing importance in the future as the choice of different commercially-available architectures widens. The starting-point for the discussion is the assertion that serious knowledge-based computing must make serious use of both pointers and parallelism, because these ideas are inherent in the processing of knowledge. This is not to say that the pointers and parallelism available in typical experimental computer architectures in 1988 have much to do with the same ideas as applied cognition. However, starting from this emphasis is a good way to distinguish between computer architectures that are likely to be useful for AI applications in the future and those that are not.

The remainder of the first volume concentrates on AI applications. Not surprisingly, this means that expert systems or rule-based systems come in for most of the attention. Because of the very wide range of these applications, one can try either to cover the whole range thinly with different samples or to concentrate. We have used the second option here. The areas that receive special attention are design and decision support. They have both been recognized for some time as being well suited to the use of rule-based systems, since many of their component pieces of knowledge are heuristic and natural to express in rules, but they have not been treated so thoroughly in print as other areas of application like diagnosis, planning or administrative law.

The second volume has two main focuses: natural language, and improvements in the use of databases by AI methods. It begins with a topic that clearly belongs to natural-language processing rather than any other part of AI, but that is not often seen in published material on AI: machine translation. The traditional separation between translation and natural-language processing in AI is a matter of history, as historical surveys like those of Hutchins (1986) show. But the aims of the subjects have enough of an overlap that people working on each subject should not ignore what is happening in the other one. For this reason the conference has included some up-to-date views of machine translation that are difficult to find elsewhere in the AI literature. Articles on natural-language processing from a more traditional AI viewpoint then follow, including one novelty (though perhaps not so novel for a Basque conference): an article dealing with aspects of processing problems for the Basque language.

The common theme of the articles in the second volume is human–computer interaction where the AI component is intended to react primarily to the special needs of the user rather than to the special features of some application area. One of these special needs is for interaction with collections of data without having to be trained in how to run database programs. The section of the second volume that deals with the coupling between expert sytems and databases shows something of the achievements of European research in this direction, and reinforces a point that has been made elsewhere (Campbell, 1987): that, while this area is of world-wide research interest, it is a particular European speciality.

The second volume ends with some coverage of a further human-oriented application that receives plenty of exposure in its own specialized conferences but is not often enough treated in general surveys of AI applications: computer-aided instruction.

The intention of the organizers of the AI conference in the Second World Basque Congress was to provide a survey which could not touch on every subject under the current umbrella of AI but which would present a representative picture of research in a coherent set of topics. This set is one that travels well, like robust wine. It does not require heavy investment in equipment or extensive existing software in order to make progress in the subjects treated here, and any such progress in research is likely to have immediate applications in places that do not have the same economic and technological advantages as Massachusetts or California. This is clearly relevant to the Basque country, Euzkadi, but it is probably equally relevant to readers in a majority of states in the USA, not to mention other countries. We are therefore pleased to offer this collection to an international audience.

REFERENCES

Campbell, J. A. (1987) Applications of artificial intelligence within the ESPRIT programme. In W. Brauer and W. Wahlster (eds), *Wissensbasierte Systeme,* Springer-Verlag, Berlin, pp. 373–379.

Hutchins, W. J. (1986) *Machine Translation: Principles and Applications,* Ellis Horwood, Chichester.

Michalski, R. S., Carbonell, J. and Mitchell, T. (eds) (1983, 1986) *Machine Learning: an Artificial Intelligence Approach,* Springer-Verlag, Berlin, vol. 1 (1983); vol.2 (1986).

Winston, P. H. and Brown, R. H. (1979) *Artificial Intelligence: an MIT Perspective,* MIT Press, Cambridge, MA.

Yazdani, M. (ed.) (1986) *Artificial Intelligence: Principles and Applications,* Chapman & Hall, London.

Part I
Machine translation

1

Machine translation: practical issues

J. Slocum, Microelectronics and Computer Technology Corporation (MCC), 3500 West Balcones Center Drive, Austin, Texas 78759, USA

SUMMARY

Many of the problems with (and consequently much of the resistance to) machine translation (MT) has sprung from ignorance: on the part of early developers, who failed to appreciate the magnitude of the problems they faced, and hence made outrageous claims; on the part of opponents, who frequently fail to understand what translation is about, and how it is (properly) performed; on the part of zealots for theoretical formalisms, who seldom if ever try to produce working systems and consequently lack appreciation of the magnitude of the practical problems to be faced; on the part of modern developers, too many of whom know little about translators' needs and other human engineering concerns; and on the part of translators, who often fail to realize the potential for improvement in the quality of their working lives when computers become able to take over much of the 'grunt work' in translation.

In this chapter we confront these and other problems. We characterize areas where knowledge has been lacking, and discuss the consequences of such ignorance; provide background knowledge enabling the reader to acquire a more balanced perspective from which to judge the developments in the field; and finally present the author's opinions, based upon his experience as an MT system developer, regarding some of the most important issues in the construction of a practical system. This will entail, in places, an exposition of certain aspects of the underlying technology; however, complete understanding of these technical matters is not a prerequisite for appreciation of the major points.

1. A BRIEF HISTORY OF MT

Translation of human languages was one of the first applications considered for digital computers. Indeed, the idea of mechanizing translation predated the invention of such machines, but it was only after World War II, when digital computers became generally available, that MT was taken up seriously, as a consequence of a memo by Warren Weaver. During its first decade, in the 1950s, interest and support was fueled by visions of high-speed, high-quality translation of arbitrary texts (especially those of interest to the military and intelligence communities, who funded MT projects quite heavily), with no need for human intervention. During its second decade, in the 1960s, disillusionment crept in as the number and difficulty of the linguistic problems became increasingly obvious, and as it was realized that the translation problem was not nearly so amenable to fully automated solution as had been thought. The climax came with the delivery of the US National Academy of Sciences ALPAC report in 1966, condemning the field and, indirectly, its workers alike. The ALPAC report was criticized as narrow, biased, and short-sighted but, nevertheless, it resulted in the cancellation of MT projects in the US and, though to a much lesser extent, elsewhere around the world.

By 1973, the early part of the third decade of MT, only three government-funded projects were left in the US, and by 1976 there were none. Paradoxically, MT systems were still being used by various government agencies in the US and abroad, because there was simply no alternative means of gathering information from foreign (Russian) sources so quickly. Private companies were also developing and selling (mostly outside the US) MT systems based on the mid-1960s technology so soundly condemned by ALPAC. However, the general disrepute of MT resulted in a rather quiet third decade.

We are now well into the fourth decade of MT, and there is a resurgence of interest throughout the world — plus a growing number of MT and MAT (machine-aided translation) systems in use by governments, business and industry. This year, as much as a million pages of text will be translated by machine, worldwide. Industrial firms are also funding M(A)T research and development projects of their own; thus it can no longer be said that only government funding keeps the field alive. Indeed, in the US there is virtually no government funding, though the Japanese and European governments are heavily subsidizing MT research and development.

2. THE MT CONTROVERSY

Machine translation of human languages is not a subject about which many scholars feel neutral. This field has had a long, colourful career, and boasts no shortage of vociferous detractors and proponents alike. In this section, we attempt to clarify the misunderstandings responsible for so much contention, and provide an initial basis for a more informed assessment. We close with a discussion of some of the psychosocial issues affecting acceptance of MT systems, and a summary of some lessons to be learned.

2.1 Early researchers' ignorance

Early MT researchers proved to be victims of their own enthusiasm and optimism. They had been convinced that producing general translation systems, able to deal with a wide range of texts without significant human intervention, and to produce high quality tranlation as output, would soon result, given nothing more than hard work. The 1954 Machine Translation Conference at Georgetown University had finished on a very optimistic note: 'mechanical translation was not only feasible but far closer to realizations than possibly the audience recognized' (Reynolds, 1954). This was not an isolated view: 'In about two years [from August 1957], we shall have a device which will at one glance read a whole page and feed what it has read into a tape recorder and thus remove all human co-operation on the input side of the translation machines. ... it will not be very long before the remaining linguistic problems in machine translation will be solved for a number of important languages' (Reifler, 1958). Obviously, it was easy for the ALPAC committee to conclude that the results achieved did not fulfil the promises made.

2.2 US critics' ignorance

In the US — a large, essentially monolingual society — it is still common to conceive of translation as simply that which any human translator does. It is generally believed that a few years' study of a foreign language qualifies one to be a translator, for just about any material whatsoever. Native speakers of foreign languages are therefore considered to be even better qualified. (In June 1986, a TV commentator, discussing President Reagan's proposed Workfare program, listed as typical positions to be filled by the otherwise-unemployed: 'clerks, street cleaners, and translators'.) Worse, fluency in one foreign language is sometimes taken to be, *ipso facto*, proof of competence in related languages; an embarrassing incident involving a former US President in Poland (whose State Department interpreter, a Russian specialist, was perceived to be insulting the audience) illustrates the folly of this position, yet it is still widely held. Thus, translation is not particularly respected as a profession in the US — it is frequently perceived as the 'last resort' of otherwise-unemployed liberal arts majors — and the pay is poor (an ironic contrast with the reviving interest in MT in the US).

In Canada, in Europe, and elsewhere around the world, this myopic attitude is not held. Where translation is a fact of life rather than an oddity, it is realized that one translator does not equal another, that any translator's competence is sharply restricted to a few domains (this is especially true of technical areas), that native fluency in a foreign language does not bestow on one the ability to serve as a translator, and that different languages deserve treatment as such. Thus, in college-level and postgraduate schools that teach the theory (translatology) as well as the practice of translation, a translation student is trained in the few areas in which he will be doing translation. True competence is expected only after years of experience beyond that training, and even then only in a few limited domains of expertise.

Of special relevance to MT is the fact that essentially all translations for dissemination (export) are revised by more highly qualified translators who necessarily refer back to the original text when post-editing the translation: unrevised translations are regarded as being inferior in quality, or at least suspect, and for many if not most purposes they are simply not acceptable.

In the multinational firm Siemens, even internal communications that are translated are also post-edited. Such news generally comes as a surprise, if not, indeed, a shock, to most people in the US.

2.3 Translator resistance

Some translators will never be torn from their dictaphones, and will finish their careers penning corrections on drafts transcribed by secretaries. Others have advanced to typing their own translations — some, even, on word processors, where they may also make corrections, though frequently resorting to marking up printed drafts. Many of these others would still not want a computer to translate for them. Thus, there is a large class of translators who could not appropriately be called potential users of MT systems. There seems to be a high correlation of youth with willingness to experiment with MT (or, for that matter, with any new technology).

A second area of resistance to MT is a fear that translation produced by computers may, in the long term, have a detrimental effect on a translator's own style and ability to translate well. Some translators who have already been exposed to working with poor MT systems may also be opposed to the idea because of such unsatisfactory experiences.

2.4 Developers' ignorance

There remain varying levels of misunderstanding among translators and MT system developers about what is involved in translation with machine aids. Translators are becoming increasingly involved in the development of MT systems, but some developers are still not fully aware of the needs and concerns of translators — the end-users of MT systems. It is important for system developers to understand that there are still translators who resist the advent of MT because they fear being replaced by a computer, although this fear does seem to have decreased somewhat in recent years as translators have become more familiar with other new technologies (word processors, on-line terminology databases and so on).

2.5 Lessons for all

It is easy to see that the 'fully automatic high-quality machine translation' standard, imagined by most US scholars past (the ALPAC committee) and present to constitute minimum acceptability, must be radically redefined. Indeed, the most famous MT critic of all, when faced with evidence of significant user satisfaction with seemingly poor translations performed by computers, eventually recanted his strong opposition to MT, admitting that these terms could only be defined by the users, according to their own standards, for each situation (Bar-Hillel, 1971). However, the US research-funding and academic communities have largely failed to notice and learn from this retraction, and for the most part remain convinced of the impossibility of successful translation by computer — ironically, often quoting Bar-Hillel's earlier 'disproofs' as authoritative.

In informed circles, it is now recognized that an MT system does not have to scan books, then print and bind the results of its translation in order to qualify as 'fully automatic'. 'High-quality' does not rule out post-editing, since such proscription would 'prove' the infeasibility of high-quality human translation. Academic debates about what defines 'high-quality' and 'fully automatic' are considered irrelevant by the users of M(A)T systems. What matters to them are two things: whether the systems can produce output of sufficient quality for the intended use (e.g., information acquisition, or revision for dissemination), and whether the operation as a whole is cost-effective or, rarely, justifiable on other grounds, such as speed. (The Georgetown Automatic Translation system, as with other installations of its type, offered the choice of translations available overnight, if produced by machine, vs. delays of several months, if done by human translators.)

There certainly exists some innate translator resistance to MT, and system developers will have to live with this fact; more, they may have to educate their potential customers, who might in ignorance consider a system to be a failure if it is not universally adopted. When we speak of translators, then, as potential users, we are talking about those whose temperament admits such a possibility. Even in this group, there are barriers to overcome, but of course translators deserve proof that MT can improve their work; some systems have admittedly not done so.

It is precisely for these reasons that it is vital for system developers to understand what is involved in the art of translation, as indeed many translators justly view their craft as a creative art. Having gained an insight into the steps involved in translation, system developers can implement MT systems in such a way that they become useful tools for translators, who need no longer view MT as a threat to their livelihood, linguistic integrity, or sanity.

2.6 A more balanced viewpoint

Existing MT systems have already proven that they hold a place in the field of industrial translation. They are powerful tools for translators, who are relieved of some of the more tedious tasks such as repetitious translation, re-typing, or cutting and pasting diagrams involving very little actual translation. In order for MT to gain widespread acceptance, however, it is important for each system to be implemented with the full range of user needs in mind and to include a full range of adaptable and user-friendly tools. An MT system may be based on highly sophisticated linguistic theories, but it will not be acceptable to users unless it is relatively simple to learn and operate, because translators will be unwilling to adapt to the new technology and will return to their individual methods of translation.

That is not to say that translators should not be ready to adapt to MT systems; indeed, they can derive the most benefit from MT by being prepared to learn the new skills required. Translators also have a great deal to offer by becoming involved in the development of systems intended for their use, and by providing continual feedback about their experiences with MT to system developers and implementers.

3. SURVEY

This section presents a cursory overview only; Slocum (1985) offers a more expanded treatment. The tutorial will expand on the general themes presented herein. We divide the MT world into the three most active regions: North America, the Far East, and Western Europe.

3.1 North America

North America, particularly the US, was until recently rather isolated, even insular. The economies were largely domestic and, in the case of Canada and the US, English was sufficient for virtually all government and commercial purposes. With the adoption of French as an official national language, the situation in Canada began to change: the amount of translation required grew dramatically, and translation bureaus soon could not cope adequately with the volume. Thus, a serious interest in MT arose in that country, resulting in part in the TAUM project at the University of Montreal.

Although, through demographic studies, one can foresee potential for the promotion of Spanish as an official national language of the US, that time is well into the future. Only with the recent shift of the US from a domestic toward an international economy has there been a growing perception of translation services as a serious need. Heretofore, US industry, to the extent that it dealt with foreign concerns at all, has generally succeeded in requiring customers to interact in English, and to accept English documentation. The 'translation bureaus' of major firms sometimes consisted of no more than a few bilingual secretaries — and those, of course, having no training as translators. As the US has begun turning to foreign markets — and meeting with stiff competition from international companies which, among other things, are willing and able to deal in customers' native languages — the interest in translation has increased.

This trend, however, is only recent, and quite small. Frequently it is not even perceived until one points out evidence such as the recent establishment of MT projects inside several US computer companies. Even in the last few years, major commercial MT vendors have reduced their domestic staffs and further increased their attenion to foreign markets. The only large academic MT project in the US, at the University of Texas, receives its entire support from Siemens, a West German firm; a related, but purely research project at the same institution, receives its funding from Hitachi, a Japanese firm.

It is a paradox, then, that — until two years ago — the major commercial MT firms had all arisen in the US, even though their markets lay elsewhere; perhaps this is a testament to the American entrepreneurial spirit. In any case, this situation too has changed. More than a dozen Japanese companies have announced commercial MT systems, or production-prototypes, since 1984, and the customer base already has numbers in the hundreds. At a time when the need for translation is finally becoming apparent, the US is rapidly losing any edge it may have had in this field.

3.2 The Far East

Unlike the US, Far Eastern countries have not enjoyed the luxury of requiring potential customers to learn their languages. Especially for Japan, whose economy is founded upon the export trade, the ability to provide documentation in the customer's language is of paramount importance. Contrary to popular belief (in the US, at least) about the propensity of the Japanese for learning foreign languages (English), most of them find it an arduous task, and even translation for information acquisition is therefore highly important.

Translation in Japan now constitutes an annual market estimated at around one trillion (1 000 000 000 000) yen, with some of the larger industrial firms reporting individual translation budgets exceeding one billion (1 000 000 000) yen; perhaps 80% of this comprises technical texts for the export market, of which English accounts for about half (Philippi, 1985). This is a staggering demand, and the prospect of a trillion-yen market, which may double in 2–3 years, is dazzling. It is quite understandable, then, that no small number of Japanese companies are interested in developing, using, and marketing MT systems.

3.3 Western Europe

Europeans have for millenia coped with language problems. Normal commerce requires the ability to communicate in several languages, and companies traditionally use both in-house and outside translators to supply documents to customers. With the establishment of the European Economic Community (EEC), and its subsequent expansion from four to nine official languages, the growth in demand for governmental translation has been staggering. In 1986 the European Parliament spent nearly half its budget for translation and interpretation services. The Council of Ministers employs over 700 translators, and the cost of translation in the Commission exceeds that of Commission-supported research.

In such an environment, it is easy to see how interest in MT can flourish as it does. Accordingly, individual European companies and governments, to say nothing of the EEC itself, are willing to invest large sums in techniques that promise to deal with translation demands more effectively. As a result, there are a number of projects scattered about Europe whose goals are to ameliorate the translation problem in one way or another. Some government-supported projects have been large, and of long standing: the Groupe d'Etude pour la Traduction Automatique (GETA), at Grenoble, and its sister group at the University of the Saar, in Saarbrücken, come to mind. Other groups, some supported by government and some by industry, have been smaller.

Some groups have been effective in the sense of producing systems admitting practical application, and others not; but failures occur in all research and development areas, not just MT. Indeed, lack of success is not always complete: one early group — CETA at Grenoble — failed in its original mission, but learned from its mistakes and, reinstituted as GETA, adopted another approach; this eventually resulted in a prototype now undergoing production implementation in the French national project ESOPE.

4. SYSTEM CLASSIFICATION SCHEMES

In order to appreciate the technologies behind machine translation systems, it is necessary to understand the broad levels of ambition by which they can be categorized, and something about the linguistic techniques that MT systems employ in attacking the translation problem. Each of these, in different ways, has a profound effect on system design. In this section we outline the major design issues.

4.1 Levels of ambition

There are three broad categories of 'computerized translation tools' (the differences hinging on how ambitious the system is intended to be): machine translation (MT), machine-aided translation (MAT), and terminology databanks (TD). Up to now, we have only discussed the first. We shall continue to concentrate on this end of the spectrum, but the reader should remember that there are these other categories. In fact most of our comments throughout this paper, though adressed at MT systems, also reflect on these others.

MT systems are intended to perform translation 'without human intervention'. This restriction does not rule out pre-processing (except for such decisions as marking phrase boundaries and resolving part-of-speech and/or other linguistic ambiguities), or post-editing (since this is normally done for human translations anyway). However, an MT system is solely responsible, without human assistance, for the complete translation process from input of the source text to output of the target text, using special programs, comprehensive dictionaries, and collections of linguistic rules (to the extent that they exist, varying with the MT system). On the scale of computer translation ambition, MT occupies the top position. All of the early work in MT addressed this goal.

MAT systems fall into two subgroups: human-assisted machine translation (HAMT) and machine-assisted human translation (MAHT), reflecting successively lower levels of ambition. In an HAMT system the computer is responsible for producing the translation *per se*, but may interact with a human monitor at many stages along the way, by asking the human to disambiguate a word's part of speech or meaning, or to indicate where to attach a phrase, or to choose a translation for a word or phrase from among several candidates discovered in the system's dictionary. In a MAHT system, on the other hand, the human is responsible for producing the translation *per se* (on-line), but may interact with the system in certain prescribed situations, for example, requesting assistance in searching through a local dictionary–thesaurus, accessing a remote terminology databank, retrieving examples of the use of a word or phrase, or performing word processing functions such as formatting. The existence of a pre-processing stage is unlikely in an MA(H)T system (the system does not need help, rather it is making help available), but post-editing is frequently appropriate.

Terminology databanks (TD) are the least ambitious systems because access frequently is not made during a translation task (the translator may not be working on-line), but usually is performed prior to human translation. Indeed, to the translator, the databank may not be accessible on-line at all, but may be limited to the production of printed subject-area glossaries. A TD offers access to technical terminology, but usually not to common words (the translator already knows these). The chief advantage of a TD is not that it is automated (even with on-line access, words can be looked up almost as quickly in a printed dictionary), but that it is up-to-date: technical terminology is constantly changing, and published dictionaries are essentially obsolete by the time they are available. It is also possible for a TD to contain more entries because it can draw on a larger group of active contributors: its users.

4.2 Linguistic techniques

We shall characterize the methodologies employed for MT along two axes: depth of analysis, and the primary source of knowledge. Regarding the depth of analysis, there are three classic categories (direct, transfer, and interlingua). Regarding the primary source of knowledge, there are four (lexical, syntactic, semantic, and cognitive). We shall consider these two axes in turn.

4.2.1 Depth of analysis

Superficially, translation may be regarded as analysing an input (text, sentence, or whatever) in the source language (SL), and synthesizing an equivalent output in the target language (TL). In designing an MT system, one must decide how 'deep', or comprehensive, the analysis is to be. This will determine where one starts when it comes time to perform synthesis, and hence the design of the entire synthesis module.

At the shallowest level, one can perform 'direct translation', which is characterized by the fact that analysis of the SL is restricted to the minimum work necessary to produce a translation in a single, specific TL. Assuming that such a shallow analysis can be sufficient for high-quality translation (and there are arguments concerning whether or not this is true), it remains the case that another translation of the same input, into a second TL, requires a complete re-analysis of that input. This is considered to be inefficient, from both the operational standpoint (performing a new analysis for the new TL) and, perhaps more importantly, the standpoint of the development project itself (since, in theory, one can use nothing from one linguistic rule base when building another, each being geared toward a single, specific language pair). Consider, for example, that a direct MT system contains in the SL dictionary details of the behaviour of the TL: for translation into a new TL, one must construct an entirely new dictionary. For translation in all directions among N languages, one would have to construct $N \times (N-1)$ entirely different MT systems: 72 of them, for the 9 EEC languages.

At the other extreme, one can opt to analyse an input into a deep, language-independent representation of meaning usually called an interlingua. From this meaning structure, one can in principle translate into multiple languages merely by synthesizing multiple outputs — without ever re-analysing the input. Thus, for translation in all directions among N languages, one need construct only N analysers plus N synthesizers. To use our dictionary example, only N dictionaries (one per language) are required. This would seem to maximize operational and development-project efficiency. One major problem with this is that linguists are not yet able to specify an interlingua: the necessary theories have not yet been devised (indeed, that one can possibly exist is mere conjecture). Another problem is that, the world being an imperfect place, there will always be some sentences that cannot be analysed — either because the sentence is truly ungrammatical or, more likely, because the machine's grammar is incomplete. In a system relying on an interlingua, a failure to analyse fully almost necessarily entails a failure to synthesize, and no translation is produced — something human users do not tolerate well.

A compromise position involves an intermediate stage called transfer. An input is analysed into a structure deeper than that required for direct translation, but not (quite) language-independent like an interlingua. Then a transfer step transforms that structure (peculiar to the SL) into an equivalent structure peculiar to the TL, and the synthesizer uses the result to produce the output translation. In our hypothetical N-language environment, this requires N analysers, and N synthesizers, plus $N \times (N-1)$ transfer modules — which seems the worst of all solutions. (One needs N monolingual dictionaries, and at least $N \times (N-1)/2$ bilingual dictionaries.) However, it is generally agreed that the transfer modules and bilingual dictionary entries can be kept sufficiently small that the research and development efficiency is acceptable. This approach also has the great advantage that it has been shown to work well in practice — better than the direct approach, which was generally abandoned years ago — whereas the interlingua approach has thus far failed to produce a workable system, and clearly will not do so in the near future. Today, essentially all serious MT system development efforts employ the transfer approach, while the few extant long-term MT research efforts tend to concern themselves with the interlingua approach.

4.2.2 Primary source of knowledge

Another design decision faced by an MT system developer is the locus of the primary source of knowledge used to guide the translation. One could locate most knowledge about language behaviour in the lexicon — as, for example, a direct translation system does. This tends to result in maximally specific rules (hence, presumably, the highest accuracy). However, it vastly increases the size of the rule base unless one is extremely clever about organizing a lexical taxonomy supporting feature inheritance — something not yet demonstrated. Worse, in practice this approach has led to many kinds of unforeseen, destructive rule interactions.

An alternative locus of the primary source of knowledge is in syntax rules. Almost all of the most promising MT systems today rely primarily on this form of knowledge. However, it is difficult if not ultimately impossible to control a purely syntactic knowledge base, and all these systems use other sources of knowledge to reduce what would otherwise be an explosive growth of interpretations as the rule base and sentence length grow. Syntax rules also suffer from problems of fragility: for example, there is little or nothing one can do to recover a full-sentence analysis of an input sentence that is structurally unsound by the standards of the syntax rules.

A third potential locus is in the semantic rules. It is claimed that these can be somewhat less fragile than syntax rules in the presence of errors, though in practice this has not been remarkably obvious. However, no semantic-rule formalism has achieved widespread acceptability, for the reason that all proposals are known to be faulty in too many respects. It is also the case that currently-proposed semantic rules tend to be rather large and time-consuming to construct, individually, with the result that the manpower investment required to produce a practical application is prohibitive.

With respect to the fourth potential locus of primary knowledge, cognitive rules (including, e.g., common-sense knowledge of the world), the same arguments apply, only to a greater extreme. They are potentially the most robust, if proponents are to be believed, but they are easily the most debated, complex, and costly form of knowledge yet proposed. It is hard to imagine constructing any large application by encoding their requisite cognitive knowledge base manually. (Consider the world knowledge subsumed by a 100 000-page telephone switching-system manual.) Rather, it is more likely that machine learning of such structures will be required before they can be used outside of 'toy' problem domains. MT systems are generally intended to be applied to hundreds of thousands, perhaps millions, of pages of text, whereas NLP systems based on cognitive rules have been 'applied' to texts measured in tens of words (that is, where any form of comprehension of the entire text was attempted: we discount what amount to augmented keyword searches posing as models of cognitive processing).

5. LOOKING AT TRANSLATION

Before one can meaningfully critique a translation, or a translation process, whether performed by man or machine, one must determine the use to which the result is being put. When considering, further, whether translation by machine is necessary, or even desirable, one must recognize the strengths and weaknesses of computers vs. humans as translators, vis-à-vis the type of text.

5.1 The purposes of translation

Consider two extreme purposes of translation: information acquisition vs. information dissemination. The classic example of the former is intelligence-gathering: with masses of data to sift through, there is no time, money, or incentive to translate carefully every document by normal (i.e., human) means. Scientists more generally are faced with this dilemma: already more must be read than can be read in the time available. Having to labour through texts written in foreign languages — when the probability is low that any given text is of real interest — many not be worth the effort. In the recent past, English has been the lingua franca of science, but it is becoming less and less dominant for a variety of reasons, including the rise of nationalism and the spread of technology around the world. As a result, scientists who rely on English are having greater difficulty keeping up with work in their fields. If a very rapid and inexpensive means of translation were available, then — for texts within the reader's areas of expertise — even a low-quality translation might be sufficient for information acquisition. At worst, the reader could determine whether a more careful (and more expensive) translation effort might be justified. More likely, his understanding of the text would be good enough to preclude the need for a more careful translation. The older MT systems were generally intended for this application. Without them most documents are never translated because, in economic terms, producing careful translations that will only be cursorily scanned (even assuming they are not outdated by the time they are available) is a waste of resources.

The classic example of the latter purpose of translation is technology export: an industry in one country that desires to sell its products in another country must usually provide documentation in the purchaser's native language, or at least a designated second language. In the past, US companies, for example, have escaped this responsibility by requiring that the purchasers learn English; other exporters (German, for example) have never had this kind of luxury. With the increase of nationalism, it is likely that monolingual documentation will be less acceptable; for this and other reasons, translation is becoming increasingly common as more companies look to foreign markets. More to the point, texts for information dissemination (export) must be translated with a great deal of care: the translation must be 'right' as well as clear. Qualified human technical translators are hard to find, expensive, and slow (translating somewhere around 4–8 pages/day, on the average). The information dissemination application is most responsible for the renewed interest in MT.

5.2 Literary vs. technical translation

Natural language texts range in 'linguistic complexity' from technical documentation through edited abstracts and scientific reports to newspaper articles, literary works, and political–sales material.

Literary and technical translations, residing as they do near opposite extremes of this range, differ with respect to both process and output. In literary translation, emphasis is placed on style, perhaps at the expense of absolute fidelity to content (most especially for poetry). In technical translation, emphasis is properly placed on fidelity — especially with respect to technical terminology — even at the expense of style. Highly polished technical translations, especially of manuals, are often not considered worth the investment required to produce them. (Indeed, highly-polished original texts are rare!) Technical accuracy is a critical consideration.

As far as MT is concerned, technical is less complex than literary translation because it is characterized by relatively less syntactic and semantic variety and more denotative as opposed to connotative content. Paradoxically, the order of complexity for human translators is essentially reversed for reasons of vocabulary: the acquisition, maintenance, and consistent use of valid technical terminology is an enormous problem. No qualified human translator has much difficulty with straightforward syntax or normal idiomatic usage, but the prevalence and volatility of technical terms and jargon poses a considerable problem. MT systems may lack good style, but they excel at terminological accuracy and speed: they are best suited for technical translation.

As it happens, there is little or no need for literary translation by machine: there is no great shortage of human translators capable of handling the load. By contrast, in many technical fields there are far too few qualified human translators, and it is obvious that the problem will never be alleviated by such measures as greater financial incentives, however laudable that may be.

The demand for technical translation is staggering in sheer volume. A single set of operation and maintenance manuals for, say, a modern telephone switching system can exceed the size of all of the works in classical Greek literature. Also, as the manuals are revised, they may require retranslation several times. The only hope for a solution to the technical translation problem lies with increased human productivity through the full range of computer technology: full-scale MT, less ambitious MAT, on-line terminology data banks, and word processing.

5.3 Advantages in technical MT

There are several reasons why computers are already effective at translating technical texts. One of theses concerns vocabulary: technical texts (hence, MT system dictionaries) tend to concentrate on one subject-area at a time, wherein the terminology (lexical semantics) is relatively consistent, and where the vocabulary is relatively unambiguous, even though it may be quite large. (This is not to say that lexical problems disappear!) Another advantage is that there is typically little problematic anaphora, and little or no 'discourse structure' as usually defined; thus MT systems can usually get away with ignoring these hard problems. Third, in accordance with current practice for high-quality human translation, revision is to be expected. That is, there is no *a priori* reason why machine translations must be 'perfect' when human translations are not expected to be so: it is sufficient that they be acceptable to the humans who revise them, and that the translation process proves cost-effective overall (including revision).

5.4 Problems in technical MT

Notwithstanding the advantages of MT for technical texts, there are definite problems to be confronted. First of all, the volume of such material is staggering: potentially hundreds of millions of pages per year. Even ignoring all cost-effectiveness considerations, the existence of this much candidate material demands a serious concern for efficiency in the implementation. Second, the emphasis in MT is changing from information acquisition to information dissemination. The demand is not so much for loosely approximate translations from which someone knowledgeable about the subject can infer the import of the text (perhaps with a view toward determining whether a human translation is desired); rather, the real demand is for high-quality translations of, e.g., operating and maintenance manuals — for instructing someone not necessarily knowledgeable about the vendor's equipment in precisely what must (and must not) be done, in any given situation. Fidelity, therefore, is essential.

In addition to the problems of size and fidelity, there are problems regarding the text itself: the format and writing style. For example, it is not unusual to be confronted with a text which has been 'typeset' by a computer, but for which the typesetting commands are no longer available. This can be true even when the text was originally produced, or later transcribed, in machine-readable form. The format may include charts, diagrams, multi-column tables, section headings, paragraphs, etc. Misspellings, typographical errors, and grammatical errors can and do appear. Technical texts are notable for their frequency of 'unusual' syntax such as isolated phrases and sentence fragments, a high incidence of acronyms and formulae, plus a plethora of parenthetical expressions. The discourse structure, if it can be argued to exist, may be decidedly unusual — as exemplified by a flowchart. Unknown words will appear in the text. Sentences can be long and complicated, notwithstanding the earlier statement about reduced complexity: technically-oriented individuals in all cultures seem to be renowned for abusing their natural languages. The successful MT system, then, will address these problems as well as those more commonly anticipated.

6. BUILDING A PRACTICAL SYSTEM

Constructing a practical MT system is extraordinarily difficult. Many questions arise to which there are few known (or at least agreed-upon) answers. Certain of these questions, being of academic interest, are discussed in considerable detail in the open literature. Matters of the parsing algorithm, the linguistic formalism, the translation strategy, etc., will thus be ignored here. One critical area, however, being of mere practical interest, has received very little scholarly attention: the user interface. By 'user' we refer, variously, to the linguist who is developing the grammar rules; to the lexicographer-terminographer who is developing the dictionary entries; and to the translator who is of course the true end-user. In our discussion below, we use the term 'linguist' to refer to anyone engaging in a strictly system-development role (e.g., grammarian, lexicographer); a 'translator' is anyone engaging in a pre- or post-editing or terminology update role.

No natural language processing (NLP) system is likely to be successful in isolation. An environment of support tools is necessary for ultimate acceptance on the part of prospective users. The following 'linguist support tools', we think, constitute a minimum workable environment for both development and use of NLP systems generally: a DBMS for handling lexical entries; validation programs that verify the admissability of all linguistic rules (grammar, lexicons, transformations, etc.) using a set of formal specifications; dictionary programs that search through large numbers of proposed new lexical entries (words, in all relevant languages) to determine which entries are actually new, and which appear to replicate existing entries; defaulting programs that 'code' new lexical entries in the NLP system's chosen formalism automatically, given only the root forms of the words and their categories, using empirically-determined best guesses based on the available dictionary database entries plus whatever orthographic information is available in the root forms; and benchmark programs to test the integrity of the NLP system after modifications (Slocum, 1982). A DBMS for handling grammar rules is also a good idea.

For MT applications, one must add 'translator support tools': a collection of text-processing programs that (semi-)automatically mark and extract translatable segments of text from large documents, and which automatically insert translations produced by the MT system back into the original document, preserving all formatting conventions such as tables of contents, section headings, paragraphs, multi-column tables, flowcharts, figure labels, and the like; a powerful on-line editing program with special capabilities (such as single-keystroke commands to look up words in on-line dictionaries) in addition to the normal editing commands (almost all of which should be invokable with a single keystroke); and also, perhaps, (access to) a 'term databank', i.e., an on-line database of technical terms used in the subject area(s) to be covered by the MT system.

The first section below deals with support tools for the linguist, which aid in the development and maintenance of any NLP system. Next we deal with tools for translators, which aid in the document preparation, translation, and editing tasks.

6.1 Tools for linguistics

There are several issues that must be addressed in the selection and implementation of natural language processors and their accompanying support environments. The computing world is slowly but surely coming to recognize the importance of what is called 'the programming environment' in research and development circles, or 'integrated software' in application circles. This is opposed to an earlier focus on, e.g., the hardware or programming language *per se*. We shall therefore open out discussion with a consideration of some man–machine interface issues relating to the dictionary–grammar production cycle. In particular, we take the position that a rule interpreter cannot be separated entirely from its system development and maintenance environment; rather, it must fit naturally into its environment so that overall productivity may be maximized.

As our canonical linguistic rule interpreter, we designate the parser, though of course there are other things one does with (other kinds of) linguistic rules. By the term 'parser', we refer to a program that interprets a 'sentence' according to a distinguished set of dictionary and grammar rules; that is, a parser does not itself incorporate the linguistic rules by which sentences are interpreted. Although adhering to good principles of modular programming may cause a parser to be somewhat divorced from its operational environment, the separation cannot be rigid. In particular, one should not consider a parser with total disregard for its operating environment. One must consider the overall NLP system, including the facilities that support the development and maintenance of the linguistic rules (dictionaries and grammars) that the parser relies on, the format and structure of the rules as seen by the lexicographer and linguist, the testing facilities that allow one to evaluate the NLP system, and the relationship of the parser to that system.

6.1.1 Rule development and maintenance

In any large software system, the problem of producing and maintaining the data sets on which the programs operate becomes important, if not critical. First of all, when there is a large volume of such material the data-entry process itself can consume a significant amount of time; second, the task of ensuring data integrity becomes an even larger time sink. We shall expand briefly on these two problems.

There are two problems associated with data entry: creating the data in the first place, and getting it entered in machine-readable form. In most applications of database management systems, the creation of data is relatively straightforward: such data items as personal name, age, job title, identification number(s), salary, etc., serve as examples to illustrate the point that the data items usually pre-exist; thus data entry becomes relatively more important. In an NLP application, however, creating the original data is the major bottleneck: one must decide, for each of thousands of words, many details of behaviour in a complicated linguistic environment. Certainly these data may be said to 'pre-exist' (in the language), but a real problem arises when humans attempt to identify them. In general, the more sophisticated the NLP system, the more of these details there are. Data entry, relatively speaking, becomes a small or insignificant issue — although it remains a significant issue in absolute terms.

In the dictionary realm, an initial solution to this problem is a 'lexical default' program that accepts minimal information (the root form of the word, and its category) and automatically encodes the features and values that specify the details of linguistic behaviour. This can be accomplished by a combination of morphological analysis of the root form of the input word, search of the existing dictionary database for 'similar' entries, and statistically-justified guessing. This amounts to automated dictionary-entry coding by analogy. Defaulted lexical entries can be created in machine-readable form to begin with, and made available for human review–revision using standard or special-purpose on-line editing facilities. This can reduce greatly both coding time and coding errors. It does not seem that any similar solutions to this problem yet exist for grammar rules, though one can imagine a system researching for grammar rules analogous to the one desired.

A potentially harder problem, however, is the maintenance of data integrity. Humans will make mental errors in creating lexical entries, and will aggravate these by making typographical errors during data entry. Even assuming a lexical default program (which, of course, does not make such 'syntactic' mistakes), the process of human revision of the defaulted entries may introduce errors. The solution to this problem would be to include a validation program that, working from a formal specification of what is legal in linguistic rules (grammatical or lexical), identifies any errors of rule format and/or syntax within each submitted entry. The formal specification could be organized by language, by lexical category within language, and perhaps by subcategorization feature.

There is also the problem of maintaining an existing database. In any NLP system, there will be a need for changing linguistic rules in the light of experience; in a system that serves as a vehicle for research in NLP, this problem is magnified by the occasional need for large-scale changes to accommodate new system features, or even theories of language. One approach to this problem is to incorporate a general database management system (DBMS) along with a group of interface routines that transform, upon entry, rules from a format optimized for human use into a format more suitable for storage by the DBMS, and which reverse the transformation when retrieving the rules.

Finally, there is the problem of trying all these modules together with a powerful, high-level user interface that optimizes the task of rule acquisition and maintenance. Programs intended to solve this problem should use the database interface, the default program (in the case of lexical entries), the formal specifications governing linguistic rules, and the rule validator, to facilitate the process of rule acquisition and maintenance. Such programs must support the usual requirements for adding, modifying, and deleting all types of rules.

6.1.2 Rule structure and format

The market for computational linguistics is growing more rapidly than the number of trained personnel who can best fill the positions. Even if this were not true, other factors would argue for the NLP system grammars and lexicons being maintained in a format optimized for use by linguists and lexicographers, rather than by programmers *per se*. The issue of overall efficiency in research, development and application precludes interest in machine efficiency alone. NLP is an exceedingly difficult problem whose optimal solution is not yet well understood: empiricial results can and will dictate that linguistic procedures proliferate and be changed. For this to be effected by linguists and lexicographers who are not sophisticated in the computer arts, the rule bases must be expressed in a formalism with which they are familiar, or at least which they can easily understand. This tends to eliminate, e.g., LISP code from consideration.

Similarly, the software component (parser) should impose no significant constraint on how the linguistic component represents interpretations of sentences. The most common representation formalism in modern linguistics in the US, for example, is constituent-structure trees; in related disciplines, other formalisms are preferred. In order to allow freedom of choice, a few specialized routines could be written for each desired representation; the parser should interface with these modules 'at the back end' in a well-defined manner. Thus the linguists could change their representation formalism at will.

6.1.3 Rule base testing and evaluation

Linguistic rules, like programs, require extensive debugging and tuning. Since the phenomena that one is trying to account for in an NLP system are generally more complex and open-ended than those encountered in other forms of programming, it can be argued that the need for debugging–tuning tools is even more acute. It is strange, then, that the field has witnessed so little discussion of such issues. Perhaps this is due to the fact that most NLP systems deal with very small subsets of natural language, so that all of the behavioural characteristics of the system can be accommodated in the computational linguist's head. At any rate, when NLP systems grow large, human memory fails; such tools then become indispensable, else the system falls apart.

Certainly, the minimal information required for debugging is a trace of the applications of all rules (lexical and grammatical). Both the input and output of each rule should be noted, including reasons for failure. In any large system, where the number of rule applications grows rapidly with the increase in rule-set size, the tracing behaviour should be selective — conditioned on, e.g., information type (lexical, syntactic, semantic), and/or such information content as category (noun phrase, clause, etc.). Otherwise, the flood of information will be more than the linguist can effectively deal with.

For tuning purposes, the needs are greater. In addition to recording the application history of all rules, special analysis programs must be written to summarize and present the data thus gathered. Data points should include such things as, for each rule, the number of applications attempted, the number of successes or failures that result in a local sense (conditioned on subcategorized features, including semantic tests), and the number of times a construction actually appears somewhere in a global (complete sentence) analysis.

6.2 Tools for translators

This section discusses the ways in which end-users interact with MT systems, and the need for MT system developers to be aware of user requirements. A collection of adaptable techniques to facilitate the operation of an MT system at each stage of interaction is proposed.

A user interacts with an MT system in four different stages:

(1) text preparation,
(2) dictionary update,
(3) execution of translation run, and
(4) post-editing MT output.

Each of these four stages requires special tools so that the relevant task may be accomplished as easily and effectively as possible.

6.2.1 Text preparation

Whenever a text is to be translated on an MT system, it is necessary for the text to be available in machine-readable form, but a text submitted for translation may be supplied as a typewritten or even hand-written document. This first step of inputting a text can prove to be more than a trivial problem: MT system developers need to be aware of this possibility, and to make available text entry facilities that are as powerful and as user-friendly as possible.

Once the text is available in machine-readable form, it must be prepared for translation. Many technical documents contain diagrams in which blocks of text do not run strictly from left to right; these must be marked and extracted as separate translation units, then re-formatted when the translated document is produced. An MT system should recognize, translate, and re-format all diagrams: if too much time is spent on manual pre-processing, the cost of translation begins to rise, the advantages of speed and cost-effectiveness when using MT begin to decline, and user-acceptability decreases.

6.2.2 Dictionary update

Once the text is available to the MT system, it is usually necessary for any new words that do not yet appear in the system's dictionary to be added. User acceptance of the dictionary update procedure tends to involve two factors:

(a) the kinds of information that a user is required to supply, and
(b) the method used to enter that information into the dictionary.

Even during the linguistic development phase, consideration should be given to the kinds of information that the user will be asked to code in dictionary entries. If the coding process becomes too complex, the user will be frustrated and the number of incorrectly-coded dictionary entries is likely to increase. It may be necessary for MT system developers to avoid a powerful but complex system, considering the ability of the user to code correctly the dictionary entries. It is important that the user be able to understand the effects of lexical coding decisions on the resulting translation: not only does this improve the quality of dictionary entries, but it also enables the user to gain more control over the dictionary and, consequently, the quality of the translation. Experience has shown that acceptance by users is enhanced when they have some control over the output of the MT system (Piggott, 1982).

6.2.3 Running the translation

Once the source text has been made available to the MT system and the dictionary update is complete, translation can begin. If users are to manage the execution of these tasks, there must be user-friendly tools, including a mnemonic means to request execution of them, to check on their status, and to be informed upon the completion of a translation. In order to gain the most benefit from an MT system, the system must accept requests for translations to be run in batch mode (e.g. overnight).

In general, the aims of developers should be to produce an MT system in which the task of scheduling translations is very simple, and in which translation jobs can be executed efficiently in order to make the best use of system resources.

6.2.4 Post-editing

An editor may need to revise a translation and, since user acceptance of MT is vital to its ultimate success, it is especially important that the system tools developed for post-editing be user-friendly and flexible. Post-editing tools should be designed so that a revisor can make changes to the draft translation with a minimum number of keystrokes: this will enable him to work rapidly, and will minimize frustration.

The translator should be able to select his preferred method for editing. Some prefer to write changes on a hardcopy printout of the translation and to input these changes into the computer later; others prefer working on-line, but with a hardcopy of the source document available for reference; still others prefer working entirely on-line, with alternating sentences of source and target text, or with two windows containing source and target text. Some prefer to re-format a text before editing, while others would re-format afterwards; this may depend on the type of text that is being post-edited, and whether it contains flowing text or a large number of diagrams and tables. An ideal MT system would allow users to edit using the method they find most comfortable.

Although there are many powerful word processing systems available, most of these were designed with text input in mind rather than post-editing. The particular changes that a post-editor needs to make to a document depend on the accuracy of the draft translation, but there are some general changes that appear to be common to all MT systems. A post-editor tends to work in units of sentences and, therefore, sentence-oriented functions that allow the cursor to be moved to the beginning or end of a sentence, as well as of a line, are necessary.

One of the most frequent post-editing changes made to translations is modifying word order. A screen editor for an MT system should, therefore, also include a full range of functions for moving–deleting words with single keystrokes. An ideal MT system would also include simple ways for entire phrases to be marked and moved from one point in the sentence to another.

Piggott (1982) noted that MT systems tend not to be totally accurate in capitalization. Even if MT systems were to commit no such errors, there would still be cases where a post-editor would break a long sentence into two shorter sentences, or combine two short sentences. Changing the case of a single letter should be implemented as a single-keystroke function; similarly for an entire word.

There will be instances in which a particular term is translated incorrectly throughout a text. The editor should have available two separate global replacement functions: an 'all-at-once' version, for when the editor is confident of the change; and an interactive 'query and replace' version, for substitution on a case-by-case basis (after confirmation).

The user should bear in mind that as much as possible of the original draft translation should be retained; otherwise, the purpose of MT is lost. There are instances, however, when the post-editor must rewrite major parts, or even all, of a sentence. The screen editor should also be able to cope with these cases in a user-friendly way, allowing the editor to overwrite, or alternately to insert new text into, the body of a sentence; ideally, the post-editor would be able to switch back and forth from overwrite-mode to insert-mode with one keystroke.

To allow even greater flexibility, an editing environment could also supply a set of user-programmable keys. These would allow individuals to program the strings of commands used most frequently. For example, if an MT system tended to make errors by inserting extra definite articles in the English target text, a post-editor could program one key to search through the document for each instance of 'the' and a second key to delete it automatically if it was superfluous.

While there is no doubt that new MT system users must learn new skills and accept different kinds of translation problems from those they have been accustomed to, their freedom to select a preferred method for editing a draft translation would enhance the acceptance of MT systems. In addition, the range of screen-editing functions outlined above would decrease the number of keystrokes required to make the necessary changes in a document. This in turn, would speed up the post-editing phase and help to minimize the final cost of working with MT by simplifying the interaction between the user and the system.

7. STATE-OF-THE-ART SUMMARY

Machine translation has long since reached the point of commercial viability: the 15–20 year longevity of some commercial vendors attests to this, as much as anything can. The feverish level of recent activity in Japan, as well as the expanding markets in the rest of the world, indicates that MT is in a growth phase. In this final section we critique the state of the art in terms of the current lines of research, areas receiving too little attention, some of the (still) controversial questions that plague the field, and some problems whose solutions, if available, would result in dramatic improvements.

7.1 Lines of research

A high level of interest has always existed for interlingual (AI) representations of meaning, and research continues along this front. There are two aspects of interlingua: structural, and lexical. So far, objectively discernible progress has been meagre, and research has been plagued by some lack of awareness of the full import of the distinction above. Poor research on interlinguas, of which there is unfortunately too much (frequently conducted by monolingual language speakers, speakers of only closely related languages, or at best linguistically naive computer scientists) indicates nothing, of course. Also unfortunate are proposals to employ a natural language as an interlingua; competent translators must derive considerable amusement from such suggestions. The best research indicates clearly that far more work will be required before this question yields an answer.

Another line of active research in MT concerns grammatical theories, and corresponding representations of grammatical knowledge. Variations on phrase-structure grammar, though criticized as weak, have been popular in the past owing to their computational tractability and relative ease of maintenance; but while useful for analysis and synthesis, there is nothing in the theory that speaks to the problem of transformation — as is required for transfer, or conversion into a semantic representation (e.g., interlingua). Tree-to-tree transducers have been equally popular because of their greater power and straightforward transformational application, but have tended to suffer computationally as well as from maintenance problems. (Since anything is possible, it is hard to know where to start fixing a problem, or extending coverage.) Recently, interest has grown in variants of functional unification grammar — especially within the EUROTRA project. Active investigation of this formalism is increasing, but it is not clear how the formalism could be used for, e.g., transfer.

7.2 Research gaps

Typically embodied in functional unification grammar theory, as well as certain other theories of language, is the notion of lexicon grammar: rules of grammatical behaviour are to be attached to lexical entries. This is all fine and well, provided that one is willing to conduct the large-scale effort necessary to identify those behaviours. Unfortunately, far too few have shown such an interest, and this represents a major gap. Such work is detailed, perhaps (to some) to the point of monotony, but it must take place before one can responsibly claim a breakthrough in grammatical formalisms, or know whether a workable approach has been found.

There have been too few (almost no) systematic contrastive studies of language; rather, it is too often the case that language differences are resolved in some *ad hoc* manner as they are encountered during the course of an MT application. The early EUROTRA work is a start in this direction, but very little of it has been published, and in any case this represents but a drop in the bucket for the nine EEC languages, to say nothing of the language families that are entirely neglected. This is another area where a large-scale, detailed effort is the only answer.

Terminology represents another research gap in the sense that too few MT groups are concerned with it. Precious few MT projects have even considered employing existing term banks, much less investigated the extent to which they might be useful. A frequently automatic assumption is that there is little if anything of value to be gained from the effort because of the naiveté of the linguistic knowledge contained. However, blindly acting on this assumption allows one to lose other perspectives — namely, that good term banks are not assembled casually: considerable attention is paid to several principles of their organization (hierarchical subject-area coding, vendor- or product-specific terminology, etc.), and MT workers would benefit from attending to them.

7.3 Controversial questions

One of the most obvious of the controversial questions surrounding MT is the matter of pre-and post-editing requirements. In the US, where ignorance of good translation practice is the rule, the very notion of post-editing a translation is anathema. Human translators are imagined to work without benefit of editing, and thus MT systems are imagined to be acceptable only in an environment devoid of editing. Even if it were not the case that human translations are typically edited, this argument would not hold. What really matters, of course, is whether MT, including any post-editing, is cost effective or justifiable on other grounds, such as speed. Undeniably it is, which accounts for the substantial and growing interest in the technology. MT research efforts are concentrated on improving the speeds of MT systems, while at the same time reducing the amount of post-editing required, in the interest of further improving the cost–benefit ratio.

A related argument concerns pre-editing. Some form of pre-editing texts to be translated by machine is typical, even if confined to marking sentence boundaries or simply excising materials not to be translated (formulas, etc.). In the case of the Japanese commercial systems, such editing is far more involved, consisting of at least manually resolving lexical and structural ambiguities, if not indeed rewriting the text. No one in MT would like to claim that rewriting a text is desirable, but — again — the relevant question concerns the cost–benefit ratio.

On less obviously practical grounds, the notion of an interlingua is controversial. First of all, there is the question of whether one can exist. Certainly none has been identified. Some Japanese systems are claimed to employ an interlingua. However, when one reads their descriptions including, most revealingly, the example-based arguments, it is clear that the Japanese 'interlinguas' are, so far, *ad hoc* rather than theoretical solutions. In some cases this is admitted; in others, the writers seem unaware of the real issues.

The second question related to the use of an interlingua concerns its desirability compared with the alternative (the transfer approach, since history has dealt with questions regarding the direct approach). The lessons of CETA should not be ignored: if an interlingual representation is actully achieved, one loses (by definition) all source-language clues about how to render the translation stylistically — critical information, as any human translator will attest. Finally, there is the matter of practicality: do any benefits of the interlingua approach actually pay for the cost incurred? This question cannot be answered definitively until a true interlingua-based system is available; meanwhile, there is no compelling reason to assume the affirmative.

A related question concerns the necessity for AI-ish techniques (e.g., world models). Whatever the arguments — and there are very good ones — for 'full understanding' being prerequisite to 'high-quality' translation, it remains the case that translators to a considerable extent work by lexical substitution and syntactic rearrangement. That is, translation is not by any means a simple matter of understanding the source text, then reproducing it in the target language — even though many translators (and virtually every layman) believe this is so. On the one hand, there is the serious question of whether, in for example the case of an article on front-line research in semiconductor switching theory, or particle physics, a translator really does fully comprehend the content of the article he is translating. On would suspect not. Johnson (1983) makes a point of claiming that he has produced translations, judged good by informed peers, in technical areas where his expertise is deficient, and his understanding, incomplete. On the other hand, it is also true that translation schools expend considerable effort teaching techniques for low-level lexical and syntactic manipulation — a curious fact to contrast with the usual AI 'full comprehension' claim. In any event, every qualified translator will agree that there is much more to translation than simple analysis + synthesis (an almost *prima facie* proof of the necessity for transfer). World models are not the solution to all translation problems, as some AI proponents would have one believe; the question is whether, and to what extent, they constituted a necessary part of the solution.

Finally, one must consider that even semi-objective MT evaluation and system comparison methods are at best suspect, and at worst nonexistent. Evaluation of translation is, to be sure, inherently subjective. However, there has been virtually no effort on the part of MT workers, commercial or academic, to standardize evaluation techniques, and meaningful comparisons have not been performed. Vendors naturally advance performance figures, including translation accuracy, showing their systems to be the best (at least in some context), but such self-serving claims are not credible. The matter of what might constitute reasonable evaluation criteria, in the context of necessarily subjective judgements about translation quality, is thus very much open to question.

7.4 Unsolved problems

One of the major unsolved problems in MT (indeed, in AI applications more generally) concerns system construction efficiency. Highly-trained experts spend much of their time trying to build these large, complex systems, while their efforts almost certainly could be simplified considerably by the existence and use of good system-building tools. Good general software development tools are just beginning to appear, as it is recognized that human costs — no longer machine costs — are the major contributing factor to system-development expense. Certainly such tools would benefit MT system developers; but equivalent tools for linguists, who are charged with developing large, complex systems of linguistic rules, do not yet exist.

A related problem concerns scale-up bottlenecks. Aside from the system maintenance aspects, discussed above, there are performance aspects. Small systems may appear to function perfectly adequately, in their limited environments; but unless there is some means of predicting behaviour in a scaled-up implementation, trying to develop a fast production version is like shooting in the dark. MT workers could make good use of techniques for predicting future system performance, but none has yet been identified for systems of linguistic rules.

For those involved in applications of current technology, there are linguistic problems related to case roles and semantic markers; specifically, which set to use. There is no standard repertoire. Ultimately the identification of such details becomes a research question, but there is a significant problem relating to the identification of a more-or-less standard collection for interim use, and each project mounts its own effort to select a set.

Finally, there is the problem of world knowledge representation–use. Not only are there no standard representation schemes, but there is no consensus concerning their practical application. Ultimately this boils down to identifying the right questions to ask, before knowing how to search for the answers, so the solution is not soon forthcoming. However, if decent world knowledge representation–use schemes were in hand, there would remain the problem confronting MT developers now: how to integrate such schemes into an MT system, where linguistic knowledge is as important as so-called world knowledge, and is of a very different kind.

REFERENCES

Bar-Hillel, Y. (1971) Some reflections on the present outlook for high-quality machine translation. In W. P. Lehmann and R. Stachowitz (eds.), *Feasibility Study on Fully Automatic High Quality Translation, Final Technical Report RADC-TR-71-295*, Linguistics Research Centre, University of Texas at Austin.

Johnson, R. L. (1983) Parsing — an MT perspective. In K. Sparck. Jones and Y. Wilks (eds.), *Automatic Natural Language Parsing*, Ellis Horwood Ltd., Chichester, West Sussex, England.

Philippi, D. L. (1985) *Japan Intelligence*, Vol. 1, Part 4, Donald L. Philippi, San Francisco.

Piggott, I. M. (1982) The importance of feedback from translators in the development of high-quality machine translation. In V. Lawson (ed.), *Practical Experience of Machine Translation*, North-Holland, Amsterdam, pp. 61–73.

Reifler, E. (1958) The Machine Translation Project at the University of Washington, Seattle. *Proceedings of the 8th International Congress of Linguistics, Oslo.*

Reynolds, A. C. (1954) The Conference on Mechanical Translation. *Machine Translation* **1** (3), 47–55.

Slocum, J. (1982) The LRC machine translation system: an application of state-of-the-art text and natural language processing techniques. *9th ICCL (COLING 82), Prague, Czechoslovakia.*

Slocum, J. (1985) A survey of machine translation: its history, current status, and future prospects. *Computational Linguistics* **11** (1), 1–17.

2

EUROTRA: the machine translation project of the European Communities

B. Maegaard
University of Copenhagen, EUROTRA-DK, Njalsgade 80, DK-2300 Copenhagen S, Denmark

1. INTRODUCTION

The EUROTRA project is the machine translation programme of the European Community. In 1982 it was decided by the Council to implement this programme, but only by late 1984 were the first contracts between the Commission of the European Communities and some countries signed. The goal of the project is to develop a pre-industrial prototype for machine translation between the nine community languages. When the decision on EUROTRA was taken there were only seven languages, but with the accession of Spain and Portugal last year we now have nine languages. The prototype should be ready in 1990.

The Council decision further states that the prototype shall work for a vocabulary of 20 000 lexical entries, for a limited subject-field and for a limited set of text types. The subject-field is not determined by the Council decision; it has been chosen to be information technology (IT). The set of text types has not been fully defined yet; the text types in question will be Commission texts, such as Council decisions, working papers, etc.

Apart from this the Council Decision of 1982 requests that the prototype be extensible: it must be possible to extend the coverage of the vocabulary to other subject fields, to extend to other languages, and to extend to other text types.

The components of the system are being developed by all the Community countries and the project is managed by the Commission in Luxembourg. So, we do not only have the task of building a machine translation system. There are two very important additional factors which have to be taken into account.

First we are faced with a very high degree of decentralization with 12 countries and the Commission, i.e. 13 participants. Furthermore, in some countries the work is further decentralized in that the EUROTRA group is made up of two or more centres. The system design has to take this into account.

Secondly, the programme is *multi*lingual, not bilingual or just comprising a few language pairs. This project is unique in that it comprises 72 language pairs. What this means for the linguistic descriptions is considered later.

2. DESIGN

EUROTRA uses a variant of the transfer model for machine translation, i.e. the translation process is broken down into three modules, analysis, transfer, generation:

$$\text{text} \xrightarrow[\text{analysis}]{} \text{IS} \xrightarrow[\text{transfer}]{} \text{IS}' \xrightarrow[\text{generation}]{} \text{text}'$$

This is generally acknowledged to be a very good scheme for multilingual machine translation, as it restricts the bilingual treatments to the transfer modules: only one analysis module is made for each language, and only one generation module. There will be transfer modules for all language pairs, i.e. 9×8=72 transfer modules in our case. (Of course an even better scheme in an environment which is multilingual to this extent would be a transfer-free, i.e. fully interlingual, approach. For the time being, however, this is not a practical possibility.)

The monolingual components are made in the various countries, Danish in Denmark etc., and the transfer components are made in collaboration between two language groups, with the target group as mainly responsible.

In the EUROTRA framework we have generalized the transfer model

$$\text{text}\rightarrow\text{R1}\rightarrow\text{R2}\rightarrow\ldots\rightarrow\text{Rn} \xrightarrow[\text{transfer}]{} \text{Rn}'\rightarrow\ldots\rightarrow\text{R2}'\rightarrow\text{R1}'\rightarrow\text{text}'$$

The mapping Rn→Rn′ is the original transfer mapping.

We are working with

(1) a base level, which will probably be broken down into more levels of representation, EBL;
(2) a constituent structure level, ECS;
(3) a syntactic relations level, ERS;
(4) a semantic relations level, IS.

Each level of representation is defined by what we call a *generator*, i.e. a grammar and a dictionary. The mapping between levels is performed by a *translator*.

A generator consists of *structure-building rules* and *non-structure building rules*. Structure-building rules are context-free rules operating over objects which are *feature bundles*. The context-free rules not only refer to categories (such as N, NP etc.) but may also mention features in the feature bundles in question. Most of the feature manipulation is done by the non-structure building rules, however.

Here is a short example to show how the generators and translators are supposed to work. The example is made according to a definition of the EUROTRA framework which was used in the spring of 1987.

Let us consider an ECS rule for a noun phase:

Structure-building rule

```
np2 = (np)
      [ ^(detp)
      *(adjp)
      (n, {case=ngen})
      ^(pp)]
```

This ECS rule will build a noun phrase out of an (optional) determiner, zero or more adjective phrases, a noun, and an (optional) prepositional phrase.

The annotations to this structure-building rule contain the following rules:

Non-structure building rules

killer:

```
aknp1 = (np)
        [ ?,*, (n, {def = df}),*]
```

strict:

```
asnp1 = (np)
        [ ^(detp, {gend=G, numb=N, def=D}),
        *(adjp, {gend=G, numb=N, def=D}),
        (n, {gend=G, numb=N, def=D}),
        *]
```

gentle:

```
agnp1 = (np, {gend=G, numb=N, def=D})
        [*,
        (n, {gend=G,m numb=N, def=D}),
        *]
```

These non-structure building rules, or feature rules, work as follows.

The killer rules will delete a structure built by the structure-building rules, if they unify, i.e. the aknp1 rule will delete an np-structure, if the noun of the np is definite. The example here is taken from a Danish grammar. For example, in Danish we may have noun phrases such as

	English translation:
forslag	proposal
forslaget	the proposal
det bedste forslag	the best proposal

The strict rules, like killer rules, can delete structures that have been built. Strict rules are typically used to check agreement: the structure will be deleted if the components do not obey the rules expressed by the strict grammar rule. In the actual case of a Danish noun phrase, agreement is required between the (optional) determiner, the (optional) adjective(s), and the noun.

Finally, the gentle rules are used for percolation etc. They do not delete anything; they only add information. In the actual case of the Danish agnp1 rule, it percolates the values of gender, number and definiteness from the noun to the resulting noun phrase.

At ERS level the corresponding rule could be

```
np3 = (–, {cat=np}
      [(gov, {cat=n})
      (^ mod, {cat=detp})
      (*mod, {cat = adjp})
      (^ mod, {cat = pp})]
```

A t-rule which translates an ECS structure built by the np2 rule into the corresponding structure at the ERS level could then be

```
tnp10 = (np)
        [$B(^ detp),$C(*adjp),
         $D(n),$E(^ pp)]
         –> np3($D,$B,$C,$E)
```

In this scheme all nodes have to be translated explicitly, and furthermore it ia already decided by the t-rule what structure-building rule to apply at the next level (np3 in the above case).

We see this as a problem when we get to bigger systems and more complicated structures. Therefore a proposal has been made for a slightly modified system where the t-component becomes a little weaker, and in particular where the generator has more power.

Basic ideas about *generators* and *translators* are now considered. Generators are context-free rules with annotations, as described above. Translators are (1) one-shot and (2) compositional.

That translators are 'one-shot' means that they map from one level of description directly to the next level of description, i.e. there can be no intermediate representation (such a representation could not be checked for wellformedness).

The basic objective of 'compositionality' is that the overall image of sentence, on translation, can be obtained from the images of its parts.

Now, if translators were totally compositional, they would be homographies in the mathematical sense, and t-rules such as the one above, which manipulates the order of constituents, would not be allowed. Consequently we are using a relaxed version of compositionality, where it is possible to change precedence between sister nodes, to change dominance, to delete nodes, and to insert nodes.

In the course of spring 1987, work on a slightly different version of the same ideas has been going on. It has resulted in a new prototype which will be used for implementation at least until the end of the second phase of the project.

The main difference of the new approach is exactly that the nature of the translators is changed: as we can see in the earlier framework, the t-rule determined the structure to be built at the next level. In the new framework this is not the case; the t-rules will in general be weaker than before, whereas the generators will have more expressive power than before. This is a sound principle as it makes the generators more autonomous, and makes the implementations more easily modularizable.

The main principle is that translators deliver as input to the next level a set of nodes, with 'soft' precedence and dominance relations between the nodes. What can be done to this 'softly structured' object by the generator, apart from just consolidating the structure, is that nodes can be inserted both in the horizontal and the vertical dimension. Thus, for example, if

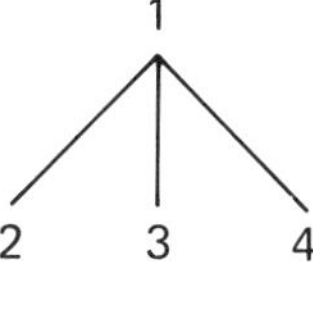

Fig. 1.

is the input from the previous level, then the shape of the object may be one of the following after application of the generator:

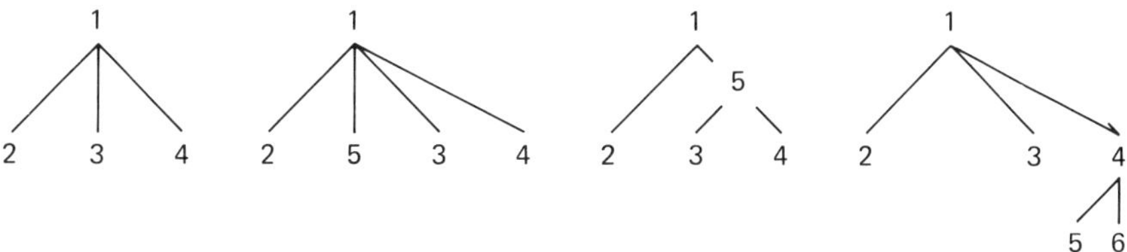

Fig. 2.

3. THE DEFINITION OF THE LEVELS

The interface structure which is the common exchange format has to be totally defined, and all language groups have to use the same definition.

For the other levels, however, this is not necessarily the case. The closer we get to surface text, e.g., the more divergent the descriptions may be. We do try to have a reasonably well-defined set of representations or set of ideas of representations that is used for all languages. This is an advantage for the communication between groups, but it is in a way not a necessary condition; only a common definition of the interface structure is necessary. Having common ideas about the lower levels as well provides a common basis of understanding for the various language groups, however, and we should therefore allow only for as much freedom as is necessary for handling the various languages adequately.

Here is a brief example of a translation of a simple sentence from Danish ECS to German IS. As can be seen (Fig. 3) the ECS structure reflects the surface word order. The Danish input sentence is 'I 1982 blev alle forslagene vedtaget af Komissionen'. At ECS the constituents are built.

At ERS level the surface order is abolished: ERS and IS both have a fixed order of constituents. At ERS the surface syntactic relations are determined (Fig. 4).

Then finally at IS level (Figs. 5 and 6), the case roles of the various constituents are determined. Surface phenomena such as argument-bound prepositions, determiners, etc., disappear structurally at the IS level — they are expressed by other means.

The case-role system which is used is very simple. It is complicated to define case roles (like ARG1, ARG2, ...) in a way that accounts for all languages; this is why for the time being we are using this very simple set of roles, which can then be supplemented by lexical semantic features. As can be seen from Fig. 6 the German IS is very similar to the Danish IS. The translation process continues from German IS to German ERS, ECS and text. (This is not shown in the figures.)

4. MORE COMMENTS ON THE IS LEVEL

For the distinction between ambiguous words, lexical features of the semantic kind are needed. For example, we require features of the type human–non-human, concrete–abstract, and all the subject-field features known from ordinary dictionaries, such as zoological, medical, etc. Here we should remember, however, that for the time being the project is working within the subject-field of information technology and distinctions involving other subject-fields, too far away, are not taken into account.

Consequently what is taken into account are word-senses that fall within the subject-field of IT and neighbouring fields, as well as the general senses. Neighbouring fields in Community terms are administration, economy, legal aspects, ...

In order to make transfer simple we disambiguate monolingually as much as is reasonable. What is reasonable can be seen from the distinguishing features. If a lexical unit can be distinguished by e.g. frame, it splits according to the semantic features of one of its constituents etc. There are words, however, that do not lend themselves in a reasonable way to a monolingual disambiguation. There are three possibilities:

(1) The disambiguation is done in transfer, i.e. with access to the two languages involved.
(2) The disambiguation is done in generation, by the target language generator and dictionary.
(3) This will be done in the eventual analysis, and will be decided in negotiation between the two language groups.

It should be stressed that the monolingual solution, i.e. either analysis or

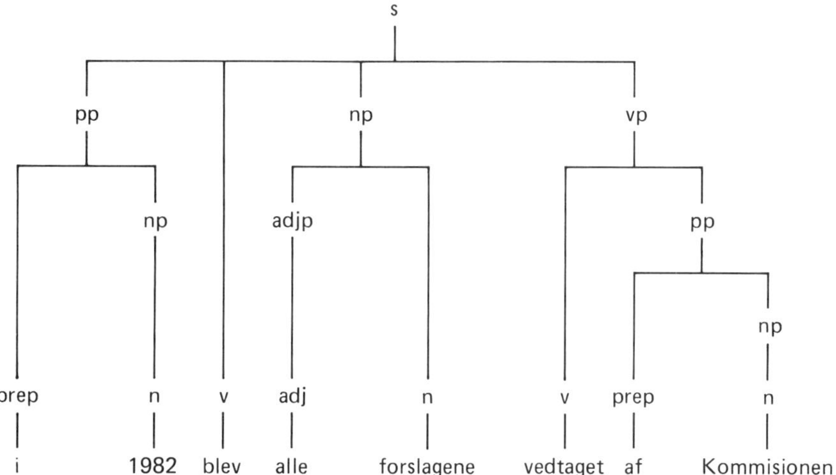

Fig. 3.

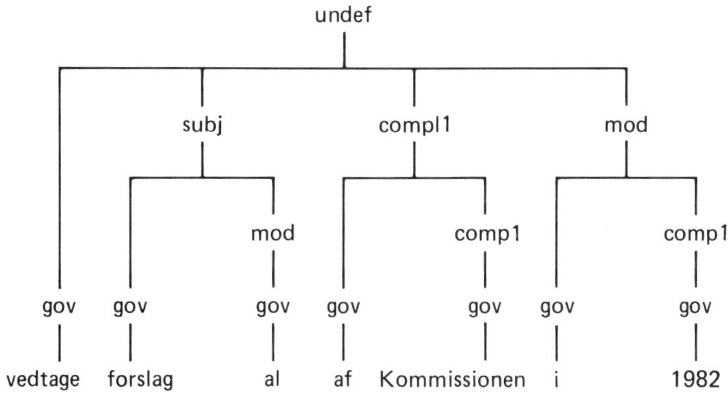

Fig. 4.

generation, is preferable, because the transfer component should be kept as simple as possible.

One of the problems in the lexical transfer is in fact what a lexical unit is: what is the unit which we want to translate and consequently which we want to list in our dictionaries?

Here the opinions in EUROTRA are quite divergent: some people would like to do the translation in the most elegant way, that in our case would be to split everything into small units which could be translated by simple transfer and then recombined by the target-language grammar in a

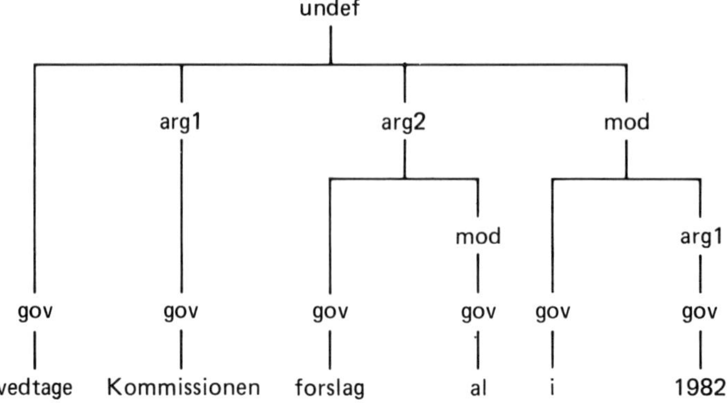

Fig. 5.

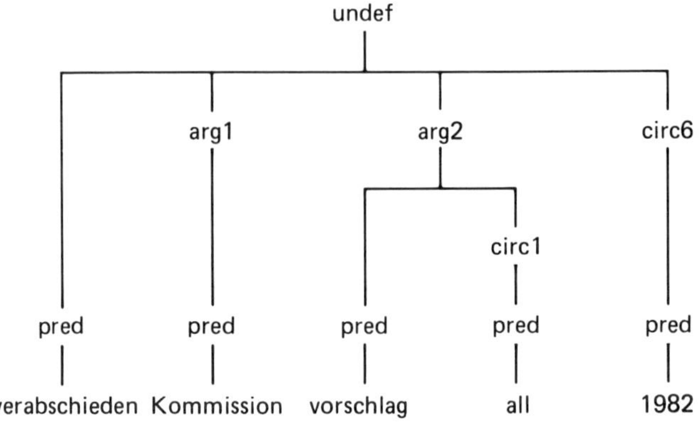

Fig. 6.

correct way. This is possible only with an interface structure which has a very high degree of interlinguality.

Consequently other Eurotrians find that the safest approach is to put bigger parts of the text into the dictionary, e.g. derivations and compounds, in so far as they are 'lexicalized' and are of course idiomatic expressions and terms. In fact nobody argues about the idioms and the terms, but it is not so easy to see when a compound is lexicalized.

For the time being we are not splitting derivations and compounds into their parts; in the future, if a good method comes up, we may do it.

One of the reasons why compounds come up as a problem is of course that Danish, German and Dutch have a compounding mechanism whereby words are glued together to form one single string. However, this is not the heart of the problem; the problem is the 'context-sensitive' translation and how to handle it. Take as an example (Danish–French).

handelsoverskud	excédent commercial
handelsminister	ministre du commerce

5. THE STATUS OF THE PROJECT, SUMMER 1987

The Council Decision of 1982 divides the project period into three phases. The first phase is preparatory; the goal of the second phase is to develop the theory of translation and to implement it in a small machine-translation system which covers all languages with a vocabulary of 2500 lexical entries. The second phase finishes in July 1988. The goal of the third phase is to extend the small system of the second phase and to cover a vocabulary of 20 000 lexical entries.

In February 1987 the first small-scale translation system was finished. It had a vocabulary of 500 words, grammars only for simple sentences, and it worked for translation between German, English and Danish. Since then the coverage has been extended, in terms of language pairs, in terms of vocabulary and in terms of grammar, and we believe that at least for the languages which were part of the programme from the beginning good results can be obtained by July 1988 — special programmes have been initiated for the Spanish and Portuguese languages, as these became part of the project only recently.

EDITORS' NOTE

We have included this survey in the current volume because of the potential interest of the EUROTRA project for natural-language specialists in AI. The scope of the project, especially with respect to the large number of language pairs involved, suggests that there will be many specific problems that can be attacked usefully by AI methods when the more conventional methods used in traditional automatic translations are not sufficient. The chapter serves partly to indicate what the present EUROTRA approach is, but mainly to spread information about the existence of EUROTRA and its goals more widely among the AI community.

3

Current projects at GETA on or about machine translation

Ch. Boitet
GETA, BP 68, Université de Grenoble et CNRS, 38402 Saint-Martin-d'Hères, France

SUMMARY

Research and development projects at GETA all concern machine (aided) translation. The majority of projects are concentrating on improving lingware and software techniques for producing quality translations without an explicit representation of the domain of discourse, and on building small to large running systems. New ideas are introduced to improve the now classical transfer approach, new languages are added, parts of modern linguistic theories are incorporated in the grammars, and better software environments for the rule-based specialized languages are constructed.

Systems of the previous kind are dynamic (computational) in nature. At GETA, some other projects also address the static representation of both grammatical and lexical knowledge. A concrete goal is to build a linguistic workstation usable by linguists, lexicographers and end users. Parts of it have already been prototyped.

Finally, several projects concern new types of MT systems, of the second, third and fourth generations.

1. INTRODUCTION

The Groupe d'Etudes pour la Traduction Automatique (GETA), led by B. Vauquois, has been studying the problem of automation of the translation process since 1972, pursuing the work done by CETA since 1962. In the course of this long period, it has developed complete and integrated machine translation systems. However, the design principles of such systems have evolved. In particular, current 'second-generation systems' are a far cry from those of the 1960s.

These experiments have been the foundation of the French M(A)T National Project. By M(A)T, we mean 'machine (aided) translation', thus stressing the fact that these techniques centre around the automation of the production of 'good enough' rough translations, rather than around machine aids for translation, although they are present in an integrated environment.

In the first part, we begin with a short presentation of the current principles and technology of second-generation M(A)T systems, such as those implemented at Grenoble. In the following three parts, we present the different kinds of research and development projects pursued by GETA, following the order presented in the summary.

2. TYPES OF MT SYSTEMS AND THE APPROACH OF GETA

2.1 What to automate?

M(A)T systems are a subset of the computer-aided translation (CAT) systems. Although it may be very interesting to investigate the subtleties involved in the translation of a set of test sentences, and how to emulate them by machine, it is even more promising to attack the real problem of automating (totally or partially) the translation of documents.

Hence, the researchers at GETA have constantly looked for techniques which might lead to a practical implementation of large-scale systems, usable in an operational setting, while at the same time looking into theoretical issues in MT and computational linguistics in general. Good M(A)T systems should offer functional aids in a working translation environment.

2.1.1 Main functions of a translation process

There are four main successive phases in the processing of a document in a translation environment:

— acquisition or creation of the document;
— rough translation, possibly done in parallel by several translators;
— revision, sometimes done in several passes. For technical documents, a technical revision by a (possibly monolingual) specialist in the field is often required;
— output of the final document, including figures, charts, etc.

(i) *Creation–acquisition: free or controlled*

A document may be created in a translation environment (as in the EC), or sent to it in its final form. As soon as some automation is envisaged, machine aids are in current use for putting the document in machine-readable form (text-processing systems, possibly coupled with OCRs).

Strictly speaking, the creation of a document is not a function of the translation process. However, if this creation could be linguistically controlled by some linguistic process, automation of the rough translation would become a lot easier.

The TITUS (Ducrot, 1982) system illustrates this point. However, this kind of system, using a 'controlled' language, neither lexically nor grammatically ambiguous, is now restricted to very specialized domains, and severe constraints are placed on the authors. As we shall see later, one of the most exciting lines of research is to generalize this approach to (good approximations of) really 'natural' languages, with their inherent ambiguity.

(ii) *Rough translation: automated or manual*
M(A)T techniques centre around the total or partial automation of the rough translation process. Two main approaches have been tried. In the first ('pure MT'), translation is done by a program, in batch or interactive mode. GETA, TAUM, SFB-100, METAL all follow the batch line. BYU (ITS), ALPS and WEIDNER have tried the interactive approach ('human-aided MT', or HAMT). As with usual human translation, there must be some (human) revision.

The second approach is generally called machine-aided human translation (MAHT). Here, emphasis is on the automation of the translator's office, with specialized text processing systems, fast access to on-line terminological data banks, spelling checkers, etc.

Within the M(A)T approach, two strategies are possible. First, one can try to **define** some subset of a given natural language as a formal language. Then, an analyser is built. If a given unit of translation is 'legal', it will be translated. If not, it will be rejected. Hence, the automatic system is a 'partial system', because it translates only $N\%$ of the input. TAUM-METEO, or the first CETA systems (before 1970) are good examples of this strategy.

The second strategy, followed in all current GETA systems, is to build a 'total system', which will always attempt to translate 100% of the input, even if it is partially ill-formed with regard to the implemented linguistic model.

(iii) *Revision: human only*
The revision of a document is usually done with the help of full-screen text processing systems, sometimes with the possibility of accessing a terminology file on-line (IBM's DTAF, WEIDNER, ALPS, TAUM).

However, the automation of the revision function itself has not yet been attempted. It seems that the level of understanding and of general knowledge required to perform even a 'linguistic' revision is higher than the one required for translation. This is even more true in the case of 'technical' revision.

2.1.2 Integrated systems
There are two other functions which should be automated in a modern CAT environment. First, the management of a large database of documents, together with a record of the actions performed on them (modifications, translations, revisions, etc.). In other words, a translation environment should interface nicely with a textual database system.

Second, in the case of M(A)T, creation, debugging, maintenance and evolution of the 'linguistic software', abbreviated here as 'lingware' ('linguiciel'), require a 'programming environment', that is, a specialized database centred around one or several programming languages. In our case, these programming languages are specialized languages for linguistic programming (SLLPs).

At GETA, we have developed such an integrated programming system, called ARIANE-78. Only the batch approach has been implemented for the rough translation phase. However, the system also supports a subenvironment for MAHT (THAM in French), used for the revision of the rough machine translations as well as for purely human translation (and revision).

2.2 Linguistic principles

2.2.1 Multilingualism and transfer approach

Contrary to general practice, the translation systems developed at GETA have been designed to be multilingual. The 'hybrid' interlingua approach previously used by CETA has been replaced by the 'transfer' approach. This means that translation must be composed of three logical steps:

— monolingual analysis;
— bilingual transfer;
— monolingual synthesis (also called 'generation').

Thus, a given analyser may be used to translate from one 'source language' into several 'target languages', and the same synthesizer ('generator') may be used to translate from several source languages into the same target language. The same division is used in modern 'multitarget' compilers for programming languages.

2.2.2 'Implicit' versus 'explicit' understanding

Everybody agrees that a very good translation requires a very deep understanding of the text. However, this is not achieved, even by good human translators, in particular in technical fields, or there would be no need for revision in the first place!

Hence, the objective of M(A)T systems may rather be set to produce **good enough 'raw' translations**, that is, translations which may be revised with less than twice the effort needed to revise an average human translation of the corresponding text, and whose (subjective) quality makes them acceptable to revisors in the first place. This goal is already met by state of the art systems, tuned to a given typology and a given domain.

By using such expressions as 'very good', 'good enough', or 'medium', we implicitly suppose the existence of some 'hierarchy' of understanding. In actual fact, understanding cannot be defined in an absolute way, but only with reference to some domain.

As we see it, the hierarchy of understanding is organized around a hierarchy of **levels of interpretation**. We distinguish between **linguistic levels** and **extralinguistic levels**.

2.2.2.1 Linguistic levels

(1) **morphology**: this is the level of the analysis of words or idioms in terms of morphemes, lexical units, potentialities of derivation, semantic features, valencies, etc.

(2) **syntax-1**: at this level, syntactic classes, such as noun, verb, etc., are associated with words, and **syntagmatic classes**, such as nominal phrase or verbal phrase, with groups of words. This gives a 'bracketing' of the text (or several in the case of ambiguity), often represented as a tree giving the 'constitutent structure'.

(3) **syntax-2**: this is the level of representation in terms of **syntactic functions**, such as subject, object, attribute, or (equivalently) of **dependency relations**.

(4) **logico-semantics-1**: at this level, the logical relations between parts of the text are identified. They are sometimes also called **inner cases**. In the GETA systems, they are usually named ARG0 (logical subject, or 'argument 0'), ARG1 (logical object), etc.

(5) **logico-semantics-2**: the **semantic relations**, such as consequence, cause, concession, measure, localization, etc., are essential to translate correctly the 'circumstants', as opposed to the 'arguments' of a predicate. On circumstantials, semantic relations are also sometimes called **outer cases**.

Of course, they may also be attached to the arguments (for example, a logical object may be interpreted as a patient). However, they are less indispensable (for translation), because the semantic relations of the arguments of a predicate are often very difficult to compute, and because, even if they are computed, a good translation may often be obtained simply by using directly the lexical unit of the predicate, plus restrictions on the (semantic features of the) arguments.

This list of levels is not exhaustive. The implemented lingwares also use the representation of a sentence's **actualization features** (surface tense or abstract time, aspect, modality, determination), type of statement (declarative, interrogative, exclamative, imperative, negative) or emphasis (theme–theme, intensification), etc. However, we consider that all of them are relative to a knowledge encoded in a formal system of a linguistic nature.

Hence, we characterize this type of understanding (at any one or all of the preceding levels) as **implicit understanding**. Systems relying only on this type of knowledge are of the second (and also first) generation.

2.2.2.2 Extra-linguistic levels

(1) **expertise**: here, we refer to some static knowledge about a particular subject matter, consisting in a collection of facts, rules and procedures. This level has also been called 'static semantics', in contrast to the '**feature semantics**', incorporated in the lingusistic knowledge, and to the '*dynamic semantics*', which is discussed below. MT systems using such an expertise of the domain have been strongly advocated, notably by the Yale school (Schank and coworkers), but no translating systems of this kind have yet been constructed. They would constitute the third generation (see below for further comments).

(2) **pragmatics**: this level is taken to be the highest level of understanding. Pragmatically understanding a document means creating a represetation of the facts, events, suppositions, scenarios, etc., described by the

text. This presupposes the ability to learn facts and structures, to reason by analogy, and to abstract. In short, pragmatics is related to the most ambitious themes of AI.

Until now, only very small illustrative computer models have been presented. Interacting intelligently with the author of a document might be a good way to enter this presently imaginary world of near-perfect fourth-generation MT (see below).

Understanding at some extralinguistic level may be called **explicit understanding**. Typical applications where it is needed include expert systems, which should be able to explain their actions.

However, **for translation purposes**, implicit understanding is often sufficient. An experimental proof of that is given by the daily practice of human translators. Of course, **at the level of a technical revisor**, explicit understanding is required.

2.2.3 'Multilevel' descriptors and fail-soft strategies

Second-generation M(A)T systems rely only on the 'linguistic' levels of understanding. In the past, and still in some current systems, these levels are mutually exclusive. By this, we mean that a given unit of translation (sentence, paragraph, or text) will have separate representations for each of the defined levels. This usually leads to a sequential strategy of processing, with all its drawbacks.

During analysis, for example, it is often difficult to compute the semantic relations for all parts of the unit of translation, especially if the size of this unit is large (one or several paragraphs). In the sequential approach, one is then forced to refuse the unit, or else to translate the complete unit at the previous level.

This is why GETA uses **multilevel interface structures** to represent all the structures computed levels on the same graph (a 'decorated tree'). Detailed examples of this kind of structure have been given elsewhere (e.g. Guilbaud, 1984).

In short, such structures are in effect **generators** of representations at different levels, and also factorize various types of ambiguities.

Incidentally, this type of structure was first proposed by B. Vauquois in 1974, during sessions of the Leibniz group, which led to the launching of the EUROTRA project by the EEC. Since then, it has been refined and tested, on a variety of applications, including Russian–French, Portuguese–English, English–Malay, English–French, English–Chinese, English–Japanese, French–English and German–French.

2.2.4 Necessary specialization to 'sublanguages'

In translation, by human or by machine, specialization is indispensable in order to obtain good quality. A literary translator is usually at a loss to translate a computer manual. This specialization follows two lines: first, specialization to a certain **typology** of texts, and second to a certain **domain**.

As humans, M(A)T systems rely on a core of knowledge, plus knowledge specific to the application. As a first approximation, we may say that grammars incorporate the typological specialization, and dictionaries the domain specialization. This is why modularity is essential in the construction of M(A)T systems. The same core should be the base of several versions, tailored to different **sublanguages**.

One might argue that specialization to a certain sublanguage amounts in fact to the incorporation of some extralinguistic knowledge in a M(A)T system. However, the **form** of this knowledge is not what is required in order to qualify as expertise, because it is expressed by some **combinatorics of classes** ('combinatoire de classes', to translate one B. Vauquois' favourite expressions). Rather, we may say that, as in Plato's cave, the real world is 'reflected' in the structure of texts and in their peculiarities. In particular, 'in-house' writing habits correspond to some sociological conditions governing document creation.

2.3 Implementation principles

Let us now give a brief introduction to the main principles that have guided the implementation of M(A)T systems at Grenoble.

2.3.1 Use of SLLPs

In principle, there are many ways to implement lexical and grammatical knowledge. In SYSTRAN and other first-generation systems, the assembler or macro assembler level is used.

In 'first and half' generation systems, the implementation language may be some high-level programming language, such as FORTRAN (SUSY I), COBOL (Saskatoon system), PL/I (ITS), COMSKEE (SUSY II), etc. The drawbacks are evident. In particular, either linguists are burdened with ancillary tasks, such as implementing data and control structures, or they require the help of some 'slave' computer scientists to translate their wishes into working programs, with the result that their desires, incorrectly formulated, are also incorrectly translated.

Nowadays, certain groups are trying to use (also directly) very high-level general programming languages, such as SETL (Novosibirsk), LISP (NTT) or Prolog. Not enough experience has yet been gained to say whether the above criticism on the use of general-purpose algorithmic languages applies or not at this level.

In second-generation systems, and in projected third-generation systems, emphasis is placed on the use of SLLPs, which offer built-in data and control structures, with an underlying powerful mechanism.

This is the case in all 'rule systems', based on (extended) CF-grammars (CETA (Vauquois, 1975), METAL (Chauche, 1974), SFB99, ETL-Lingol), adjunction grammars (LSP,LADL), Q-systems (TAUM), ATNs (BBN (Woods, 1970), TAUM), (extended non-deterministic) finite-state transducer (GETA-ATEF), tree-transducers (Friedman, Petrick, GETA-ROBRA, SFB99-TRANSFO). The built-in data structures are usually particular classes of graphs or hypergraphs, such as decorated trees, Q-graphs, 'charts' (MIND), etc.

Choosing one or more implementation languages for SLLP is another matter. The highest and most efficient level should be selected. There is an inherent conflict in this dual goal. Hence, compromises are made, sometimes by using several implementation languages. For example, ARIANE-78 is implemented in ASM360 (macro assembler) and PL360 for the compilers and interpreters of the SLLPs, Pascal and EXEC2–XEDIT for the other tools, the management of the data-base and the interactive interface ('monitor').

2.3.2 Balance between combinatorial and heuristic methods

As in other fields of AI, the declarative and procedural approaches are in competition. The declarative approach leads to rule systems with an underlying 'combinatorial' algorithm, which produces a set or a subset of 'solutions' in some fixed way. It is best exemplified by analysers built on (extended) CF-grammars, or by Q-systems. The main advantage is the relative ease of programming. However, it is almost impossible to implement powerful heuristics, because, in essence, there is no way to control explicitly the computations of several possibly interdependent solutions.

The procedural approach has been followed in the more recent second-generation systems ('second and a half'?). For example, the TAUM-Aviation system uses REZO, a Q-graph transducer based on the ATN model. In ARIANE-78, ATEF and ROBRA give even more possibilities of heuristic programming. This added power, however, requires more programming skill.

2.3.3 User-oriented programming environment

SLLPs are designed to be easy to use by linguists and terminologists who have almost no computer science background. Hence, they must be integrated in some 'user-friendly' environment.

In ARIANE-78, this environment is implemented on any user space (a VM/CMS 'virtual machine') as a specialized database of lingware files (grammars, dictionaries, procedures, formats, variables) and of corpuses of texts (source, translated, revised, plus intermediate results and possibly 'hors-textes' — figures, etc.). A conversational monitor interfaces the database with the users (in French or in English).

Subenvironments are defined to permit the preparation, testing, debugging and maintenance of the lingware, to manipulate the texts, to check the spelling of a list of corpuses (or of individual texts), to produce mass translations, and to revise the translations. The database system ensures the coherence and integrity of all the applications and texts in a given user space (since the system is multilingual, it is perfectly possible to have several translation systems in the same user space, sharing one or several analysers or generators).

It is interesting to note that the needs of linguists led to the creation of such a 'programming system' before this type of system became a main theme of research and development in software engineering.

A parallel can be made between this sort of CAT system and compiler-

compiler systems for programming languages. The various SLLPs are in effect tools used to build morphological analysers, structural analysers, transfers and generators.

ATEF, for instance, may be compared with LEX, used to write lexical analysers for programming languages. Of course, the richness of the information contained in each word, and the inherent ambiguity of language, make such a tool more complex: it is necessary to handle large dictionaries (as opposed to small sets of reserved words and of identifiers with no *a priori* content) and to offer advanced control structures, such as non-deterministic programming with or without heuristic functions.

3. DEVELOPMENT OF (CLASSICAL) MT SYSTEMS

The ideas exposed above have been and are tested in a variety of MT systems, developed as laboratory experiments, in the framework of various academic cooperations, or for industrial purposes, in the context of the French M(A)T National Project (MAT-NP). The experience gained has also triggered an interesting new idea concerning a way to reduce the apparently inherent quadratic cost of transfer-based multilingual MT systems.

These linguistic developments are accompanied by parallel work on the basic software, which is in constant evolution.

3.1 Experiments with MT systems

3.1.1 MT systems developed as laboratory experiments

3.1.1.1 Types and aims of such systems

MT systems are developed in the laboratory for four main reasons.

(1) To validate the linguistic methodology for multilingual systems by attacking various languages, preferably pertaining to different groups or families. This is why we started long ago with Russian–French, and are now working on French–Chinese.

(2) For training and testing purposes. This is or was the case for Portuguese–English (POR–ENG), French–English and English–French 'for the example' (BEX–FEX and FEX–BEX), English to Chinese and Japanese (IN1–HAN, JAP), Chinese into five other languages (HAN–ENG, FRA, GER, RUS, JAP), and now French–Russian.

(3) To prepare further large-scale development, by developing methods and tools for lingware engineering, and making real experiments. This has been the case for Russian–French since 1982.

(4) To support linguistic research on some language(s) or pair(s) of languages (e.g., German–French, English–Arabic).

Let us give some more details on the two most developed systems.

3.1.1.2 Russian–French: a real-size operational prototype

This system is being constantly developed, improved, and used on real texts, in the framework of an operational translation unit (since April 1982). An immediate project is to evaluate it in cooperation with an independent research institute.

The various dictionaries contain some 7500 lexical units in Russian and 5000 in French, which amounts to roughly 30 000 terms in usual dictionaries (remember that a lexical unit is a family of 'lemmas', which may correspond to simple or complex terms), because of the richness of the derivational systems used for the two languages.

The grammars cover a (perhaps too) wide range of typologies, ranging from titles and technical abstracts to scientific articles. Technical abstracts are by far the most difficult, owing to the poor quality of writing, the length of sentences, the abundance of apocopes (e.g. 'the abund. of apoc.'), and the presence of figures and mathematical formulae.

As the texts do not come on magnetic media, it is necessary to type or read them in. In 18 months (April 1984–October 1986), around 200 000 running words, or 1.5 million characters, were inputted in the textual database, half of them using an OCR (in cooperation with the Paris-based CERTAL research group).

In one month (September 1986), around 835 abstracts and texts, or 97 000 running words, were translated or retranslated on a shared minicomputer (IBM 4331–2 with 4Mb under VM/CMS), to present a set of coherent results in the final report of a contract with the Ministry of Defence.

This system is also used as support for contrastive studies by its main author, N. Nedobejkine.

Some examples of machine translations with manual on-screen revisions are given in the appendix. In the first, long example, some words appear between brackets, e.g. ⟨"m_AMX-30⟩. This is because their lexical unit was not in the Russian dictionaries. However, in most cases, the morphological sub-grammar for unknown words has analysed them correctly. Here, the special prefix "m_introduces a trademark, hence, an inanimate proper noun.

The second, shorter example, exemplifies the improvement obtained by modifying the lingware. Here, three or four dictionary items have been corrected in transfer and generation. For example, 'introduction dans' is replaced in the second translation by 'introduction à', and 'golografia', having been indexed, is no longer decomposed in 'golo-' (nude) and 'grafia' (graphy), and is correctly translated as 'holography'.

The virtual CPU time used for translating one word is about 1.4 Mipw (million operations per word). In terms of elapsed time on a shared 4331–2 (4 Mb, 0.4 Mips), it amounts to 15 min per page of 250 words, or $3.50 if taking all computer-related costs in consideration. On-screen revision of the long example (TANK2) has taken less than 15 min, including terminological discussion, and using the standard ARIANE-78 REVISION subenvironment (XEDIT in two or three-windows configuration, with some useful macros associated with certain keys).

3.1.1.3 German–French: a feasibility study supporting linguistic research

This system uses the same generation of French as the former one. The German side (analysis and transfer) is still a prototype, covering a restricted typology and based on a small lexicon (around 2000 lexical units, or 4000 terms for German).

A particular feature is its development by two independent researchers, one in Paris (G. Stahl) and the other in Grenoble (J. Ph. Guilbaud). The first author has developed the structural analysis, and the second the morphological analysis and the transfer.

No large-scale development is planned for the moment. Rather, J. Ph. Guilbaud is now using this system as support of a study on the possibility of integrating some results of the linguistic research pursued by J. M. Zemb (Collège de France, Paris), mainly on the contrastive French–German grammar, but also on the fundamental notions underlying the grammatical descriptions.

3.1.2 MT systems developed in academic cooperation

3.1.2.1 Aims of such systems

B. Vauquois has always sought international cooperation, in order to confront different points of view on natural language processing, and to try them experimentally, MT being perhaps the best benchmark.

In the 1960s, permanent contacts were established with scholars from the USA, the USSR, Japan, Czechoslovakia, and almost all West-European countries. Long stays by Czech and Japanese colleagues strengthened those links, but no common systems, or even mockups, were built.

In the 1970s, GETA developed a truly language- and theory-independent software environment for building multilingual MT systems, ARIANE-78. This tool (or its preceding versions) supported the development of a series of experiments, all done in cooperation with foreign colleagues: several analyses of French (J. Weissenborn and E. Stegentritt, Saarbrücken), an analysis of Portuguese with a mockup transfer and generation into English (P. Daun Fraga, Campinas), a structural analysis of Japanese (R. Shimamori), and prototypes from or into Chinese (Feng Zhi Wei, Yang Ping, Beijing).

From 1979 onwards, a long-term cooperation was started with Malaysia and Thailand, producing two prototypes sharing the same analysis (English–Malay and English-Thai). We give more details about these systems below.

3.1.2.2 English–Malay

This effort started in 1979, after a visit of Professor B. Vauquois to Malaysia, at the initiative of Professor Tan Wang Seng (USM, Penang). The outline of the project was defined and some common understanding on the methodology was reached during a one-month stay of Professor Tong Loong Cheong and Dr Chang May See. The ARIANE-78 system was installed at USM.

In 1980, B. Vauquois, P. Daun Fraga and Ch. Boitet stayed at USM for two months. Starting only from previous desk research (specifications), B. Vauquois, P. Daun Fraga and our two Malaysian colleagues produced a working English–Malay prototype in 6 or 7 weeks, while the author was busy producing an English version of ARIANE-78. At the end of August, an international seminar convened at USM, and the prototype was used extensively for demonstrations and experiments.

Since then, the group at USM has grown and become permanent. By the end of 1985, the English–Malay system had reached the stage of laboratory prototype. It was systematically evaluated, with a resulting acceptability rate of 76% (Tong, 1986). The stage of operational prototype should be reached at the end of 1988s. The system aiming mostly at translating computer-related technical material.

3.1.2.3 English–Thai

Initiated during the 1980 USM seminar, this cooperation started effectively in 1981. Several Thai universities participate in this effort (Rakhamhaeng, Chulalongkorn, Prince of Songkhla, etc.). The stage of laboratory prototype should be attained at the end of 1987.

Of course, the peculiarities of the Thai writing system have been a challenge. However, the computer scientists from Chulalongkorn have connected the ARIANE-78 system to special I/O (input/output) devices, so that translations can be produced in Thai characters.

3.1.3 MT systems developed for industrial purposes

3.1.3.1 The French MAT-NP (National Project)

The French Machine (Aided) Translation National Project (MAT-NP) started in November 1983, and ended in February 1987. Financing of the project was 50% public and 50% private. Public financing and control was centralized by ADI (Agence de l'Informatique), while the private firm SG2 and its subcontractors (including the SONOVISION and B'VITAL firms) invested the rest and built the system. The first official presentation of CALLIOPE-AERO was made at EXPOLANGUES (Paris) in February 1986.

For the first development, it has been decided to build a French–English system tailored to aviation manuals of the kind produced by SONOVISION, which are in machine-readable form, and for which the appropriate terminology exists in both languages.

After EXPOLANGUES, it has been decided to begin the development of CALLIOPE-INFO (English to French for computer-related material), which was until then only an option of the project. A first version was obtained at the end of the MAT-NP, and should be expanded, if adequate funding can be found. The first translations were produced in February 1987.

The core of the architecture of the lingware and the software comes from previous work done at GETA, but new tools and techniques have been added. The use of SCSGs is quite notable.

Use of SCSGs for static specification of dynamic grammars
B. Vauquois and S. Chappuy developed a formal model '**static grammars**' (Chappuy, 1983; Vauquois and Chappuy, 1985) before the start of the MAT-NP.

A SCSG (structural correspondence static grammar) describes the correspondence between the strings of a natural language and the corresponding interface structures. Such a description is neutral with respect to analysis and generation, and does not express any particular strategy for computing the correspondence.

During the first phase of the MAT-NP, from November 1983 until November 1984, only SCSGs of French and English were developed, and no procedural grammars. Special care was taken to describe a reasonable core grammar and to study in detail the particularities of the considered typology. As for any sublanguage, it offered grammatical constructions which would be judged ungrammatical in other contexts.

These SCSGs have been used later as reference and documentation while writing the very large dynamic grammars.

3.1.3.2 CALLIOPE-AERO (French–English)

The size of grammars and dictionaries is obviously heavily dependent on the considered application. In the case of CALLIOPE-AERO, the typology of the manuals includes almost all normal syntactic constructions, with the exception of interrogative clauses, relative clauses introduced by 'dont' and imperative forms of verbs (replaced by the infinitive form), and a lot of special phenomena.

As far as the lexicon is concerned, a preliminary study of the corpus had led to the estimation that 6000 general terms and 15 000 terminological terms would be necessary for the system to be usable.

The dictionaries comprise now around 8000 lexical units in the running system (more in the lexical database), or about 12 000 terms, in both languages. Counting the source lines (written in ATEF for morphological analysis, TRANSF for lexical transfer and SYGMOR for morphological generation), we arrive at a total of about 55 000 lines.

As far as the grammars are concerned, there are about 175 rules for morphological analysis (AM), 600 for structural analysis (AS), 90 for structural transfer (TS), 200 for syntactic generation (GS), and 20 for morphological generation (GM). In terms of source lines, we find, for the grammatical part of the same phases, a total of around 4500 (AM), 18 000 (AS) 2300 (TS), 5600 (GS) and 470 (GM).

If we compare this with the size of a compiler for some programming language, written in metalanguages such as LEX and YACC, we see that the lingware engineering effort required to create and maintain such an MT system exceeds by far what is required for a compiler. This is made even worse by the fact that natural language is not fixed by decree, but changes, and is not defined by our grammars, but only approximated. Contrary to the case of a compiler, the grammars and dictionaries of an MT system must be easily modifiable, by linguists and not by computer scientists. Hence, modularity in the SLLPs and user-friendliness of the programming environment are essential.

3.1.3.3 CALLIOPE-INFO (English–French)

This system aims at translating computer manuals. The SCSGs of French and English are of course reused, and enriched for two reasons:

— the typology changes, hence, more grammatical phenomena must be accounted for;

— ambiguity 'boards' ('planches', or two-dimensional representations of rules in a SCSG) are being constructed for English, as they have been for French. They are useful for analysis, where they help design the disambiguation (dynamic) rules.

The dynamic grammars for the analysis of English and for the generation of French are offshoots from those developed by GETA, in-house or in cooperation.

Indexing of the terminology has been done by the SONOVISION firm, as for CALLIOPE-AERO. Around 3000 specialized terms have been incorporated in the first version.

3.1.4 A way to reduce the cost of transfer-based multilingual systems

In the context of the Russian–French, German–French and English–French systems, a unification of the generators of French has been attempted, as they had diverged somewhat from their common root, the generator of Russian–French. This unification is accompanied by a deep restructuring of the syntactic generation phase, with the aim of making **composition of machine translators** possible in the context of multilingual transfer-based MT systems.

The main disadvantage of the transfer approach is that $N(N\text{-}1)$ transfers must be written to translate between N languages, as opposed to the N analysers and N generators.

Of course, one might envisage attempting to translate everything into a natural language, which would act as 'pivot'. However, structural ambiguities would multiply. An artificial 'natural' language such as Esperanto is even worse, because of the need to build a **complete** technical vocabulary. A satisfactory 'logical' language, in which everything would be disambiguated, has yet to be devised and equipped with the appropriate 'universal' vocabulary.

An idea, then, is to 'compose' transfers. However, this cannot be done immediately. As a matter of fact, the input to a generator is a **target interface structure** which is not in general of exactly the same type as the **source interface structure** produced by an analyser. This is because the final form of the text to be generated is not yet fixed (paraphrases are possible), because polysemies not reduced by the transfer may appear as a special type of enumeration, and because the transfer may transmit to the generator some advice or orders (relative to the possible paraphrases), by encoding them in the structure.

Instead of producing directly the surface tree (to be passed to the morphological generator), the new technique consists of **producing a source interface structure of the target text** as an intermediate result, which may be sent to a transfer going from the target language to still another language.

For example, consider the four main Romance languages (French, Spanish, Italian, Portuguese). Taking any one of them as 'stopover', it would only be necessary to build 6 transfers instead of 12.

Note that, in general, a minimum of *N* transfers would be enough. However, the associated 'ring' organization leads to an average of (*N*-2)/2 stopovers (and a maximum of *N*-1) for a language pair. With a unique 'stopover', 2 (*N*-1) transfers are necessary, but the number of stopovers in a given translation is always 0 or 1 (an average of 1-2/*N*).

A pragmatically better organization can be envisaged. For instance, consider the nine languages of the European Community, and divide them in three groups: four Romance languages, four Germanic languages, and Greek. Instead of constructing 72 transfers, it might be enough to construct only 16: 6 in each group of four, and 4 between the 'pivots' of the groups, e.g. English–Greek, Greek–French, French–English, English–French. No translation would then require more than two stopovers.

3.1.5 Projects in basic software for MT

3.1.5.1 ARIANE-78.4 and ARIANE-85.2 on mainframes and micros

ARIANE-78.4 has been chosen as support for all developments of the MAT-NP (CALLIOPE) project. Its successor ARIANE-85.2 is beginning to replace it, with the advantage of added modularity and better handling of big dictionaries (Boitet *et al.,* 1985).

Until recently, this system ran only on mainframes and minis. However, the compactness and relative speed of the code have made it quite easy to adapt the complete ARIANE-78.4 system to the IBM PC/AT-370 (under VMPC). ARIANE-85.2 will soon follow. Exactly the same programs run on the micro and on the mainframe. The minimal configuration uses a fixed 20 Mb disk, the 370 kit (two cards), and a 3278/79 emulation card. A memory extension of at least 1.5 Mb may be added and used for paging, which speeds it up considerably.

Of course, the speed of the 370 card (0.1 Mips) does not yet make it possible to consider such a configuration for the **production** of translations. However, it is quite adequate to build MT prototypes, and may be used as low-cost hardware for academic cooperation.

In order to use the PC for producing translations, it would be necessary for IBM to modify VMPC in such a way that the memory extension could be used **directly** as real memory (as Lotus does with the EEMS extension). Now, only the basic 512 Kb can be used as real memory. Available memory cards might then be used to get a real memory of 4 Mb (VMPC limit for the virtual memory). Also, it is likely that faster 370 cards will be produced, and perhaps adapted to the faster hardware of the new PS/2 series.

3.1.5.2 Work on ARIANIX

In the framework of the French MAT-NP, it was decided to push ahead a project which had been prepared at GETA over recent years, but advanced slowly, due to the lack of resources. This new basic software for MT is constructed in Le_lisp, a French dialect of LISP produced by INRIA and converging toward Common Lisp. Here are the main features of this future system:

— A unified SLLP, called TETHYS for the moment, will replace the four SLLPs of the previous systems. It will contain several 'rule engines', in order to make it upward-compatible with ARIANE.85, and also to open it to rule systems developed elsewhere (such as Q-systems).
— The system will be basically multilingual, down to the level of characters.
— Access to the implementation language will be possible from within the rules written in TETHYS.

A very large set of characters has been defined. Several properties are attached to each character. Among them, the natural language (neutral, or Math, French, English, Spanish, Japanese, . . .), the name of the (usual) character set (keywords, special, Roman, Greek, Cyrillic, Thai, hiragana, kanji, hanze, hangul, . . .), its case and diacritics, if any, and some information about 'stress' (italic, bold, underlined).

These properties have been selected because of their importance for linguistic processing. They are all important for defining the dictionary order of words. For example, the information on the natural language permits one to consider 'ch' as one letter in Spanish, and also to display a TETHYS keyword, considered as one character, in the appropriate language.

Two preliminary implementations have been prepared on a SM-90 under SMX (a version of UNIX), one in Le_lisp, using property lists, and one in Pascal, using a 32-bit representation.

Also, a norm for representing multilingual documents has been defined, in order to be able to use information relative to the logical structure of a text in the linguistic processors. For example, a table containing textual elements in its cells should not be represented as a sequence of lines, each made of fragments of textual elements separated by tab characters, but as a construct of matrix type, where each textual element appears contiguously.

4. BUILDING A LINGUISTIC WORKSTATION

A lot of work has been done on translator workstations (Melby, 1982). Such stations always appear as extensions of classical text-processing systems, with extremely limited linguistic capabilities. By contrast, a linguistic workstation would be centred around non-trivial linguistic capabilities, and offer powerful extensions to existing, programmable text processors of various kinds.

The basic capabilities envisaged relate to the specification of dynamic grammars by static grammars, to the construction of multitarget integrated dictionaries, and to the structural study of corpuses, translator's aids being seen as subproducts.

4.1 Grammatical specification with SCSGs

Recently, a first environment for building SCSGs has been designed and implemented on a Macintosh+ by Y. F. Yan in 1987, under the guidance of F. Peccoud. It incorporates a methodology for writing the different components of an SCSG (attributes, axioms, boards), while handling at the same time the corpus investigated and the examples from the corpus appearing in the boards.

There is still much work to be done in this direction, before a complete environment can be offered to linguists. In particular, it would be useful to relate directly a dynamic grammar being executed on a text to the boards containing the specification of the partial correspondences computed by the executed dynamic modules or individual rules of the dynamic system. For this, AI workstations and software tools are envisaged.

4.2 Construction of lexical databases (MIDs)

Ultimately, the cost of MT systems lies essentially in their dictionaries, which are quite difficult to construct and to maintain. Since 1982, GETA has been working on **fork integrated dictionaries**, now called **multitarget integrated dictionaries** (MID). They integrate the terminological and the integrated dictionaries' grammatical aspects, as well as the 'usual' and 'coded' information used in computer applications. A given dictionary contains terms in one language, with the information concerning that language, and the translations of the different meanings in one or several languages.

In the prototype version, an item is a tree, structured according to a grammar, from which an analyser is derived automatically, using a tool developed by Y. Lepage, as well as the definition of the image database structure, in the DDL (data definition language) of a commercial DBMS (now CLIO from SYSECA, but others could be added). From a given item, a DML (data manipulation language) program is generated automatically, to load the image of the item in the DBMS. There is an ongoing project to build a complete user interface, written in Prolog, and easy to interface with any reasonably powerful DBMS.

In order to get some practical experience, 3000 terms in telecommunications have been written in MID format in 1986, in three languages (French, Japanese, English), in cooperation with the French Telecommunications (DGT) and with KDD (Japan). The corresponding 9000 entries have been keyed in on a Macintosh+, using Kanji-Talk.

The work to be done remains immense, in practice and in theory. It is comparatively easy to generate MT dictionaries from MIDs. However, the reuse of existing lexical information encoded in machine dictionaries developed for computer applications is a very difficult task.

We have begun to study how to extract the lexical information from our Russian–French system and to put it in MID format. The preliminary results obtained so far show this to be more difficult than we imagined at the beginning, because some information is implicit or absent from the codes, and has to be added (in the form of comments) in order to be accessible by a program.

4.3 Structural study of corpuses

This line of research has been hardly touched by GETA until now. Some elementary tools (concordances) have been constructed, and some methods used elsewhere in particular at the Bureau of Translations (Ottawa), have been tested in experiments.

However, we are trying to get researchers to explore this further, in the context of such a linguistic workstation. The idea is to use a tree editor equipped with pattern-matching facilities to explore linguistic trees (source interface structures, for example) associated with the units of text (paragraphs, sentences, . . .) under consideration.

A powerful tree transformational editor, TTEDIT, has recently been developed by J. C. Durand in REXX–XEDIT. The rules look like simplified ROBRA rules, with an addition to move a cursor in the edited forest. Commands may be grouped in packages analogous to usual editor macros. The fact that left-hand sides are schemas with variables gives TTEDIT considerably more power than graphic editors with which one manipulates only the drawing of a tree (or a graph).

Such a tool might also be used for exploring and modifying intermediate results produced by an existing analysis or transfer step, in the context of the validation of dynamic grammars constructed from SCSG specifications.

5. DESIGNING NEW TYPES OF MT SYSTEMS

Fianlly, several projects concern new types of MT systems. Grafting an expert system onto a second-generation MT system can produce an expert translator system of the third-generation type. Replacing the usual purely automatic analyser by a linguistic editor interacting with the author should lead to fourth-generation systems. Finally, second-generation systems might be completely reshaped as expert systems relying only on static linguistic knowledge. These three approaches are or have been followed concurrently by small teams.

5.1 Going to third generation by accessing domain-specific expertise

The linguistic and paralinguistic knowledge incorporated in modern second-generation MAT systems is quite enormous. Unless the knowledge of a given domain is extremely limited, it is not feasible to put this information directly into such systems. We have proposed (Boitet and Gerber, 1984) to graft corrector expert systems onto existing MT systems. The corrector system would detect 'problem patterns' in the source interface structure, convert them into questions on the domain (represented as a knowledge base, an expert system, or as a simple database), and modify the structure according to the answer.

A small prototype has been built by Gerber (1984) connecting a small

English–French system to such a corrector system, written in Prolog. The problem here is that developers of MT systems have no time and no competence to build knowledge bases for technical domains. However, significant improvements in translations cannot be obtained if the knowledge base is too small. To continue this line of research, we are looking for a situation where both an adequate knowledge base and texts to be translated would be available.

5.2 Going to fourth generation by interacting with the author

Even if a large knowledge base is available, no machine analysis of a text can be 100% correct, because **new** knowledge is usually introduced by the translated text. However, no adequate learning method has yet been devised to modify and enrich the knowledge base dynamically. Even if one did exist, the communicative character of texts, their **pragmatic aspect**, would not be handled satisfactorily.

As an alternative or complement to the method above, we propose to return to the interactive approach. The essential difference from previous schemes such as that of ITS (BYU, Provo) is to consider an interaction with the author of a document, and not with a specialist of both the domain and the MT system, without imposing a too restricted controlled language, as in the TITUS system (Ducrot, 1982).

In his thesis, Zajac (1986a) has proposed an organization of the dialogues with the author, in an MT system using a traditional morphological analyser, but where the structural analyser would be replaced by a **syntactico-semantic editor** parametrized by the SCSG used to specify the usual purely automatic editor-analyser. The structure of the dialogues is partly an elaboration of Tomita's methods for handling ambiguities (reduction of the number of questions asked (Tomita, 1984)), and partly original (paraphrases are proposed, and no questions are asked in terms of the grammar).

There are many situations where documents are produced within a computerized environment, and where the editor must follow some norm of writing (e.g., the AECMA norm for aircraft manuals written in English). Such an approach might lead to very good translations, transfer and generation being done with no interaction, as now. Of course, not all polysemies and ambiguities can be reduced in this way, because some are of a contrastive nature. Hence, revision would still be necessary to obtain 'guaranteed' translations, as is the case with very good human translations of high importance.

5.3 Organize the linguistic knowledge as in expert systems

The new types of MT systems just presented pertain respectively to the third and fourth generations. However, it is also interesting to investigate new approaches to the purely linguistic part of the MT process, even of the second generation. We have already mentioned a new design of the generators permitting us to compose translators. A more ambitious goal is to reshape completely the grammars and dictionaries, in order to represent the linguistic knowledge as in an expert system.

In all existing systems, much procedural knowledge is included in the rules and in the control of their application. The main part of the procedural knowledge is concerned with solving class and structure ambiguities. Usually, ambiguities are eliminated or ignored rather than handled.

In first-generation systems, they are eliminated as soon as they are encountered. In second-generation systems using the 'filter' technique, their number is reduced by the combinatorial application of the rules, and one final solution is arbitrarily chosen (Veillon, 1970). Sometimes (Slocum, 1984) a weighting device is used to rank them, but it is extremely difficult to assign weights in a meaningful way. In other systems (GETA, or Kyoto), heuristic programming is used to follow one or a few solutions at a time, with the possibility to backtrack (locally) or to 'patch' later (Vauquois, 1979, 1983). Programming in this way is quite delicate, although it makes it possible to get some direct handling of the ambiguities.

What seems to be needed is a way to represent ambiguities such that the major part of the linguistic programming could be expressed without bothering about them, through rules of a declarative nature (like the 'boards' of the SCSGs), and that ambiguities might appear as **problems** treated by a separate mechanism of **metarules** which would describe solutions to individual problems and be used by the linguists at appropriate points.

A first effort in this direction has been made (Verastegui, 1982), before SCSGs were introduced. A promising line of research consists of using the boards of the SCSG as the declarative rules of a (combinatorial) analyser, and to **precompute** as many ambiguity cases as possible, much in the same way as is done when testing that a context-free grammar is LL(1). Then, there would be some variant of the SLLP to describe how to solve those identified problems. Some default solution might be used in the absence of a good enough expert rule, and for the ambiguities which could not be precomputed.

Note that this scheme might be used in second-, third- and fourth-generation systems, as the solutions described might involve a call to some knowledge base or an interaction with a human.

6. CONCLUSION

The tradition of GETA has always been to pursue at the same time fundamental and applied research on machine translation or related topics. Big experimental systems have been built, and techniques linked with AI and modern linguistics are being investigated.

However, and this is also true of almost all work in computational linguistics (CL), they are just techniques. CL, of which MT is a part, could only attain the status of an experimental science if experiments would be made in order to prove or disprove scientific hypotheses, or to discover new phenomena, calling for new hypotheses, etc., very much like in physics. However, things built nowadays, such as MT systems or natural-language interfaces, do not seem to give any new insight into scientific questions, even if they are useful in practical settings.

From this point of view, building a linguistic workstation of the kind described above would be a very important goal.

REFERENCES

Bachut, D. and Verastegui, N. (1984) Software tools for the environment of a computer-aided translation system, *Proc. of COLING-84, ACL, Stanford, July 2–6, 1984,* pp. 330–334.

Bennett, W. and Slocum, J. (1984) *METAL: The LRC Machine Translation System,* Linguistic Research Center, Austin, Texas, USA. September 1984.

Boitet, Ch. (1976)Un essai de réponse à quelques questions théoriques et pratiques liées à la Traduction Automatique. Définition d'un système prototype. *Thèse d'Etat,* Grenoble.

Boitet, Ch. (1984) Research and development on MT and related techniques at Grenoble University (GETA). *Lugano Tutorial on Machine Translation,* April 1984.

Boitet, Ch. and Gerber, R. (1984) Expert systems and other new techniques in MT. *Proc. of COLING-84, ACL, Stanford, July 2–6, 1984,* pp. 468–471.

Boitet, Ch. and Nedobejkine, N. (1981) Recent developments in Russian–French machine translation at Grenoble. *Linguistics* **19**, 199–271.

Boitet, Ch. and Nedobejkine, N. (1983) Illustration sur le développement d'un atelier de traduction automatisée. *Colloque "l'informatique au service de la linguistique", Université de Metz, France, juin 1983.*

Boitet, Ch., Guillaume, P. and Quezel-Ambrunaz, M. (1978) Manipulation d'arborescences et parallélisme: le système ROBRA. *Proc. of COLING-78, Bergen, August 1978.*

Boitet, Ch., Guillaume, P. and Quezel-Ambrunaz, M. (1982) ARIANE-78: an integráted environment for automated translation and human revision. *Proceedings COLING-82, Prague, July 1982,* North-Holland, Linguistic Series No. 47, pp. 19–27.

Boitet, Ch., Guillaume, P. and Quezel-Ambrunaz, M. (1985) A case study in software evolution: from ARIANE-78 to ARIANE-85. *Proc. Conf. on Theoretical and Methodological Issues in MT, Colgate University, Hamilton, N.Y., August 1985.*

Chappuy, S. (1983) Formalisation de la description des niveaux d'interprétation des langues naturelles. *Thèse de 3è cycle,* Grenoble.

Chauche, J. (1974) Transducteurs et arborescences. Etude et réalisation de systèmes appliqués aux grammaires transformationnelles. *Thèse d'Etat,* Grenoble, décembre 1974.

Chauche, J. (1975) Les langages ATEF et CETA. *AJCL Microfiche* **17**, 21–39.

Clemente-Salazar (1982) Etudes et algorithmes liés à une nouvelle structure de données en TA: les E-graphes. *Thèse de Docteur-ingénieur,* USMG & INPG, Grenoble, May 1982.

Clemente-Salazar (1982) Une structure de données intéressante en TA: les E-graphes. *Proc. of COLING-82, Prague, 1982,* North-Holland.

Ducrot, J. M. (1982) TITUS IV. Proc. of the EURIM-5 Conf., Versailles. In: P. J. Taylor (ed.), *Information Research in Europe,* ASLIB, London.

Gerber, R. (1984) Etude des possibilités de coopération entre un système fondé sur des techniques de compréhension implicite (système logico-syntaxique) et un système fondé sur des techniques de compréhension explicite (système expert). *Thèse de 3è cycle,* Grenoble, January 1984.

Guilbaud, J. Ph. (1984) Principles and results of a German–French MT system. *Lugano Tutorial on Machine Translation,* April 1984.

Melby, A. (1982) Multi-level translation aids in a distributed system. *Proceedings COLING-82, Prague, July 1982,* North-Holland, pp. 215–220.

Mozota (1984) Un formalisme d'expressions pour la spécification du contrôle dans les systèmes de production. *Thèse de 3è cycle,* Grenoble, juin 1984.

Slocum, J. (1984) METAL: The LRC Machine Translation System. *Lugano Tutorial on Machine Translation,* April 1984.

Tomita, M. (1984) Disambiguating grammatically ambiguous sentences by asking. *Proc. of COLING-84, ACL, Stanford, July 2–6, 1984,* pp. 476–480.

Tomita, M. and Carbonell, J. (1986) Another stride towards knowledge-based machine translation. *Proc. of COLING-86, IKS, Bonn, August 25–29,* pp. 639–642.

Tong, L. C. (1986) English–Malay translation system: a laboratory prototype. *Proc. of COLING-86, IKS, Bonn, August 25–29, 1986.*

Vauquois, B. (1975) La Traduction Automatique à Grenoble, Document de Linguistique Quantitative 29, Dunod, Paris.

Vauquois, B. (1979) *Aspects of Automatic Translation in 1979.* IBM-Japan, Scientific Program, July 1979.

Vauquois, B. (1983) Automatic Translation. *Proc. of the Summer School on the Computer and the Arabic Language, Rabat, October 1983,* Chapter 9.

Vauquois, B. and Chappuy, S. (1985) Static grammars. *Proc. Conf. on Theoretical and Methodological Issues in MT, Colgate University, Hamilton, N.Y., August 1985.*

Vauquois, B. and Boitet, Ch. (1985) Automated translation at GETA (Grenoble University). *Computational Linguistics* **11**(1) 28–36.

Veillon, G. (1970) Modèles et algorithmes pour la traduction automatique. *Thèse d'Etat,* Grenoble, 1970.

Verastegui, N. (1982) Etude du parallélisme appliqué à la traduction automatisée par ordinateur. STAR-PALE: un système parallèle. *Thèse de Docteur Ingénieur,* USMG & INPG, Grenoble, May 1982.

Woods, W. (1970) Transition network grammar for natural language analysis. *CACM* **13**(10) 591–606.

Zajac, R. (1986a) Etude des possibilités d'interaction homme–machine dans un processus de traduction automatique. Spécification d'un système d'aide à la rédaction en vue d'une traduction par machine. Definition d'un langage de spécification linguistique. *Proc. of COLING-86, IKS, Bonn, August 25–29, 1986, pp. 393–398.*

Zajac, R. (1986b) SCSL: a linguistic specification language for MT. *Proc. of COLING-86, IKS, Bonn*, August 25–29, 1986, pp. 393–398.

APPENDIX: EXAMPLES OF TRANSLATIONS

Russian–French is designed to produce 'crude' translations, not necessarily revised, but good enough to give the content of the source text in an intelligible and reliable way.

We give two examples, as they are produced by the ARIANE-78 system, on our IBM mainframe, using the SCRIPT–DCF formatter. ARIANE's result has been transmitted to the Macintosh used to produce this document by Kermit, over an SM-90. This explains why the columns are not as well aligned as on the IBM 3262 printer used in the laboratory, in spite of Yan Yong Feng's valuable aid.

A long example, with source text, machine translation and human revision

LANGUES DE TRAITEMENT: RUB - FRB

----- (TRADUCTION DU 24 SEPTEMBRE 1986 9H 31MN 26S) -----

VERSIONS : (A : 21/07/86 - T : 21/07/86 - G : 21/07/86)

----- (REVISION DU 6 NOVEMBRE 1986 10H 58MN 54S) -----

-- TEXTE SOURCE --

Na tanke ustanovlen 12-cilindrovyij mnogotoplivnyij dizelq s turbonadduvom i zhidkostnyi oxlazhdeniem "m_HS-110. Mexanikheskaya transmissiya "m_5SD_200D vklyukhaet v sebya pyatistupenkhatuyu korobku peredakh, avtomatikheskoe centrobezhnoe sceplenie s yelektroprivodom, mexanizm povorota, tormoz s gidroprivodom i planetarnyie bortovyie peredakhi. Podveska opornyix katkov torsionnaya. Na pervom i pyatom katkax ustanovlenyi gidroamortizatoryi . Tank oborudovan sistemoj zathityi ot oruzhiya massovogo porazheniya , avtomatikheskoj sistemoj pozharotusheniya. OPVT pozvolyaet tanku preodolevatq po dnu vodnyie pregradyi glubinoj do 4 m

-- TEXTE TRADUIT --

Sur le char on a installé un diesel polycarburant à 12 cylindres avec la suralimentation par turbosoufflante et le refroidissement par liquide <"m_HS-110>. La transmission mécanique <"m_5SD_200D> comprend la boîte à cinq étages de vitesses, embrayage centrifuge automatique avec la commande électrique, mécanisme de direction, le frein avec la commande hydraulique et les engrenages de bord planétaires. La suspension de galets porteurs est à barre de torsion. Sur les galets premier et les galets cinq on a installé les amortisseurs hydrauliques. Le char est équipé du système de protection contre l'arme de destruction massive, le système automatique de lutte contre incendie. Le schnorchel permet au char

-- TEXTE REVISE --

Sur le char, on a installé un diesel polycarburant à 12 cylindres avec suralimentation par turbosoufflante et refroidissement par liquide HS-110. La transmission mécanique 5SD_200D comprend une boîte de vitesses à cinq étages, un embrayage centrifuge automatique avec commande électrique, un mécanisme de direction, un frein avec commande hydraulique et des engrenages de bord planétaires.

La suspension de galets porteurs est à barre de torsion. Sur les premier et cinquième galets, on a installé des amortisseurs hydrauliques. Le char est équipé d'un système de protection contre l'arme de destruction massive, et d'un système automatique de lutte contre

Na baze tanka "m_AMX-30 sozdanyi mostoukladkhik "m_AMX-30PP remontno-yevakuacionnaya mashina "m_AMX-30D, samoxodnaya zenitnaya ustanovka "m_AMX-30SA, samoxodnyij zenitnyij raketnyij kompleks "m_AMX-30R, samoxodnaya puskovaya ustanovka raketyi "Pluton" i samoxodnoe orudie "m_AMX-30GT.

S 1982 g. v vojska nakhal postupatq modernizirovannyij obrazec tanka, polukhivshij oboznakhenie "m_AMX-30B2. V otlikhie ot svoego predshestvennika on snabzhen vmesto 12,7-mm pulemeta 20-mm avtomatikheskoj pushkoj, kotoraya po uglu vozvyisheniya takzhe imeet nezavisimyij privod. Tank "m_AMX-30B2 osnathen sovremennoj sistemoj upravleniya ognem "m_APX-M581. V sostav eevxodyat lazernyij pricel-dalqnomer, yelektronnyij ballistikheskij vyikhislitelq, yelektrogidravlikheskij stabilizator vooruzheniya , teplovizionnyie priboryi nokhnogo videniya. V boekomplekt pushki vklyukhen novyij bronebojnyij podkalibernyij snaryad , broneprobivaemostq kotorogo na dalqnosti 2000 m sostavlyaet okolo 350 mm po normali. Podvizhnostq modernizirovannogo tanka ulukhshena blagodarya ustanovke gidromexanikheskoj transmissii "m_ENC-200. V xode rabot po dalqnejshemu sovershenstvovaniyu tanka "m_AMX-30 byil sozdan osnovnoj tank

de franchir sur le fonc' les obstacles fluviaux de la profondeur jusqu'à 4 m.

Sur la base du char <"m_AMX-30> on a créé pontonnier <"m_AMX-30PP>, véhicule de dépannage <"m_AMX-30D>, canon antiaérien automobile <"m_AMX-30SA>, un ensemble de fusée antiaérien automobile <'::_AMX-30R>, rampe de lancement automobile de la fusée <"Pluton"> et canon automobile <"m_AMX-30GT>.

Dès 1982 dans l'armée a commencé à entrer modèle modernisé du char qui a reçu le nom <"m_AMX-30B2>. Contrairement à son prédécesseur il est équipé au lieu de la mitrailleuse de 12,7 millimètres du canon mitrailleur de 20 millimètres qui sur l'angle d'élévation aussi a une transmission indépendante. Le char <"m_AMX-30B2> est équipé du système moderne? actuell (Genre?)? de commande du feu <"m_APX-M581>. De sa composition font partie les viseurs télémètre à laser , un ordinateur balistique, un stabilisateur électrohydraulique de l'armement, les instruments infrarouges d'une vision nocturne. Un nouvel obus sous-calibré perforant don. la force de pénétration sur la distance de 2000 m constitue près 350 mm selon les normes est incorporé? branché? dans la dotation en munitions du canon. La mobilité du char modernisé est améliorée grâce à

l'incendie. Le schnorchel permet au char de franchir sur le fond les obstacles fluviaux de profondeur jusqu'à 4 m.

Sur la base du char AMX-30, on a créé le pontonnier AMX-30PP, le véhicule de dépannage AMX-30D, le canon antiaérien automobile AMX-30SA, l'ensemble de fusée antiaérien automobile AMX-30R, la rampe de lancement automobile de fusée "Pluton" et le canon automobile AMX-30GT.

Dès 1982, l'armée a commencé à être dotée d'un modèle modernisé du char qui a reçu le nom AMX-30B2. Contrairement à son prédécesseur, il est équipé, au lieu de la mitrailleuse de 12,7 millimètres, du canon mitrailleur de 20 millimètres, qui a aussi une transmission indépendante selon l'angle d'élévation. Le char AMX-30B2 est équipé du système moderne de commande de feu APX-M581. De sa composition font partie des viseurs télémètre à laser, un ordinateur balistique, un stabilisateur électrohydraulique d'armement, des instruments infrarouges de vision nocturne. Un nouvel obus sous-calibré perforant dont la force de pénétration à une distance de 2000 m constitue près 350 mm selon la normale est incorporé à la dotation en munitions du canon. La mobilité du char modernisé est améliorée grâce à l'installation de la

"m_AMX-32. On osnathen 120-mm gladkostvolqnoj pushkoj, imeet nezavisimuyu stabilizaciyu polya zreniya panoramnogo pricela komandira, bolee sovershennyie priboryi nokhnogo videniya. Krome togo, blagodarya primeneniyu mnogoslojnogo bronirovaniya perednej khasti korpusa i bashni , a takzhe falqshbortov znakhitelqno povyishen urovenq zathithennosti	l'installation de la transmission hydraulique et mécanique <"m_ENC-200>. Pendant les travaux selon le perfectionnement ultérieur du char <"m_AMX 30> on a créé un char de base <"m_AMX-32>. Il est équipé d'un canon à âme lisse de 120 millimètres, il a une stabilisation indépendante champs de la vue de la lunette panoramique du chef champs les instruments plus parfaits? perfectionnés (Genre?)? d'une vision nocturne. En outre grâce à l'utilisation du blindage multicouches de la partie avant de la carcasse et de la tour ainsi que des carènes considérablement on a augmenté le niveau de protection.	transmission hydraulique et mécanique ENC-200. Pendant les travaux sur le perfectionnement ultérieur du char AMX-30, on a créé le char de base AMX-32. Il est équipé d'un canon à âme lisse de 120 millimètres, il a une stabilisation indépendante du champ de vision de la lunette panoramique du chef, des instruments plus perfectionnés de vision nocturne. En outre, grâce à l'utilisation du blindage multicouches de la partie avant de la carcasse et de la tour ainsi que des carènes, on a considérablement augmenté le niveau de protection.

Improving the lingware: a short example

Source text and translation before correcting the dictionaries

LANGUES DE TRAITEMENT: RUB - FRB

----- (TRADUCTION DU 6 NOVEMBRE 1986 8H 40MN 41S) -----

VERSIONS : (A : 21/07/86 - T : 21/07/86 - G : 21/07/86)

-- TEXTE SOURCE --	-- TEXTE TRADUIT --
Cifrovaya obrabotka signalov v optike i golografii. Vvedenie v cifrovuyu optiku.	Traitement numéral des signaux dans l'optique et la graphie nue. Introduction dans une optique numérale.
Izlagayutsya osnovyi naukhnogo napravleniya, izukhayuthego ispolqzovanie cifrovyix processorov v optikheskix i golografikheskix sistemax Rassmatrivayutsya voprosyi optimalqnogo cifrovogo predstavleniya i modelirovaniya optikheskix signalov i ix preobrazovanij, yeffektivnyie vyikhislitelqnyie algoritmyi i adaptivnyie metodyi obrabotki izobrazhenij, gologramm i interferogramm, sinteza gologramm i yelementov optikheskix sistem.	On expose les bases de la direction scientifique qui étudie l'utilisation de processeurs numéraux dans des systèmes optiques et nu (Genre-Nombre?) graphiques. On examine les problèmes de la représentation numérale optimale et du modelage de signaux optiques et de leurs transformations, algorithmes de calculateur efficaces et méthodes adaptables du traitement des représentations, des grammes nus et des interférogrammes, de la synthèse des grammes nus et des

Dlya naukhnyix rabotnikov, specializiruyuthixsya v oblasti informatiki , v khastnosti zanimayuthixsya obrabotkoj izobrazhenij, optikoj, golografiej i cifrovoj obrabotkoj signalov.

éléments de systèmes optiques.

Pour les chercheurs spécialisés dans le domaine de l'informatique, en particulier les représentations qui s'occupent au traitement, optique, graphie nue et le traitement numéral des signaux.

Translation after correcting the dictionaries and revision

LANGUES DE TRAITEMENT: RUB - FRB

----- (TRADUCTION DU 6 NOVEMBRE 1986 14H 27MN 22S) -----

VERSIONS : (A : 9/10/86 - T : 6/11/86 - G : 9/10/86)

----- (REVISION DU 6 NOVEMBRE 1986 14H 29MN 54S) -----

-- TEXTE TRADUIT --

Traitement numérique des signaux dans l'optique et l'holographie. Introduction à une optique numérique.

On expose les bases des axes de recherche scientifiques qui étudie l'utilisation de processeurs numériques dans des systèmes optiques et holographiques. On examine les problèmes de la représentation numérique optimale et de la modélisation de signaux optiques et de leurs transformations, les algorithmes de calculateur efficaces et des méthodes adaptables du traitement des représentations, des hologrammes et des interférogrammes, de la synthèse des hologrammes et des éléments de systèmes optiques.

Pour les chercheurs spécialisés dans le domaine de l'informatique, en particulier les représentations qui s'occupent au traitement, l'optique, l'holographie et un traitement numérique des signaux.

-- TEXTE REVISE --

Traitement numérique des signaux en optique et en holographie. Introduction à l'optique numérique.

On expose les bases des axes scientifiques de recherche pour l'étude de l'utilisation de processeurs numériques dans des systèmes optiques et holographiques. On examine les problèmes de la représentation numérique optimale et de la modélisation des signaux optiques et de leurs transformations, les algorithmes de calcul efficaces et des méthodes adaptatives du traitement des représentations, des hologrammes et des interférogrammes, de la synthèse des hologrammes et des éléments des systèmes optiques.

Destiné aux chercheurs spécialisés dans le domaine de l'informatique, en particulier à ceux qui s'occupent du traitement des représentations, de l'optique, de l'holographie et du traitement numérique des signaux.

Part II

Natural language processing (NLP)

4

A morphological parser for Basque verbs' inflection

J. Carroll and **J. Abaitua**
University of Manchester Institute of Science and Technology, Centre for Computational Linguistics, PO Box 88, Manchester M60 1QD, UK

1. INTRODUCTION

Basque auxiliary verbs can be thought of as posing an exceptional case of resourceful inflectional productivity. The comprehensive nature of agreement phenomena in Basque means that as many as three arguments' person and number information (depending on the valency of the verb) can be reflected on the auxiliary, ranging over the various moods and tenses. This triggers an explosion of different possible combinations. Yet, the inflectional morphemes employed in the auxiliary formation show a consistent patterning across moods, tenses and valencies.

In this chapter we present a morphological parser which handles the complete range of auxiliary forms, as contained in Euskaltzaindia's 1973 *Aditz laguntzaile batua*. This shows that the parser covers well above the 2000 forms considered for standard Basque or *euskera batua*. Dialectal variations have not been taken into account, but their incorporation into the model, or the refomulation of the parser in order to accommodate them, would not be a difficult task given the parser's modular design.

The parser captures as many generalizations as possible by focusing on the consistent patterns borne by inflectional morphemes, and by filtering out special cases using comprehensive feature co-occurrence restrictions. The general approach uses a unification-based grammar, on which the relevant functional information is encoded. Such information as number, person, valency, mood or tense is represented by pair of features and values.

Since we both work in a feature-based unification phrase structure grammar formalism such as LFG, such a formalism was the natural choice for us to attempt this task. We hence express the morphotactic rules as (a) rewrite rules (although in practice these are equivalent to a finite-state machine) and (b) feature co-occurrence restrictions (see Section 3.5).

In this work it became clear that a linguistically well-motivated choice between an allomorphic explanation (i.e. with spelling rules) and a morphotactic explanation (i.e. with feature specifications and rewrite rules) would result in substantially greater clarity. This has some similarity with the distinction betwen phonemic and morphemic contexts of Jappinen and Yilammi (1986).

The parser has been implemented in Edinburgh Prolog running on a Sun workstation, and it is compatible with the syntactic analyser for Basque built upon work by Abaitua (1985) and Carroll (1986).

2 SOME LINGUISTIC REMARKS

Few issues in the Basque specialized literature have received as much attention as the morphology of finite verbs. A detailed discussion of the linguistic problems involved with it lies outside the scope of this paper and has been dealt with in various other publications, in particular Trask (1981).

Basque finite verbs show mood and tense features and bound morphemes which can agree with up to three verbal arguments: the absolutive, the ergative and the dative. The main morphotactic generalizations captured in the implementation are derived from a partition of the finite verb into roughly the following:

(i) An initial preverbal affix, *ba-*, which is a conditionality marker.

(ii) A column containing bound morphemes for first and second person, singular and plural, *n-*, *h-*, *g-*, *z-*; and the third-person markers (or empty markers, *d-* (present), *z-* (past), *b-* (imperative), *l-* (conditional).

These prenominal morphs generally correspond to the absolutive noun phrase, which can function as either the subject of the intransitive verb or the object of the transitive verb, showing the ergative nature of the Basque verb's morphology. However, some transitive forms in the past tense (e.g. *nuen, geneun,* etc.) take this morph pattern to indicate the person of the ergative noun phrase, in what is known as the 'split ergativity' of the Basque verb morphology. This irregularity is accounted for in terms of a variable feature **a**, whose case value is assigned by unification with the subcategorization frame of the stem (see section 3.6).

These bound morphemes are followed by various affixes (see Table 1, columns 3, 4, 5) with different values, depending on their combination with the other affixes, for example the morph *-nd-* co-occurs with first and second persons, when the feature **a** stands for an absolutive and the tense is past, etc. This part of the finite verb is the part where most of the idiosyncratic phonological irregularities occur and hence its complexity.

(iii) A list of 'stems' provided with subcategorization frames, that is, with a specification of the arguments (i.e. ergative, absolutive or dative) selected by each particular form. 'Stems' also indicate whether the auxiliary is indicative or not (Table 1, column 6).

(iv) A bound pronominal morpheme column that indicates the person for the dative argument (Table 1, column 8).

Table 1

1	2	3	4	5	6	7	8	9	10	11	12
ba	n	e	n	it	tzai	zki	t	ke	te	t	en
—	h	a	nt	e	ki	z	k	—	—	k	n
	g	i	nd	—	u	—	n			n	
	z	ai	r		za		da			da	
	d	—	—		i		ha			ha	
	b				ieza		a			a	
	l				te		o			—	
	—				di		gu			gu	
					'tzate'[a]		zu			zu	
							zue			zue	
							e			te	
							—				

[a]'tzate', the indicative absolutive stem, has gross spelling irregularities dealt with in the stem dictionary by feature specifications.

(v) A bound pronominal morpheme column indicating the person for the ergative argument (Table 1, column 11).
(vi) A postverbal suffix, *-n*, that co-occurs with past tense.

The above is just a schematic classification of the main partitions, and not a comprehensive one. Other affixes, such as *-ke-* (Table 1, column 9), which marks the verbal form as mooded, are also taken into account. How all these different morphemes and affixes combine to provide with the correct specification is a matter which largely depends on the feature co-occurence restriction component, which is explained in detail in section 3.5.

3. THE ANALYSER–GENERATOR

3.1 Context

Given the apparent complexity of the problem the solution was implemented in a surprisingly short amount of time (about two man-weeks). The main reason for this was the large number of basic tools for computational development of natural language available in the Centre for Computational Linguistics, UMIST, and our familiarity with their use. The particular tools chosen were the feature handling and grammar tools written in Prolog (Edinburgh Prolog) which were initially developed for an English–Japanese translation project (Whitelock *et al.*, 1986). We have used these tools before in Abaitua (1985) and Carroll (1986). The key tools were (i) f-structure facilities (see section 3.2), (ii) grammar rule compilers and (iii) a customized debugger. Also included in the tool-kit were a large number of basic Prolog utilities which additionally aided development.

These tools have not been used for any morphological treatment before (except an elementary treatment of English morphology), yet only two significant developments of them were necessary: (i) modification of the grammar rule compiler and (ii) extension of the feature co-occurrence restriction facility.

3.2 Feature–value pairs, f-structures and unification

In various grammar formalisms LFG (Bresnan, 1982) GPSDG (Gazdar *et al.*, 1985), PATR-II (Shieber, 1984), etc., a fundamental concept is unifiable objects consisting of feature–value pairs. We use the LFG term f-structures for these: as an example the f-structure for *hintzakedan* is

stem	**za**	
tense	**past**	
mood	**pot**(ential)	
ind(icative)	**no**	
postauxed	**yes**	
moded	**yes**	
erg(ative)		
	per(son)	**1**
	num(ber)	s(in) **g**(ular)
	case	**erg**
abs(olutive)		
	per	**2**
	num	**sg**
	case	**abs**
	superpl(ural)	**no**
a	<**abs**>	
choosetense	**yes**	

The key features for incorporation in a comprehensive grammar are the agreement features for person and number on the absolutive and ergative substructures. Many of the features are used during the morphological analysis and this is their only motivation, e.g. **mooded=yes** indicates the presence of the '-ke-' morph. **a**=<**abs**> means that the value of a is the valuer of **ABS**. (<**abs**> is a pointer).

The feature **a** carries the agreement indicated by the '**h-i-nt-**' which is not always absolutive but sometimes ergative as in '**hintzakeen**'.

3.3 The basic rewrite grammar

As the rewrite grammar is too long to list we simply give a diagrammatic representation (Table 1). Also allowed are 'zai' followed by appropriate parts of columns 7–12 for 'zaio' etc. (absolutive third person and dative present tense) and the letter from the second constituent followed by one of nine special cases ('naiz' through to 'dira', and 'zen', 'zatekeen' and 'bitez').

The next step is to filter the simple rewrite grammar equivalent to Table 1 to allow only the correct forms. This is done by spelling rules and feature rules.

3.4 Spelling rules

These account for some of the simpler allomorph contrasts, notably the past marker '-en'/'-n' (depending on the immediately preceding morph) and the singular-person markers in columns 8 and 11 '-t'/'-da-' etc. (depending on whether the string has terminated or not).

3.5 Feature specifications and co-occurrence restrictions (FCRs)

The key method of restricting the generative capacity of the rewrite grammar is through the feature system. The grammar builds up an f-structure of the auxiliary through **feature=value** specifications on the rule, e.g.

anum 2 --> " ", a/superpl=no
anum2 --> +"te", a/superpl=yes

(corresponding to column 10).

The specifications give either the value **no** or **yes** to the **superpl** feature of the substructure which is the value of the **a** feature. By this and similar feature–value specifications this information (which is effectively the meaning of the morph) is then related to the rest of the information incorporated in the f-structure by means of pre-compiled implications called FCRs. The real second-person plural indicated by **superpl=yes** requires that the substructure given by **a** should have **num**(ber)=**pl**(ural) and **per=2**. This is expressed by an FCR:

fcr(superpl=yes, (num=pl, per=2)).

This is interpreted as 'whenever the feature **superpl** is given the value of **yes** then the feature **num** is given the value **pl**, and the feature **per** is given the value **2**'. (In practice with this rule the **num** and **per** features are already instantiated and the FCR checks that they have the permissible values).

This is not quite sufficient since there are a few exceptions when the '-te-' can denote a third-person plural. These are exactly the times when the **a** constituent is ergative and so the FCR was extended to:

fcr(superpl=yes, (num=pl, per=2;
num=pl, per=3, case=erg)).

The ';' denotes an alternative. (This use of alternative feature co-occurrence patterns was the extension made to the implementation of FCRs over the Entran system.) To introduce the feature **case** three more FCRs are necessary:

fcr(abs=_, abs/case = abs).
fcr(erg=_, erg/case = erg).
fcr(dat=_, dat/case = dat).

3.6 The stem

The '_' and capital letters in program material in this section represent Prolog variables.The underline character stands for the 'anonymous variable', which can match any value.
Most of the rewrite rules are similar in form to those above for **anum2**; the major exception is that for the stem (column 6) which has a number of specially-marked features interpreted from a stem dictionary. The key special feature can be thought of as a subcategorization frame, e.g. **[abs, dat]**, and **[erg]** where the head of the list is the case of the **a** constituent given by the morphs preceding the stem and the tail indicates the cases(s) to be found after the stem. So the frame **[abs, dat]** for say '-tzai-' indicates that the value of the **a** feature is to be unified with that of the **abs**, and that column 8 for the dative is to be used. The frame **[erg]** which is one of the possibilities for '-u-' indicates that the feature **a** is to be unified with **erg** for say 'n-u-ke', and that neither column 8 nor 11 is relevant.

Another of the special features indicates the type of agreement shown in column 7. Either it is null (e.g. for 'za') or it indicates absolutive number, with '-z-' or -zki-' denoting plural and '-' denoting singular. Which of these three possibilities is relevant depends on the stem and hence this information is included in the stem dictionary.

The behaviour of the auxiliary most lacking regularity is of the co-occurrences of the morphs listed in columns 3, 4 and 5, with the stem. The permissible combinations and the corresponding feature-specifications are listed separately in a procedure **checkmorphs**, which for example shows the combination: 'i', 'nd', -, 'u' from say 'hindukeen' (By this and similar feature–value specifications on the rewrite rules the information corresponding to the morphs is built up in the f-structure):

```
checkmorphs([i,nd,-,u],F).
```

For this the number and person agreement patterns and the non-present tense have already been specified by the rules of 'nd' and 'i' respectively. There is a similar rule:

```
checkmorphs([i,nt,-,S],F):-
        S=u,evalfd([F/(abs/num)=pl]);S=za.
```

In this rule the two alternative stems 'u' or 'za' are specified. In the case when the stem is 'u' the **abs/num** is restricted to **pl**, although there is no such restriction when the stem is 'za'. There are a total of nine clauses for **checkmorphs** corresponding to about 30 different co-occurrence patterns. Most of these clauses are significantly more complicated than the two quoted, yet operate on the same principle of giving a fully adequate description in terms of feature–value pairs of the cases when the patterns occur. (FCRs indicate the only possible value co-occurrence pattern between different features. Their syntax is **fcr(feature0 = value0, (implications))**, where **implications** consists of other necessary feature–value assignments. The meaning of this is that whenever **feature0=value0**, then the implications must hold under unification.)

3.7 The feature choosetense

There is one special feature that deserves a separate mention. This is **choosetense** which is given the value **yes** at the end of the main rewrite rule for **aux**, the start category. The purpose of this feature is to invoke the co-occurrence pattern specified by its FCR. This ensures that the f-structure has appropriate values for **tense** and **mood**. The FCR is given by:

```
fcr(choosetense=yes,
        (mood = ind,
              (tense=pres,moded=no,postauxed=no;
              tense=past, mooded=no;
              tense=if;
              tense=then_pres;
              tense=then_past);
        mood=pot,
              (tense=pres, postauxed=no;
              tense=past;
              tense=hyp);
        moos=subj,
              (tense=pres;
              tense=past);
        mood=imp,
              (stem=za, (abs/per=1;abs/per=3),
                        (erg/per=2;erg/per=3);
              stem=ieza;
                (stem=ki;stem=di;stem=te),
                  (abs/per=2;abs/per=3) ) ) ).
```

By following through the alternatives it can be seen that this FCR effectively lists the ten possible mood and tense combinations. In most cases, e.g. **tense=past**, the necessary correspondence with features that relate to the morphs found in the word are handled by other FCRs driven off the **tense** or **mood** features. For example,

fcr(tense=past,(postauxed=yes,a/thirdmarkertype=z)).

This ensures that the past-marker '-n' occurs and that if the **a** constituent is third person it uses 'z' in column 2 rather than the alternative third person markers: 'd' (present), '1' (conditional), 'b' (imperative). In some cases, e.g. the present tense, it is more efficient† to list the feature implications here

† The mood marker '-ke-' in particular occurs with a variety of tenses and moods. Two of the implications required in the FCRs are:

tense=pres & moos=ind --> mooded=no
tense=pres % mood=pot --> mooded=yes

As the '-a-' and '-ai-' morphs in column 3 indicate present tense, the possible FCR:

fcr(tense=pres, (mood=ind, mooded=no;
mood=pot, mooded=yes))

causes an alternative depending on the morph in column 9, and hence requires extensive backtracking. By putting these two implications in the FGCR for choosetense=yes and mood=pot, this backtracking is avoided.

than elsewhere. This is particularly clear with the complicated rules over the imperative. These more logically correspond with the stem dictionary entries, but by listing the alternative patterns in the **choosetense** feature which is invoked last, it is not necessary to use the non-deterministic properties of the implementation to prohibit otherwise possible forms such as 'bitzagu'.

4. GENERATION

We do not use any declarative statements in the grammar, which is hence monotonic. Generation of auxilaries with correct agreement patterns and tense markers is reduced to running the same program, with the f-structure partially instantiated and the string being a variable. Then Prolog does all the rest of the work. The only complication is over spelling rules, where the **lookahead** facility for testing on the next letter(s) had to be written carefully to handle generation as well as analysis.

5. FUTURE POSSIBILITIES

As this work is written in the same framework as our previous work it is easy to incorporate both the specific rules into the Basque parser of Abaitua (1985) and the general principles (i.e. the extended FCR compiler) into the grammar development system of Carroll (1986). It is hoped that the latter will allow the development of a Turkish grammar (with its rich morphology) as part of an English–Turkish translation system.

ACKNOWLEDGEMENTS

We wish to thank Brian Chandler and Pete Whitelock who developed most of the basic utilities for the Entran system, which were also used here. Jeremy Carroll receives a grant from the Science and Engineering Research Council (grant 85309520). Joseba Abaitua receives a grant from the Department of Education, Universities and Research of the Basque Government.

REFERENCES

Abaitua, J. (1985) *An LFG parser for Basque*. University of Manchester M.Sc. thesis.

Bresnan, J. (ed.) (1982) *The Mental Representations of Grammatical Relations*. MIT Press, Cambridge, Mass.

Carroll, J. (1986) *A Prolog workstation for grammar development in LFG*. University of Manchester M.Sc. thesis.

Gazdar, G., Klein, E., Pullum, G. and Sag, I. (1985) *Generalized Phrase Structure Grammar*. B. H. Blackwell Ltd., Oxford.

Jappinen, H. and Yilammi, M. (1986) Associative model of morphological analysis: an empirical inquiry. *Computational Linguistics,* **12**(4), 257–272.

Shieber, S. (1984) Design of a computer language for linguistic information. *Proc. of COLING-84, ACL, Stanford, July 2-6, 1984.*

Trask, R. L. (1981) Basque verbal morphology. In Euskaltzaindia (ed.), *Iker-1*, 285–309.

Whitelock, P. J., McGee-Wood, M., Chandler, B. J., Holden and Horsfall, H. J. (1986) Strategies for interactive machine translation: the experience and implications of the UMIST Japanese project. *Proc. of COLING-86, IKS, Bonn, August 25-29, 1986.*

5

Integrating temporal reasoning in a frame-based formalism

Nuria Castell Ariño,
Universitat Politècnica de Catalunya, Facultat d'Informàtica de Barcelona, Department de Programació de Computadors, Pau Gargallo 5, 08028 Barcelona, Spain

SUMMARY

This chapter describes a knowledge-acquisition system whose aim is to map natural-language texts into an information system for subsequent retrieval. In particular, it applies to the processing of news from the Economics section in the 'El País' newspaper. Each news item describes events such as company creation, company shutdown, or merging of companies, as well as their state and some outstanding financial activities: investments, accounts of results, capital enlargements, etc.

In our work two main problems arise: the understanding of the news items and the integration of their meaning into the information system. We use a frame-based formalism to define the two essential elements of the representation: a knowledge base and a temporal system. The central goal of our research is the second element, intended to represent the temporal information of the news. For this reason we focus on the study of the linguistic expression of time and on the comprehension of the temporal relations present in an explicit or referenced way in the described events. Efficient mechanisms for the reasoning and the propagation of relations are needed to incorporate the temporal information and to deduce new ones at retrieval time.

1. INTRODUCTION

To understand natural language, both depth and variety in knowledge and reasoning are required. While general text-processing is beyond the current state of the art, some well-defined applications are currently being explored.

We are developing a system to analyse restricted Spanish narratives conveying temporal information. Texts are taken from the Economics section of the 'El País' newspaper. Our aim is to build a knowledge-based framework, general enough to deal with similar tasks in other domains. Temporal information is a key feature in our application domain. Our NL-knowledge acquisition system performs in two steps: first, understanding news; second, integrating its meaning into an information system formed by two related components, a knowledge base and a temporal system.

The problem of understanding news has been partially studied in the context of the *sketchy scripts* theory (DeJong, 1979), which allows us to extract basic events from news items and to infer causal relations among them. We extend this approach in order to consider the temporal information conveyed in the text.

In the first step, our system carries out a syntactic–semantic analysis to obtain a representation of the meaning, similar to a case grammar. The linguistic expresssion of time is also analysed to obtain the temporal information attached to the described events, in an explicit or referenced way.

In the second step, the system integrates those new data with the information already known. After verifying of their mutual consistency, the new economic information is incorporated into the knowledge base, and the temporal information is incorporated into the temporal system. During these updates, new elements and new relations are created.

In this chapter we focus on the study of the linguistic expression of time, the reasoning process to infer temporal relations from the text, and the design of an expressive and efficient temporal system. Section 2 describes the application domain. A brief exposition of the knowledge base can be found in section 3. A description of temporal information in our domain is detailed in section 4. Section 5 exposes the relation between time and language. Elements of the temporal system are explained in section 6. Finally, section 7 is devoted to an overview of the system's behaviour.

2. APPLICATION DOMAIN

The text source for our system is the news from the Economics section in the 'El País' Spanish newspaper. Each news item informs about events such as company creation, company shutdown, company purchase, merging of companies, as well as their state and some outstanding financial activities such as investments, accounts of results, capital enlargements, prices in the stock market.

As an example, a text (dated January 18, 1986) about the purchase of two companies by a third one follows.

> Hunter Douglas amplía su grupo con la compra de dos empresas
>
> Madrid
>
> Hunter Douglas ha ampliado su grupo de empresas con la compra de dos compañías, Filtrasol, S.A., de Francia, y Stilsound Holding Limited, del Reino Unido.
>
> Filtrasol ocupa a una plantilla de 380 empleados y posee un volumen de ventas de unos 4.200 millones de pesetas anuales.

Stilsound Holding, por su parte, emplea a 160 personas. Sus ventas anuales se sitúan en torno a los 1.300 millones de pesetas.

El grupo Hunter Douglas está especializado en la fabricación de productos de aluminio para la decoración y la arquitectura, y está representado en Espana a través de su filial Hunter Douglas España, S.A.

In the first paragraph the news item informs us that Hunter Douglas has purchased two companies: Filtrasol, SA (France) and Stilsound Holding Limited (UK); the second paragraph talks about these companies, and the third paragraph is devoted to the purchaser.

3. KNOWLEDGE BASE

The knowledge base is defined using a frame-based formalism. It contains representations of general objects, such as persons, integers, sets, sequences, or characters, and of specific domain objects, such as companies, purchases, creations, or capital enlargements.

Objects are organized into hierarchies of different kinds (generalization, specialization, instantiation). Mechanisms of structural inference and inheritance of properies, defined over these hierarchies, are used to incorporate or deduce new information.

Two kinds of objects are considered: classes and instances. Classes are generic descriptions of predefined concepts (character, integer, string, temporal-element, set, temporal-sequence) and of user-defined concepts (company, purchase, person, investment). Instances are realizations of the classes, i.e. the data.

An object is a composed element formed by a declarative part and a set of associated procedures. The declarative component (1) specifies its hierarchy relationships and (2) defines its structure by means of a collection of slot–value pairs. Procedures can be associated either with a slot or with an object. They express how to evaluate default values or to propagate side effect modifications.

A description of class look like:

```
CLASS : Purchase
SUPERCLASSES : Economic-activity
SLOTS :
    FINAL-PURCHASER : company
    SELLER : company
    OTHER-PURCHASERS : set of company
    INTERMEDIATE : company OR organism OR person
    SUPERVISOR : organism OR company
    OBJECT : company
    REQUEST-MOMENT : temporal-element
    ACT-MOMENT : temporal-element
        Associated procedures:
        Put-act-value. {Default value for this slot is "before"
                        request-moment is defined}
```

SELLER-MOTIVE : string
PURCHASER-MOTIVE : string
PROCEDURES :
Modify-possessions-purchaser.
{Activation when final-purchaser and act-moment slots have values}
Modify-possessions-seller.
{Activation when seller and act-moment slots have values}

4. TEMPORAL INFORMATION

Time is an essential feature in our application domain. Every news has a date of publication, and describes events that happened or will happen at a particular moment. These temporal data may be given a reference to other events. In addition, the knowledge base contains time-evolving information.

There are three types of temporal information: the point, the interval, and the chain.

— A point is equivalent to a day, and is our smallest time unit. For instance, the company price in the stock market or the signature of a purchase agreement are associated with a day.
— An interval is a sequence of consecutive days. It can be a predefined interval, such as a month or a week, or defined by the initial and final points. For instance, a capital enlargement is always associated with an interval.
— A chain is an ordered sequence of intervals, but they are not required to be consecutive. For instance, the set of investments in the economic history of a company is associated with a chain.

Among the few existing works in this domain, the most important ones emphasize temporal intervals (Allen, 1981; Kandrashina, 1983; Ladkin, 1986; Yip, 1985) and consider the point as a degenerate interval (initial point=final point). However, in our system the point plays such an important role that we consider it a differentiated concept as in Vilain (1982) and Vilain and Kautz (1986).

5. TIME AND LANGUAGE

With regard to the linguistic expression of time in Spanish, we take into account the theory developed by Norbert Hornstein (Hornstein, 1977) about the associable points for each sentence:

— S (speech moment): news date in our application.
— R (reference point): reference moment for the event.
— E (event moment): instant when the event happens.

The only relations we can establish between these three points are 'before' and 'before or equal'.

This theory has been extended in other works (Yip, 1985; Arnold *et al.*, 1985) to consider S, R and E as temporal intervals. In this case, the possible relations are the seven ones defined in (Allen, 1983): 'equal', 'before', 'overlaps', 'during', 'starts', 'finishes' and 'meets' (there are thirteen if we consider the inverse relations). In our system, S, R, and E can be points or intervals, according to need.

For instance, the sentence:

> Hunter Douglas ha ampliado su grupo de empresas con la compra de dos compañías, Filtrasol, S.A. (Francia) y Stilsound Holding Limited (Reino Unido).

has, according to Hornstein, the temporal representation E, R, S where S is the moment of the news (publication date, January 18, 1986), R is the reference point ('before' S) and E is the purchase moment ('equal or before' R). Considering temporal intervals also, its representation format is E 'during' R and R 'before' S.

The three descriptors are represented in our temporal system. In this example, the representation of S (point) is needed to situate R (interval) and E (point). In other sentences, S is used only for documentational purposes.

In order to define these temporal descriptors, the linguistic elements we must take into account are verbs, temporal adverbs, and locutions. Characteristics of the verb such as tense and aspect fix the action as finished or not, present, past, or future,.... The order relation between E, R and S is defined using the verb. Temporal adverbs (today, yesterday, always) and locutions (May 15, July 1987, from January 1987 to March 1987) give specific values to the three temporal descriptors. Sometimes adverbs and locutions modify the temporal meaning of the verb ('Tomorrow we open at nine o'clock').

Depending on the linguistic expression we obtain different temporal elements for our system: points (today, May 15), intervals (from January 1987 to March 1987) or references (before 1975, after the capital enlargement). Vague expressions (some years, a few months) have not yet been studied.

6. TEMPORAL SYSTEM

Interconnected with the knowledge base, we have a temporal system. The domain knowledge is represented in the knowledge base, and the associated information about time is represented by references to the temporal system.

Two requirements must be satisfied: expressivity, i.e. ability to represent the linguistic expression of time, and efficiency in the reasoning mechanisms (mainly the propagation of relations). Our temporal system consists of (1) a network whose nodes are instances of basic temporal units (point, interval, chain) and (2) a calendar where every year is represented by a tree. An object of the knowledge base may have several associated temporal instances. In turn, when instances in the network contain specific temporal information (a date, a month, . . .), they have associated elements of the calendar.

In contrast with previous works, we distinguish two kinds of temporal instances: the open and the closed ones. A temporal instance is closed if it has direct reference to the calendar, otherwise is open. Relations maintained in the temporal network, as we explained in section 5, are those proposed by Allen extended to deal with mixed cases: point ↔ interval, point ↔ chain, interval ↔ chain. A set of relations between two nodes can be maintained in cases where the information provided is not enough to discriminate between them.

Whenever two temporal instances have associated elements of the calendar then no relations between them appear in the temporal network. As we shall see, this criterion improves efficiency. We consider links between elements of the calendar easily computable; therefore the only relations explictly maintained in the network are the relative ones, i.e. obtained from the news and not computable from the calendar.

When a temporal instance is created, the algorithm for updating the temporal network is activated. The first step establishes whether a propagation of relations is needed. If the new instance is closed, or is open but without new relations to incorporate, then no propagation is needed. When a temporal relation is created, the propagation algorithm is activated to make explicit all the possible relations that are not computable using the calendar. This process needs a transitivity table to calculate the relation between any nodes A, C from the relations between A, B and B, C.

In order to explain the updating algorithm, we define:

- Rab: One relation between the nodes A and B
- Mab: Set of relations maintained in the temporal network between the nodes A and B
- TR(R1, R2): The entry in the transitivity table for the relations R1 and R2
- X: The new temporal instance
- RDxk: A relation or set of relations detected in the text between X and a temporal element K

The process to calculate Mac from Mab and Mbc consists in applying TR(R1, R2) to every pair where R1 belongs to Mab and R2 belongs to Mbc.

Algorithm Temporal-Network-Updating

```
if X closed then STOP endif;
if X open and not detected-relations-in-text then STOP cndif;
{Here the situation is X open and detected-relations-in-text}
for each detected RDxK do
    if (RDxk ∩ Mxk) ≠ RDxk then
        RDxk ← RDxk − (RDxk ∩ Mxk);
        Mxk ← Mxk ∪ RDxk;
        propagate (X, K, RD)
    endif
```

```
endfor
end

Action Propagate (A, B, NEW)
Add-queue-NEWab;
while queue-not-empty do
      take-NEW ab-from-queue;
      for each C related to B do
            NEWac ← Mac ∩ T̄R̄ (NEWab,Mbc);
            if (NEWac ∩ Mac) ≠ NEWac then
                  NEWac ← NEWac − (NEWac ∩ Mac);
                  Mac ← Mac ∪ NEWac;
                  add-queue-NEWAac
            endif
      endfor;
      for each C related to A do
            NEWcb ← Mcb ∩ T̄R̄ (Mca, NEWab);
            if (NEWcb ∩ Mcb) ≠ NEWcb then
                  NEWcb ← NEWcb − (NEWcb ∩ Mcb);
                  Mcb ← Mcb ∪ NEWcb;
                  add-queue-NEWcb
            endif
      endfor
endwhile
end
```

The running time of the previous algorithm is shorter than, or at most equal to, that of the case where all relations are maintained explicitly. This is because (1) the process stops when instances are closed and (2) the number of relations to consider in the propagation algorithm is smaller. In the worst case, when all the instances are open, the running time is equal. In the best case, when all instances are closed, the relations are quickly calculated in retrieval time using the calendar. Our application domain seems to be near the best case because its temporal information frequently provides direct references to the calendar.

Relations between closed instances are obtained whenever they are needed, using the following algorithm to compute relations through the calendar.

```
Function Relation (X,Y) return answer
if X closed and Y closed then return compute-Mxy-in-calendar
                                   endif;
if Mxy ≠ ∅ then return Mxy endif;
if X closed or Y closed then if X closed then return third-instance
                                   (X,Y)
                                       else return third-instance
                                   (Y,X)
                                   endif
```

```
endif;
{Here the situation is X open and Y open and Mxy=∅}
find (X,P)
find (Y,Q);
if P and Q exist then compute-Mpq-in-calendar;
                      Mxq ← TR (Mxp,Mpq);
                      return TR (Mxq,Mqy)
                 else return false
endif
end
```

```
Function Third-Intance (C,O) return answer
{The first parameter is a closed instance and the second is an open
 one}
find (O,Z);
if Z exists then compute-Mzc-in-calendar; return TR (Moz,Mzc)
            else return false
endif
end
```

The previous functions use a 'find' action that looks for a closed instance (second parameter) connected with an open one (the first parameter). This action does not consult the transitivity table because, if the closed instance exists, the relations between these two instances have been already explicated by the propagation algorithm.

In summary, the temporal system consists of the combination of the temporal network, the algorithm for updating this network (run at instance creation time), the calendar, and the algorithm for computation of relations (run at retrieval time).

7. SYSTEM BEHAVIOUR

The system processes news in two steps (Fig. 1). First, it carries out a syntactic–semantic analysis of the text to obtain a meaning representation. In a second step, the new information is incorporated into the knowledge base and temporal system.

The goal, in the first step, is to understand the news. The parser operates by performing:

(1) A preprocessing analysis in order to select an adequate *sketchy script.*
(21) An expectation-driven analysis in order to instantiate events and the relations between them (including temporal information).
(3) An inference process to resolve references.

In the second step, the system incorporates the new information into the knowledge base. This process applies verification rules to prevent inconsistencies in the stored information. Structural inference mechanisms as well as procedures associated with objects perform the update of the knowledge base. At the same time, new elements are created in the temporal network.

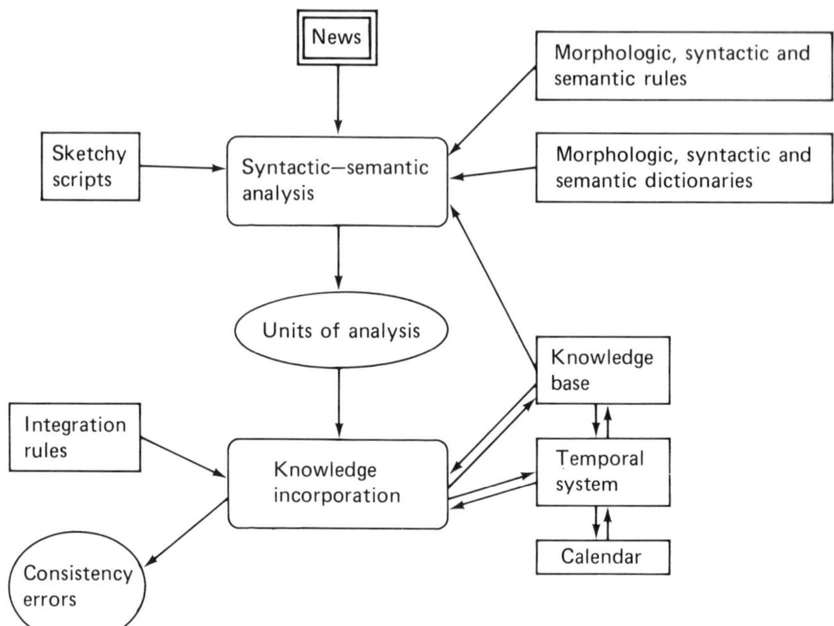

Fig. 1.

Propagation of relations takes place when both open instances and new relations are added to the network.

For example, the final knowledge representation for the text reproduced in section 2 is the following. (Let us suppose that the text is denoted by N860118, and that the system had no information about the three mentioned companies before processing it.)

The new elements incorporated to the temporal system are:

(1) A closed temporal instance (D) for the date of publication, i.e. January 18, 1986.
(2) An open temporal instance (R) for the reference point of the purchase. It is an interval.
(3) An open temporal instance (P) for the purchase moment. It is a point.
(4) The three relations P 'during' R, R 'before' D and P 'before' D. Other relations can be created during the propagation of relations.

New instances in the knowledge base are:

1) COMPANY1

Name	Hunter Douglas {doc: N860118, D}
Activity	fabrication of aluminium products {doc: N860118, D}
Possessions	{what: Company2, how: Purchase1} & {what: Company3, how: Purchase2} & {what: Company4, how: {doc: N860118, D}}

Category	holding {doc: N860118, D}
2) COMPANY 2	
Name	Filtrasol, S.A. {doc: N860118, D}
Nationality	French {doc: N860118, D}
Human-factor	380 {doc: N860118, D}
Sales-by-year	4200 millions of pesetas {doc: N860118, D}
Owner	{who: company1, why: purchase1}
3) COMPANY3	
Name	Stilsound Holding Limited {doc: N8960118, D}
Nationality	British {doc: N860118, D}
Human-factor	160 {doc: N860118, D}
Sales-by-year	1300 millions of pesetas {doc: N860118 D}
Owner	{who: company1, why: purchase2}
4) COMPANY4	
Name	Hunter Douglas España {doc: N860118 D}
Nationality	Spanish {doc: N860118, D}
Owner	{who: company1, why: {doc: N860118, D}}
5) PURCHASE1	
Purchaser	Company1 {doc: N860118, D}
Object	Company2 {doc: N860118, D}
Act-moment	P {doc: N860118, D}
6) PURCHASE	
Purchaser	Company1 {doc: N860118, D}
Object	Company3 {doc: N860118, D}
Act-moment	P {doc: N860118, D}

8. CONCLUSION

We have described an NL knowledge-acquisition system integrating a temporal framework. Source texts are news from a Spanish newspaper, financial activity being the application domain.

The linguistic expression of time in Spanish has been studied extending previous formalisms such as the Hornstein theory. *Sketchy scripts* augmented with temporal descriptors guide the parsing process.

Financial information is maintained in the knowledge base while temporal information is represented in a temporal system formed by two components: a network of temporal instances and a calendar. Nodes of the network have a twofold characterization: (1) points, intervals or chains; (2) open or closed. According to the second criterion, relations are or are not explicitly maintained.

Our approach provides an expressive formalism, with efficient algorithms for temporal reasoning. The system presented is applicable for processing descriptive texts in technical domains where temporal information plays an important role.

REFERENCES

Allen, J. F. (1981) An interval-based representation of temporal knowledge. *Proceedings 7th IJCAI,* pp. 221–226.

Allen, J. F. (1983) Maintaining knowledge about temporal intervals. *Communications of the ACM* **26,** (3).

Arnold, D. J., des Tombe, L. and Jaspaert, L. (1985) *ELS-3 Eurotra Linguistic Specification. Version 3,* Commission of European Communities, Luxembourg.

DeJong, G. F. (1979) Skimming stories in real time: an experiment in integrated understanding. *Research Report 158,* Department of Computer Science, Yale University.

Hornstein, N. (1977) Towards a theory of tense. *Linguistic Inquiry* **8** (3).

Hornstein, N. (1981) The study of meaning in natural language. In *Explanation in Linguistics,* Longman.

Kandrashina, E. Yu. (1983) Representation of temporal knowledge. *Proceedings 8th IJCAI,* pp. 346–348.

Ladkin, P. B. (1986) Time representation: a taxonomy of interval relations. *Proceedings AAAI-86,* pp. 360–366.

Vilain, M. B. (1982) A system for reasoning about time. *Proceedings AAAI-82,* pp. 197–201.

Vilain, M. B. and Kautz, H. (1986) Constraint propagation alogorithms for temporal reasoning. *Proceedings AAAI-86,* pp. 377–382.

Yip, K. M. (1985) tense, aspect and the cognitive representation of time. *Proceedings 10th IJCAI,* pp. 806–814.

6

GUAI: a natural language interface generator

Horacio Rodriguez Hontoria
Facultat d'Informàtica de la UPC, Pau Gargallo 5, 08028 Barcelona, Spain

1. INTRODUCTION

Current research in natural language interfaces (NLI) focuses on transportability conditions, i.e. how to design tools allowing, in a fast and easy way, interfaces working on different environments to be generated. TEAM (Grosz, 1982) DATALOG (Hafner and Godden, 1985) or HAM-ANS (Hoeppner *et al.*, 1985) are some well-known examples.

GUAI (generator universal automático de interfaces) is a natural language interfaces generator (N.L.I.G.), i.e. a system able to obtain, by an acquisition dialogue, the features a specific interface must have and then to generate it. Once created, the interface acts as a natural language front-end for a given computer application.

The organization of this chapter is the following. In section 2 the purposes of the system are presented. Section 3 is devoted to an overall description of the system architecture. Section 4 presents the knowledge representation formalism. Section 5 deals with the knowledge-acquisition phase. Sections 6 and 7 present how an interface generated by the system works. In particular, section 6 describes the NL dialogue structure built by the interface while section 7 describes the interface in a functional way. Finally, section 8 presents some conclusions and further development guidelines.

2. OBJECTIVES

Three main objectives are attempted by our system. First, to build a suitable environment for developing and testing different kinds of interfaces. The second is concerned with the approach to natural language understanding, based on a cooperative process between different specialists, each one working on a descriptive level (superficial, morphological, syntactic, etc.). Finally, the third one is the use of Spanish as the communication language.

The development of NLI has undergone an important growth in recent years, and this increase will probably continue. There are many examples of NLI in different states of development. There are interfaces applied to database query and/or update, NL dialogues with expert systems, NL access to operating systems and so on. Some commercial systems are already available (Wahlster, 1986). The conceptual and linguistic coverages of such systems are being extended continuously.

In our opinion, the main guidelines in the evolution of NLI technology are (see for instance Rissland, 1984, or Hayes and Reddy, 1983)

— development of system transportability features;
— improving the quality of dialogue;
— integration of NL with other kinds of man–machine communications;
— development of more efficient physical communicative devices (especially improvement of speech-understanding systems).

Taking away the last one, an NLIG offers an excellent framework to develop and test theories and techniques related to these guidelines.

A friendly NLI must have a high degree of language understanding. As a consequence, a complex interaction between large amounts of linguistic and extralinguistic knowledge has to be considered. There are three general approaches to this problem:

— The unifying approach expresses all kinds of knowledge using a unique formalism. Models based on logic are a typical example.
— The syntax-oriented or semantics-oriented approaches, where a kind of knowledge drives the parsing process. In syntax-oriented systems the contribution of semantics is, in most cases, reduced to the use of semantic features at lexical level. On the other hand, in semantics-oriented systems (frames, semantic grammar, . . .) syntax frequently appears only as valency restrictions placed at slot level.
— The integrated approach, in which each kind of knowledge has its own formalism and is managed by its own tools. This implies a distributed parsing process with several levels of description communicating between them.

High quality of language understanding together with transportability requirements lead us to select the third approach.

3. ARCHITECTURE OF THE SYSTEM

GUAI is composed of two modules, an acquisition module (AM) and a generation module (GM). The knowledge-acquisition process is carried out by means of a menu-based dialogue. Four types of knowledge can be entered:

— general knowledge (including metaknowledge and control knowledge)
— operative environment (OE) knowledge, i.e. knowledge about the system for which the interface is built
— domain knowledge, i.e. knowledge about the application domain

— linguistic knowledge (structured in lexical, morphological, syntactic and semantic levels)

The AM is composed of four independent submodules, each one managing the corresponding type of knowledge. This independence is important because the acquisition can be restricted to the scope of expertise of each user concerning the relevant field of knowledge.

Once the knowledge has been acquired the generator performs three tasks:

— Verifying knowledge consistency (in cases where it has not been done previously).
— Transforming the acquired information into a representation that can be used efficiently by the interface.
— Generating the interface.

4. KNOWLEDGE REPRESENTATION

The system uses a frame-based mechanism for knowledge representation. Generic objects (classes) and specific instances are both represented by structured objects. An object is formed by a collection of descriptors (slots) with attached values belonging to certain types.

Objects are related by means of descriptors (an object can be the value owned by a descriptor of another object) or by relations such as 'is-a', 'instance-of', 'subsumes', 'composed_by' or referenced_by'.

Information attached to objects can be declarative or procedural. The usual inheritance mechanisms are provided.

It is important to emphasize that objects used by the generator are not the same as the ones used by the generated interface. Legibility and friendliness to the human expert are qualities to preserve in the formalism used by the generator. On the other hand, objects managed by an interface are for internal use and then priority is given to efficiency criteria.

5. KNOWLEDGE-ACQUISITION MODULE

Knowledge to be incorporated is classified as follows:

— General level:
  — Parameters to tailor the interface.
  — Formulation of general strategies, heuristics and control mechanisms.
    — Control rules for parsing.
    — Referent resolution rules (definite reference, anaphora resolution, ellipsis, . . .).
    — Inheritance rules.
    — Focusing rules.
  — Metaknowledge about the other knowledge levels.
— OE level:

  - Semantics and syntax of messages that interface and OE can exchange.
- Domain level:
  - Concepts in the domain of application and their relationships.
  - Taxonomic hierarchies.
- Linguistic level:
  - Lexical knowledge: roots, suffixes and lexeme dictionaries.
  - Morphological knowledge: rules and models.
  - Syntactic knowledge.
    - Context-free rules.
    - Transformation rules.
  - Semantic knowledge.
    - Semantic rules.
    - Correspondence between concepts and their lingusitic coverage.

Some excerpts of acquisition dialogue follow, corresponding to different knowledge levels. All the examples presented in this paper are taken from a stock-market database query system.

Let us suppose the user wants to define the concept '**Morphological-Interpretation**'. First, he selects the **General-Acquisition-Menu** option, then the **Linguistic-Metaknowledge** option and finally the **Create-New-Object** option. At that point the dialogue is the following:

System	>	Nombre del objeto	{object name}
User	>	interpretación morfológica	{morphological interpretation}
S	>	posibles sinónimos	{possible synonyms}
U	>	nil	
S	>	posibles roles	{possible descriptors}
U	>	(unidad-léxica categoría-morfológica género número persona rasgo-semántico)	{lexical-unit morphological-class} {gender number person semantic-feature}
...			
S	>	número aún no definido, ¿desea hacerlo?	{number not yet defined, do you want to do it?}
U	>	no	
S	>	¿obligatorio? [si no]	{obligatory? [yes no]}
U	>	no	
S	>	tipo	{type}
U	>	(or sing pl)	
...			

The user now wants to define the concept '**Database-Relation**'. In this case, he selects the **OE-Menu** option, and then the **Create-New-Object** option. The dialogue is as follows:

S	>	nombre del objeto	{object name}
U	>	relación de base de datos	{database relation}

S	>	posibles sinónimos	{possible synonyms}
U	>	nil	
S	>	posibles roles	{possible descriptors}
U	>	(atributos directorio documentación formato clave implementación almacenamiento)	{attributes directory documentation} {fomat key implementation} {storage-structure}
		{These descriptors reproduce the EXPLORER RTMS relation structure used by the system}	
...			
S	>	relaciones con otros objetos	{relations with other objects}
U	>	(is-a concept)	
...			

Other acquisition dialogues follow the same patterns.

6. DIALOGUE-STRUCTURE DESCRIPTION

A specific interface handles two kinds of knowledge: global knowledge, provided by the acquistion step, and dynamic knowledge, bound to the dialogue and in some sense inferred from it. Global knowledge was described in the previous section. Let us now characterize dynamic knowledge.

We assume the presence of three possible participants: the user (U), the interface (I) and the operative environment (OE). The superficial structure of a dialogue is a sequence of participant's interventions, formed by utterances that can be formal or NL expressions. However, at a logic level the structure is more complex. The organization we use is roughly based on Wachtel (1986) and Ferrari and Reilly (1986).

A **conversation** is **composed-by** dialogues. Each **dialogue** is about some **subject**. Our concept of dialogue is bound to the superficial utterances exchanged by participants. In this case it seems reasonable to structure a conversation as a sequence of dialogues. Examining kinds of dialogue connections (extensions, generalizations, lateral moves and so on) appearing in normal man–machine interactions, we think that **subject** should be represented as a hierarchical structure. Under this assumption we shall speak of subject and subsubject and, consequently, dialogue and subdialogues.

Subject acts like a defining mechanism for objects referred to by the dialogue. It is used both as a search space in the process of reference resolution and as an illocutionary and conceptual expectations generator in the process of NL understanding. The **subject** consists of a collection of objects eventually related. Mechanisms for its updating are provided in the acquisition phase and widely used by the interface, as we shall see in the next section.

Furthermore, a **dialogue** is structured as a sequence of **exchanges** between participants. An **exchange** has an **objective** (any illocutionary act the interface could perform) and is **composed by** interventions (not always consecutive) of two participants. Between **interventions** other **exchanges** may be nested. A typical **exchange** pattern begins with a user **intervention** towards the interface, for instance asking for something, follows with another **exchange** between I and OE, to obtain the answer, and ends with an interface **intervention** communicating the answer to the user (see Fig. 1).

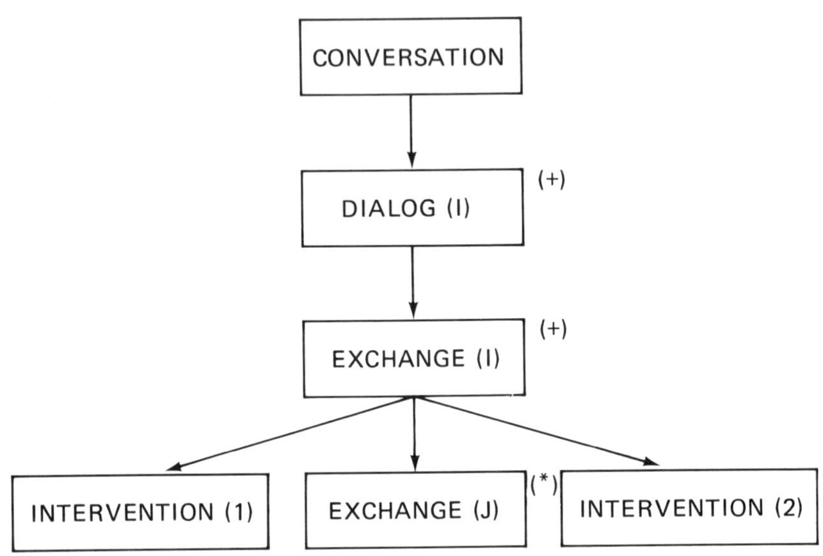

Fig. 1.

Each **intervention** is described in terms of the following descriptors:

Sender The participant who produces the intervention.
Receiver The participant to whom intervention is sent.
Moment Time of the intervention.
Focus A subset of subject containing object and relations referred to directly (although not always explicitly) by the utterances that form the intervention.
Illocutionary-description The atomic components are illocutionary acts (together with their actants of conceptual type). Its compositive relations are sequential and parallel compositions, and disjunction.
Illocutionary-expectation

Not all the combinations of participants are able to form an intervention. In fact only four kinds of interventions are well-formed: user to interface, interface to user, OE to interface and interface to OE. Interventions where the sender or the receiver is the OE consist of formal expressions whose semantics and syntax were provided at acquisition level. Interventions from and to the user use NL and have in addition the following descriptors:

Superficial-description The content is the full NL utterance. Atomic constituents are words. The only compositive relation is concentration of atoms.

Morphological-description Its atomic units are morphological interpretations (see section 5). The compound forms are morphological segments (sequences of morphological interpretations with the same lexical unit) and morphological chains (sequences of morphological segments).

Surface-syntax-description It is based on the idea of syntagmatic decomposition of a morphological chain guided by a phrase-structure grammar. Its atomic constituents are syntagms and the compositive relations are adjunction and substitution.

Deep-syntax-description From the representation point of view this level is the same as the previous one. The difference between them is nevertheless important: surface syntax is based on words appearing in a sentence and their order. This is a basic point in the phrase-structure formalism. However, syntactic relations are more general. The purpose of including this additional level is to unify expressions with the same syntactic relations but different surface appearance. Passing from surface to deep syntax expressions takes place through tree-transformations. Some features involved in these transformations are explicitation of ellipses, obtaining of a canonical form, changing passive to active, conjunctions, ...

Conceptual-description At this level atomic constituents are concepts. The compositive relations are made explict by means of descriptors and relations.

Superficial-expectation
Mophological-expectation
Surface-syntax-expectation
Deep-syntax-expectation
Conceptual-expectation

See Fig. 1 for an overall view of this structure.

7. INTERFACE FUNCTIONAL DESCRIPTION

An interface performs two different but related tasks.

(1) For each intervention
   (a) transforming a superficial description to an illocutionary one (when the interface is receiving an intervention, i.e. the analysis phase).
   (b) transforming an illocutionary description to a superficial one (when the interface is sending an intervention, i.e. the generation phase).
(2) Chaining the different interventions in order to generate or fill higher structures of the dialogue.

The rest of this section is devoted to explaining the analysis (or understanding) phase. Generation needs further study and will be covered in the near future.

Although the static description of interventions is stratified the analysis process is not. Analysis is performed by a set of procedures (parsers) working as transducers between the abovementioned description levels. Nevertheless, neither does the activation of procedures follow a pre-established order (bottom-up or top-down) nor does the transduction process effect a full level description.

Parsing is a double play of expectation generation (not necessarily between contiguous levels) and instantiations satisfying these expectations. Both expectations and instances are attached to the corresponding descriptors of current intervention.

A blackboard-like organization is used to implement the parsing process. Control rules (provided by the user in the acquisition phase) govern hypothesis and knowledge-source selection. In turn each knowledge source has its own control mechanism.

Next, a simplified example of the understanding process is given. Let us suppose the following dialogue:

S > Buenos dias, está Vd. accediendo al Sistema de Información Bursátil.
{Good morning, you are accessing the Stock Market Information System}
U > ¿Cuál es el índice de hoy?
{Which is today's index?}
S > Aún no ha acabado la sesión en la Bolsa de Barcelona
{The session at Barcelona Stock Market is not yet finished}
U > ¿y el de ayer?
{and yesterday's one?}
S > El índice general del día 16 de julio de 1987 fue 156.03
{General Index of July 16, was 156.03}
. . .

The system begins by creating objects for **conversation**, **dialogue**, **exchange** and **intervention**:

CONVERSACION-1	
instance-of	Conversation
participants	(U I O.E.)
composed-by	DIALOGO-1
DIALOGO-1	
instance-of	Dialog
subject	nil
composed-by	INTERCAMBIO-1
part-of	CONVERSACION-1
INTERCAMBIO-1	
instance-of	Exchange
objective	nil
achieved?	nil
composed-by	INTERVENCION-1

part of	DIALOGO-1
INTERVENCION-1	
instance-of	Intervention
sender	U
receiver	I
moment	{filled by a demon at creation time}
superficial description	nil
. . .	
illocutionary expectation	EXP-INL-1
EXP-INL-1	
instance-of	Illocutionary-expectation
expectation	(or Request-For-Information Salutation Good-bye)
kind	closed

The illocutionary-expectation slot of INTERVENCION-1 contains the three current interface expectations. At this point control allows a top-down expansion of these expectations. In this case several refinements take place. For instance 'Request-For-Information' is further refined in 'Request-For-Value-Of-Descriptor', being satisfied, as we shall see later. At the same time the system shows a prompt requiring a user intervention. Once the user has entered his input, the system assigns to the superficial-description slot of INTERVENCION-1 the utterance read (in this case, '¿Cuál es el índice de hoy ?').

The morphological analyser is then activated, producing different results: a morphological description of the utterance (built and placed in the corresponding slot), the generation of two conceptual expectations (fired when finding a semantic feature attached to the words 'índice' and 'hoy') and, finally, the generation of a syntactic expectation (on finding the superficial interrogative marks '¿' and '?').

EXP-SINT-1		
instance-of	syntactic-expectation	
expectation	Interrogative-phrase	
subsumes-from	(1 1)	
subsumes-to	(8 8)	
kind	closed	
EXP-CONC-1		
instance-of	Conceptual-expectation	
expectation	Indice	{index}
reference	EXP-SINT-2	
kind	closed	
EXP-CONC-2		
instance-of	Conceptual-expectation	
expectation	fecha	{date}
reference	EXP-SINT-4	
kind	closed	

EXP-SINT-2

instance-of	syntactic-expectation
expectation	NP
subsumes-from	(1 5)
subsumes-to	(5 8)
core	EXP-SINT-3
kind	open

EXP-SINT-3

instance-of	syntactic-expectation
expectation	N
subsumes-from	(5 5)
subsumes-to	(5 5)
kind	closed

EXP-SINT-4

instance-of	syntactic-expectation
element	EXP-SINT-5
subsumes-from	(1 7)
subsumes-to	(7 8)
kind	closed

EXP-SINT-5

instance-of	syntactic-expectation
expectation-from	(7 7)
subsumes-to	(7 7)
kind	closed

A further expansion process of conceptual expectations identifies 'indice' as an instance of the class conceptual-attribute whose domain can be either a 'Sesión-de-Bolsa' or a 'Sector-bursátil'. The expecation corresponding to the first possibility follows:

EXP-CONC-3

instance-of	Conceptual-expectation
expectation	Sesión-de-Bolsa {Stock Market Session}
kind	closed

The syntactic analyser instantiates several objects, some of them satisfying existing syntactic expectations. For example:

N-1

instance-of	N
subsumes-from	5
subsumes-to	5
syntactic-attributes	(gen masc num sing)
semantic-attributes	indice

NP-1

instance-of	NP
subsumes-from	4
subsumes-to	7
composed-by	(LN-1 N-1 RN-1)

syntactic-attributes	(gen masc num sing det art)
semantic-attributes	indice

N-1 and NP-1 satisfy EXP-SINT-3 and EXP-SINT-2 respectively. Obtaining deep syntactic descriptions from superficial ones is easy in this case because no transformation can be applied.

The conceptual analyser builds concepts combining deep syntactic representation and conceptual expectations. In our example four objects are created: FECHA-1, an object belonging to 'Fecha' (date) class, corresponding to today's data and satisfying EXP-CONC-2. SESION-DE-BOLSA-1 of class 'Sesión-de-Bolsa' satisfies EXP-CONC-3. INDICE-1 of class 'Indice' satisfies EXP-CONC-1. Finally SER-1 of class SER (to be) is created directly from the syntactic representation without any expectation.

Instantiation of different objects activates processes such as inheritance, filling of slots by default values and so on. In this case, FECHA-1 fills the slot 'Sesión' in SESION-DE-BOLSA-1. 'Bolsa' and 'Indice' slots are filled respectively by BOLSA-DE-BARCELONA and INDICE-1. In the same way, the descriptors subject and object of SER-1 are filled by an unknown object X and INDICE-1.

The conceptual description of INTERVENCION-1 can be paraphrased as 'X is the Index of today's session on the Barcelona Stock Market'. This conceptual description does not take into account the interrogative form of the syntactic description. Conceptual and syntactic descriptions are both combined to instantiate a request-for-value-of-descriptor:

VALOR-DE-ROL-1

instance-of	Request-For-Value-Of-Descriptor
descriptor	Indice
Object	SESION-DE-BOLSA-1

INTERVENCION-1 is fulfilled once VALOR-DE-ROL-1 is attached to its illocutionary-description slot. In turn, the objective slot in INTERCAMBIO-1 is filled with VALOR-DE-ROL-1.

The system now makes a plan to achieve the objective. For this intervention the plan has two steps: obtain the answer and communicate it to the user.

The first part of the plan instantiates a new exchange (INTERCAMBIO-2), belonging to the same dialogue, DIALOGO-1, and with the same objective. As a consequence, two new interventions INTERVENCION-2 and INTERVENCION-3 are created. The former is sent by I to OE and has as illocutionary description a sequence of RTMS actions to obtain the requested value. Then the answer generated by OE is placed as the illocutionary description of INTERVENCION-3 (see Fig. 2).

The second part of the plan produces a new intervention, INTERVENCION-4, that starts the generation process to communicate the answer to the user. This marks the end of INTERCAMBIO-1.

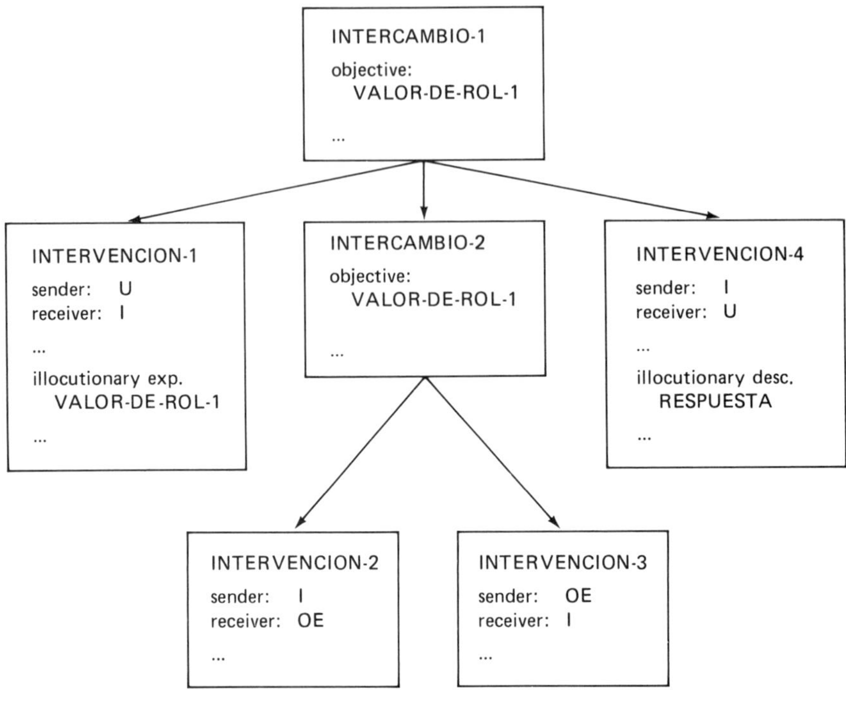

Fig. 2.

The interface now produces another exchange, INTERCAMBIO-3, for the moment attached to the same dialogue, allowing the continuation of the process.

8. CONCLUSIONS

A natural language interfaces generator has been presented. The system is based on a strict separation, both in organization and access, of different types of knowledge to allow its modular acquisition.

The main contributions of this work concern the following points:

(1) The acquisition phase provides a uniform mechanism to enter all types of knowledge, simplifying user interaction.
(2) All components related to the interface can be described in a declarative way, improving system transportability. In particular, the incorporation of the operative environment's knowledge level provides a modelling of the system for which an interface is built.
(3) A parsing process based on a cooperative control model to achieve NL understanding. This allows a more extensive use of linguistic knowledge giving a more efficient parsing than using traditional approaches.

Further development guidelines include:

(1) Testing the system in other environments in order to improve transportability capabilities and linguistic coverage.

(2) Trying alternative syntactic theories (and their corresponding parsers).
(3) Developing better generation procedures applying the same knowledge already used by analysis procedures.

REFERENCES

Ferrari and Reilly (1986) A two level dialogue representation. *Proc. of COLING-86, IKS, Bonn, August 25–29, 1986.*

Grosz, B. (1982) TEAM: a transportable natural language interface system. *SRI Tech. note 263R.*

Hafner, C. and Godden, K. (1985) Portability of syntax and semantics in datalog *ACM Tr. OIS* **3** (2).

Hayes, D. J. and Reddy, R. (1983) Steps toward a graceful interaction in spoken and written man–machine interaction. *IJMMS* **19** 231–284.

Hoeppner *et al.* (1985) The HAM-ANS project. *Artificial Intelligence Newsletter* **2** (1).

Rissland, E. (1984) Ingredients of intelligent interfaces. *IJMMS* **21** 377–388.

Wachtel, T. (1986) Pragmatic sensitivity in N. L. interfaces and the structure of conversion. *Proc. of COLING-86, IKS, Bonn, August 25–29, 1986.*

Wahlster, W. (1986) Natural language interfaces, ready for commercial success? *Proc. of COLING-86, IKS, Bonn, August 25–29, 1986.*

7

A practical natural language interface to databases

T. Yoshino, Y. Izumida, A. Makinouchi
Software Laboratory, Fujitsu Laboratories Ltd., 1015 Kamikodanaka, Nakahara-ku, Kawasaki 211, Japan

1. INTRODUCTION

A natural language interface should be easy to transport, extend, and maintain. With these goals in mind we designed a Japanese-based natural language interface using an object-oriented language called MINERVA (Sato and Sugimoto, 1986). A two-tiered approach was used to meet the goal requirements. A language model was created which contains linguistic knowledge and a world model was created which contains domain-specific information. The first model covers all three goals of transportability, extendability and maintainability, while the second model's primary function is to facilitate transportability between different domains. This approach leads to the development of a practical interface.

The user interface is a very important consideration in the development of an interactive information-processing system. Many studies have been done on the feasibility of natural language interfacing as a means of making it easier for users to communicate within their computers (Hendrix *et al.*, 1978; Walts, 1978). Parsing strategies such as entity-oriented parsing and word expert parsing have been developed (Hayes, 1984; Small and Rieger, 1982; Marcus, 1980). Some recent studies have also dealt with natural language interfacing as a front-end component for decision support and expert systems.

Vital to the success of a natural language interface is its 'transportability' — both from one application domain to another and from one user group to another. Domain-to-domain transportability is related to the semantic representation of an application for understanding a natural language. Group-to-group transportability is related to the natural language's syntactical expression. One of the problems hindering the development of natural language interfacing is the sheer difficulty of anticipating all of the user utterance and expression patterns, even in a single application domain, and establishing a set of syntactic rules that is capable of accepting these patterns. This is, of course, further aggravated by the fact that the expression of ideas is heavily influenced by the knowledge, customs, and other factors peculiar to each user group.

Another important consideration in the success of a natural language interface is the extendability and maintainability of its language-analysis component. Syntactic rules must be extended so the user can adjust the rules for individual application domains and user groups. Syntactic rules must be modularized and the number of the rules reduced. Extendability and maintainability also require that semantic analysis must be transparent. Debugging tools must be powerful enough and explanatory functions developed enough that the system gives the reason why, for example, it does not accept a sentence input by the users. It is on the basis of the information and explanation given by the system that the user guesses how to modify a rule or to rephrase a rejected sentence, and thereby to communicate with the system. Without at least that minimum explanation capability, the system cannot be satisfactory to the user.

In designing our Japanese-language interfacing system, we adopted a knowledge-engineering approach to the above problems, encapsulating linguistic knowledge into a language model (LM) and domain-specific knowledge into a world model (WM). The LM enables group-to-group transportability, extendability, and maintainability by modularizing syntactic rules and reducing their number. The WM enables domain-to-domain transportability because users need only add domain-specific knowledge to the WM to transport the system to a new domain. The WM is quite simple, and easy for users to define and understand. This simplicity is the key to transportability. The WM semantically analyses sentences input by the user, basing its analysis on two simple rules — specialization and connection — that help users understand how the system processes their sentences.

2. SYSTEM FEATURES

Japanese-language query processing can be divided into three phases. In the first, the system uses the dictionary to divide the input sentence into a list of words with grammatical and semantic features. In the second phase, the system uses the LM and WM to analyse the word list and to construct an intermediate 'meaning structure', together with a parse tree. In the third phase, the system translates the meaning structure into the query language of the database management system (DBMS) and executes it. Fig. 1 gives an overview of this process.

2.1 Morphological analysis

Unlike English, for example, sentences in Japanese are composed literally of 'character strings'. The system therefore must segment a sentence into its component words. The system must also resolve syntactic ambiguities, using the connection information for each word. To enable the system to do this, we classify words into two categories; content and function. Content words such as nouns, verbs, adjectives, and adverbs are application-dependent and are defined by the user. Function words such as auxiliaries and conjunctions

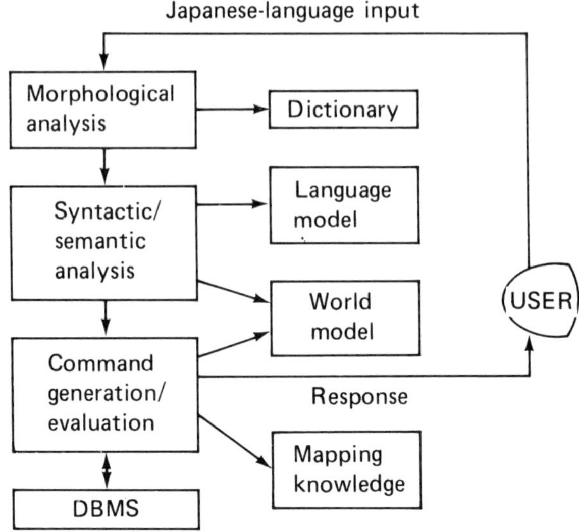

Fig. 1 — System overview.

are domain-independent. Connection information for content words depends on parts of speech. Connection information for function words depends on detailed classification as a part of speech. This classification leads to correct segmentation. The particle 'no' is classified into four categories — adnominal, paratactic, end-form and nominal postpositional. Based on connection information the system can determine, for example, that 'no' in the sentence 'Utsukushii no ha nan desu ka' ('What is the beautiful thing?') is a nominal postpositional particle.

Our system selects the segmentation candidate with the least number of 'bunsetsu', a clause-like structure consisting of an independent word accompanied by from none up to a few dependent words. This bunsetsu method (Yoshimura *et al.*, 1983) is better than the longest matching method previously used. We improved the performance of Yoshimura *et al.*'s methods by using the optimum graph search algorithm A^* (Nilsson, 1980) to search a list of word candidates.

2.2 Syntactic–semantic analysis

In the syntactic–semantic analysis phase, our system references the LM and WM to analyse the result of morphological analysis and to construct a meaning structure together with a parse tree. The meaning structure is related to part of the WM representing the meaning of an input query.

A major problem in syntactic–semantic analysis is ambiguity. To help solve this problem, we adopted nondeterministic parsing. When syntactic ambiguities occur, our system produces different parse trees. The parse tree has multiple meanings to handle semantic ambiguities so this process extracts all of the ambiguities that an input sentence implies.

This method has a drawback, in that it often leads to a combinatorial explosion in the number of possible parses. Our goal is to interpret semantically user queries without causing this sort of explosion. Rules in the LM consist of both syntactic and semantic components, including conditions and actions. That is, possible modification relationships between phrases must pass both syntactic and semantic conditions; once both sets of conditions are satisfied, syntactic action produces the partial parse tree and semantic action produces the meaning for the modification. This greatly reduces the number of possible intermediate parses, eliminating any combinatorial explosions.

For example, take the query 'Tokyo no biiru wo uru mise no namae wa' ('What is the name of the retailer who sells beer in Tokyo?'). Syntactically, the noun phrase 'Tokyo no (in Tokyo)' may modify the noun phrase 'biiru wo (beer)', the noun phrase 'mise no (of the retailer)', or the verb phrase 'uru (sells)'. Semantic ambiguities may also arise when phrases can have more than one meaning. For example, the noun phrase 'Tokyo no (in Tokyo)' corresponds to a geographical location, but it could be either a factory address or a retailer's address, depending on the context. In this case, the noun phrase 'Tokyo no (in Tokyo)' modifies the noun phrase 'mise no (the retailer)'.

2.3 Command generation–evaluation

In the last phase of processing, our system translates the meaning structure into DBMS query language and executes it. Query languages differ from system to system, so we have separated domain-specific knowledge and mapping knowledge, as previously reported (Ishikawa *et al.*, 1986).

3. LANGUAGE MODEL

3.1 Overview

The language model (LM) is a hierarchical arrangement of linguistic concepts, such as words, phrases, and sentences, classified according to their attributes. At the same time, it is also a hierarchical set of rules for parsing an input sentence. Fig. 2 shows part of the language model, which consists of class-level objects, each of which represents a linguistic concept. Dashed arrows indicate sub–super relationships.

The class 'linguistic concept' (LC in Fig. 2) has three subclasses; word (WORD), phrase (P), and sentence (S). These are basic concepts recognisable as units that form Japanese sentences.

Japanese words are classified by their grammatical category. That is, the LM has, as subclasses of the word class, a verb subclass (VB), a noun subclass (N), and a postpositional particle subclass (Pa). A Japanese word such as 'shohin (merchandise)' is represented as the 'shohin class' linked as a subclass to the N class.

Phrases are classified according to the independent word in the last bunsetsu. The phrase class (P), followed by its subclasses — the noun phrase (NP), verb phrase (VP), and adjective phrase (AP) — reflects the classifica-

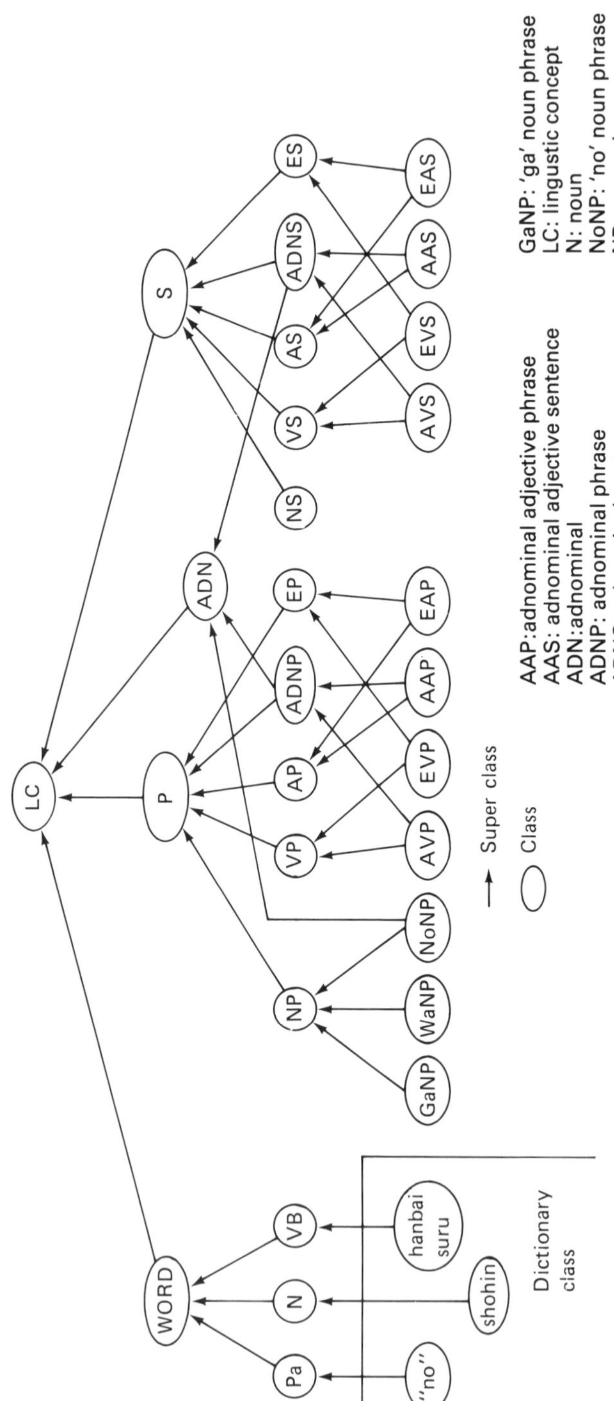

AAP: adnominal adjective phrase
AAS: adnominal adjective sentence
ADN: adnominal
ADNP: adnominal phrase
ADNS: adnominal sentence
AP: adjective phrase
AS: adjective sentence
AVP: adnominal verb phrase
AVS: adnominal verb sentence
EAP: adnominal phrase with end-form
EAS: adnominal sentence with end-form
EP: phrase with end-form
ES: sentence with end-form
EVP: verb phrase with end-form
EVS: verb sentence with end-form

GaNP: 'ga' noun phrase
LC: lingustic concept
N: noun
NoNP: 'no' noun phrase
NP: noun phrase
NS: noun sentence
P: phrase
Pa: postpositional particle
S: sentence
VB: verb
VP: verb phrase
VS: verb sentence
WaNP: 'wa' noun phrase
WORD: word

Fig. 2 — Part of a language model.

tion. Phrases are also classified according to the conjugation of the words that end them. Thus, the system has an adnominal phrase class (ADNP) and a phrase with end-form class (EP). The noun phrase (NP) is classified into a 'ga' noun phrase (GaNP), 'wa' noun phrase (WaNP), or 'no' noun phrase (NoNP) — that is, the particle (ga, wa, or no) that terminates a phrase. For example, the part of the sentence 'kawasaki-shi no koujou ga' ('a factory in Kawasaki City') is classified as a 'ga' noun phrase because its last bunsetsu 'koujou ga' consists of a noun 'koujou' followed by the particle 'ga'.

A set of syntactic rules is linked to some LM classes. Such a class usually contains two or three rules. A rule consists of two components — a conditional component that checks whether the rule can be applied to the input parse tree having a meaning structure and an action component that transforms the input parse tree and produces a new meaning structure. Figs. 3 and 4 give examples of LM class rules.

```
("no"-noun-phase
    (meta class     (rule:set))
    (super class    (noun-phrase) (adnominal))
    (control        (doall))
    (rule
        ("no")noun-phrase-with-L1¬=adnominal ;RULE NAME
          (if       (and (L1 ¬= adnominal)
                         (R1  = noun-phrase)
                         (semantic check between C and R1)))
          (then     generation of a new state
                    transformation of a syntactic tree
                    setting a parse priority))
        ("no"-noun-phrase-with-L1=adnoun     ;RULE NAME
          (if       (and L1   = adnominal)
                         (R1  = noun-phrase)
                         (semantic check between C and R1)))
          (then     generation of a new state
                    transformation of a syntactic tree
                    right shift for buffer
                    setting a parse priority))))
```

Fig. 3 — Rules in the 'no' noun-phrase class.

```
(noun-phrase
        . . .
    (rule
            (noun-phrase                          ;RULE NAME
                (if       (there is noun phrase ahead))
                (then     creation of a new state
                          left shift for buffer
                          setting a parse priority))))
```

Fig. 4 — Rule in the noun-phrase class.

3.2 Rule inheritance

There are two types of rule inheritance. In the first, the system will search for rules in its superclass if there are no rules in an activated class object. In the second, rules of a particular class are combined with those of its superclass. Rule inheritance is explained below using an example.

The input sentence used in the example in Figs. 5–8 is 'kawasaki-shi no

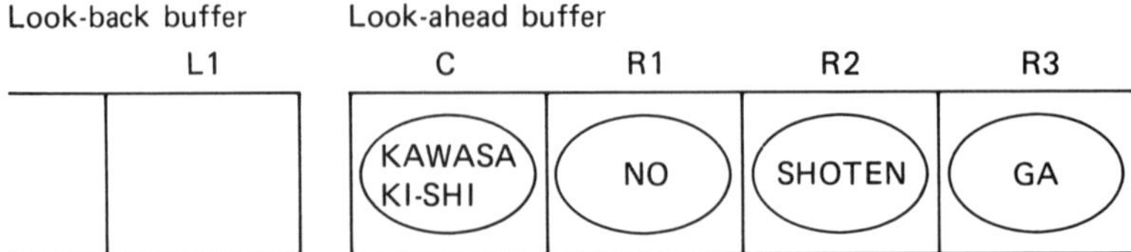

Fig. 5 — State after morphological analysis.

shoten ga hanbaisuru shohin wa' ('which merchandise does the retailer in Kawasaki City sell?'). Morphological analysis transforms this sentence into a string of instances of classes of constituent words (Fig. 5).

In Fig. 5, the nodes in the buffer are instances of the dictionary class. Here, the system sends a message to node C (the 'kawasaki-shi' instance) to execute the rule. This instance and the 'kawasaki-shi' class object do not have rules, so the rules of the noun-class objects, which is a superclass of the 'kawasaki-shi' class object, are activated. Such rules are generic and can be applied to all instances in subclasses of the noun class. In this example, the rules referring to node R1 form an instance object for the 'no' noun phrase and transform the parse tree (Fig. 6). This type of rule inheritance is also

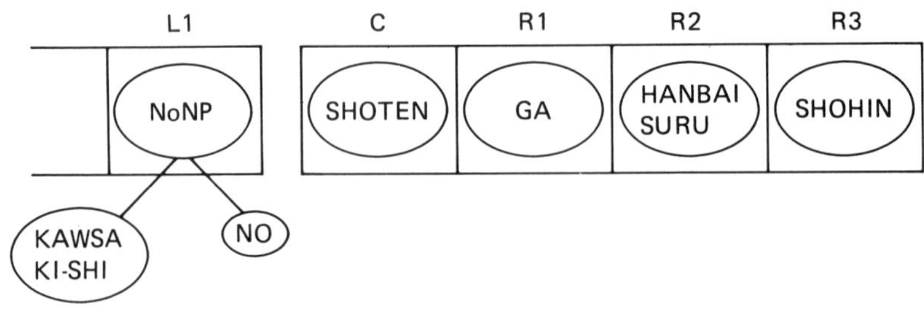

Fig. 6 — State after application of noun-phrase rule.

implemented in the adnominal sentence class and its subclasses such as the adnominal verb sentence and adnominal adjective sentence. The same rules as those for the adnominal sentence class are used for different parts of speech, reducing the overall number of rules.

Fig. 4.7 shows a state in the parsing process — after bunsetsu processing

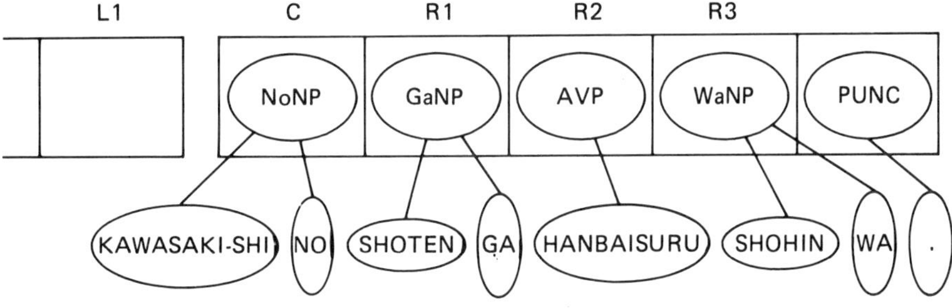

Fig. 7 — State after completion of the 'bunsetsu' process.

has been applied. The 'no' noun-phrase class has two rules (Fig. 3). When this object is activated, its rules and its superclass rule (Fig. 4), which is in a noun-phrase class, are merged to form a set of rules. The rule in the noun-phrase class is also used for the 'ga' and 'wa' noun-phrase classes which, having no rules, inherit the rule in the noun-phrase class. Applying rules in the 'no' noun-phrase and noun-phrase classes to the state in Fig. 7 forms the two states in Fig. 8.

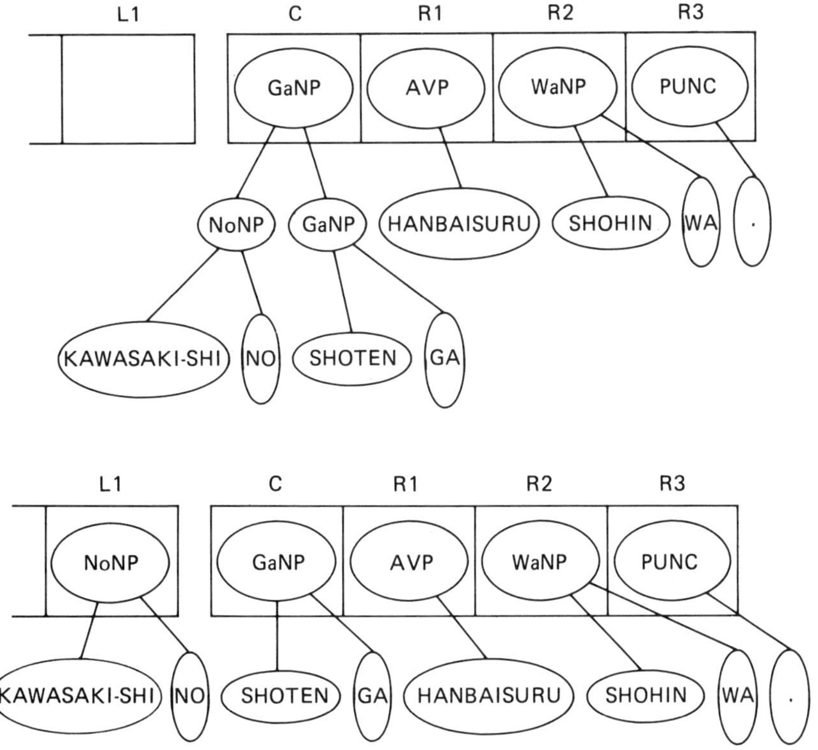

Fig. 8 — States after 'no' noun-phrase class rule application.

3.3 Attribute inheritance

The inheritance of grammatical attributes simplifies the syntactic pattern of the rule's conditional component. For example, an expression in the 'no' noun-phrase class. L1=adnominal, shows that L1 is a subclass of the adnominal class. Using this expression eliminates the need for a disjunctive expression such as

L1='no' noun phrase OR adnominal phrase OR . . .

4. SEMANTIC ANALYSIS USING A WORLD MODEL

4.1 Overview

The world model (WM) represents the user's image of the application domain — that is, classes and how they are related. A class is represented as an object in the object-oriented programming sense (Bobrow and Stefik, 1981), which describes a thing or an event in a domain. There are only two types of relationship; attribute and sub-super. This model matches the user's image and is very simple, making model design and editing easy. Fig. 9 shows the part of the world model for a sales domain. The commodity class has two attribute classes, commodity name and fixed price. The beer and whisky classes are subclasses of the commodity class and inherit its attributes.

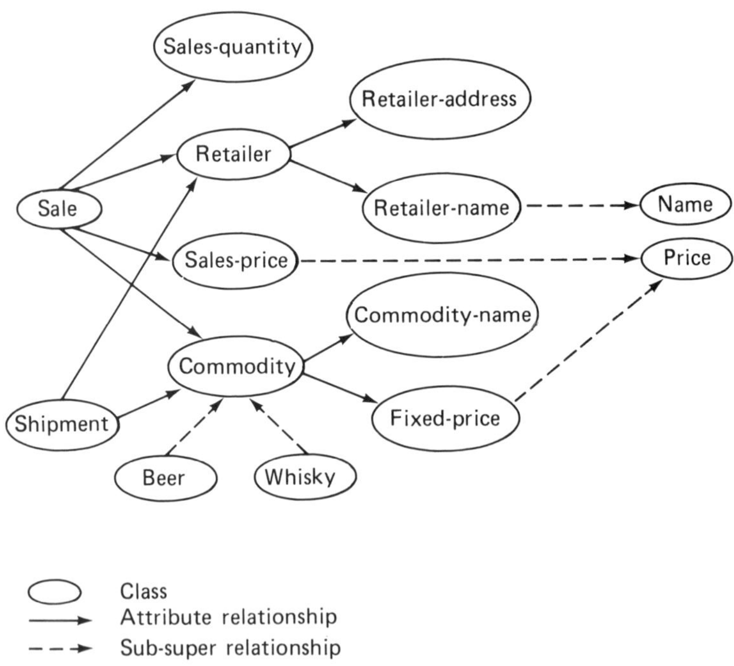

Fig. 9 — Part of the world model for sales.

4.2 Representation of meaning and rules for semantic analysis

We use the WM model not only as a knowledge base for semantic interpretation, but also as a meaning structure for user queries. Semantic interpretation identifies WM classes in the user's query, instantiates them, and makes a network of the instances isomorphic to WM classes as a meaning structure. This isomorphic structure enables users to verify clearly the results of semantic interpretation.

Semantic interpretation has two basic rules; specialization and connection. These rules check the relationship between the classes corresponding to phrases and interpret the meaning of a new unified phrase which has the phrases as its subtrees.

The specialization rule corresponds to a sub–super relationship. If two classes, corresponding to two phrases, are connected by a sub–super relationship, the specialization rule selects the subclass as the meaning of the unified phrase, because the subclass has a more specific and restricted meaning than the superclass. Fig. 10 is an example of the specialization rule

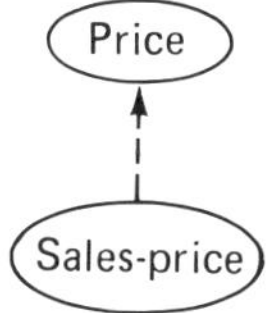

Hanbaikakaku ga 200 yen
(The sales-price is 200 yen)

Fig. 10 — Example of specialization rule.

in which the phrase 'hanbaikakaku' corresponds to the sales price class, and '200 yen' corresponds to the price class. The specialization rule selects the sales price class as the overall meaning.

The connection rule corresponds to an attribute relationship. For two classes connected by such a relationship, this rule selects the class of modified phrase as the meaning of the unified phrase. Fig. 11 is an example of the connection rule, in which the phrase 'hanbaiten' corresponds to the retailer class, and 'namae' corresponds to the name class. The connection rule selects the retailer-name class as the overall meaning. Fig. 12 shows the meaning structure of an input sentence.

5. DEBUGGING TOOLS

As a result of nondeterministic parsing, bugs may affect the system in unexpected ways, which makes debugging difficult. To avoid this problem,

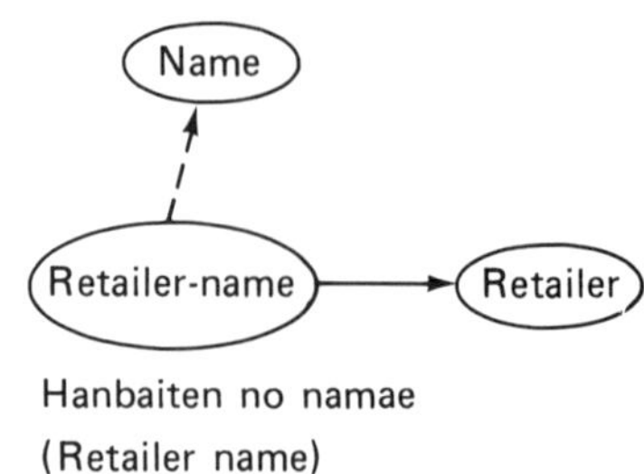

Fig. 11 — Example of the connection rule.

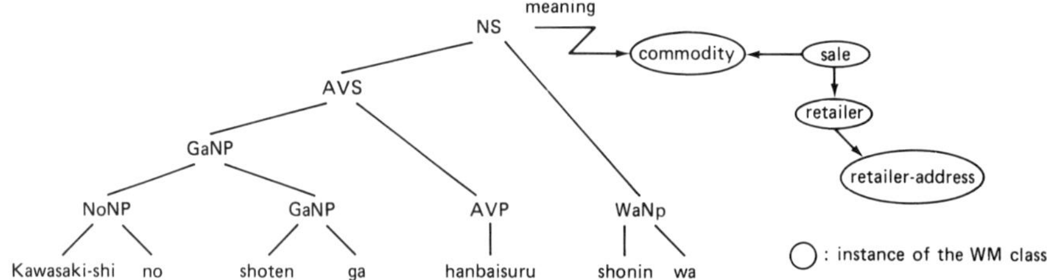

Fig. 12 — Example of a meaning structure and a parse tree.

the system keeps all parse trees produced in a parsing process. A parse tree represents a parse state in the process, enabling users to do the following:

(1) Follow the state transition of the parsing process.
(2) Rerun the analysis process from any parse state after syntactic rules have been updated.
(3) See, step by step, what happens in the system.

6. CONCLUSION

We have described a Japanese-language interface system that demonstrates good transportability, extendability and maintainability. Linguistic knowledge is encapsulated in the language model, domain-specific knowledge is implemented in the world model. The language model plays an important role in the transportability, extendability, and maintainability of syntactic rules. The world model makes it easy to transport the system from one application domain to another.

The system was implemented in an object-oriented language MINERVA. MINERVA has three level layers of objects — metaclass,

class, and instance objects — a hierarchical class–level link, and a rule-oriented mechanism. The language model and the world model are implemented by using class-level objects. The language model has 172 classes that contain a total of 142 rules.

Our system has been used in experiments as the interface for supermarket information, library, and real-estate information retrieval systems. We tested the system's transportability using a medical database differing greatly from the three databases used in experiments. The interface to the database can be implemented into the new domain in less than a month, which underscores the system's good transportability.

REFERENCES

Bobrow, D. G. and Stefik, M. (1981) *The LOOPS Manual: a Data Oriented and Object Oriented Programming System for Interlisp*, Xerox PARC, Knowledge-based VLSI Design Group Memo.

Hayes, D. J. (1984) Entity-oriented parsing. *Proc. 10th Intl. Conf. Computational Linguistics*, pp. 212–217.

Hendrix, G. G. *et al.* (1978) Developing a natural language interface to complex data. *ACM Trans. Database Syst.* **3**(2), 105–147.

Ishikawa, H. *et al.* (1986) A knowledge-based approach to design a portable natural language interface to database systems. *Proc. IEEE COMPDEC Conf.*, pp. 134–143.

Marcus, M. P. (1980) *A Theory of Syntactic Recognition for Natural Language*, MIT Press, Cambridge, Mass.

Nilsson, N. J. (1980) *Principles of Artificial Intelligence*, Tioga, Palo Alto, California.

Sato, S. and Sugimoto, M. (1986) Artificial Intelligence. *Fujitsu Sci. Tech. J.* **22**(3), 139–181.

Small, S. and Rieger, C. (1982) Parsing and comprehending with word experts: (a theory and its realization). In: *Strategies for Natural Language Processing* (eds. M. D. Ringle and W. Lehnert), Lawrence Erlbaum Associates, Hillside, New Jersey.

Waltz, D. L. (1978) An English language question answering system for a large relational database. *Communications of the ACM* **21**(7), 526–539.

Yoshimura, K. *et al.* (1983) Morphological analysis of non-marked-off Japanese sentences by the least bunsetsu's number method. *Transactions of Information Processing Society of Japan* **24**(1), 40–46 (in Japanese).

Part III
Databases

8

Integration of artificial intelligence techniques into existing database management systems

A. Illarramendi, R. Demolombe[†] and **J. M. Blanco**
Euskal Herriko Unibertsitatea, Informatika Fakultatea, 649 PK, 20080 Donostia, Spain
†Centre de'Etudes et de Recherches de Toulouse, 2 Avenue Edouard-Belin, 31055 Toulouse Cedex, France

SUMMARY

Using a combination of technologies for database management systems (DBMS) and artificial intelligence (AI) may prove beneficial to future management information systems. A DBMS can be used more intelligently and efficiently if enhanced with AI technology, while artificial intelligence techniques, particularly expert systems (ES), can effectively access very large databases through existing DBMS technology.

1. INTRODUCTION

When the requirements for advanced business applications such as decision support for managerial users are considered, current database management systems display a number of weaknesses. In this area, artificial intelligence approaches, particularly expert systems, are more interesting. On the other hand, it is also interesting to improve the ability of expert systems to access and use existing very large databases as extensions of their own knowledge base. Using a combination of technologies for database management systems and artificial intelligence may prove beneficial to future management information systems.

The interaction between DBMS and AI can be organized according to three different architectures (Fig. 1).

In this chapter we are going to present one application of the AI architecture, specifically in the query optimization area.

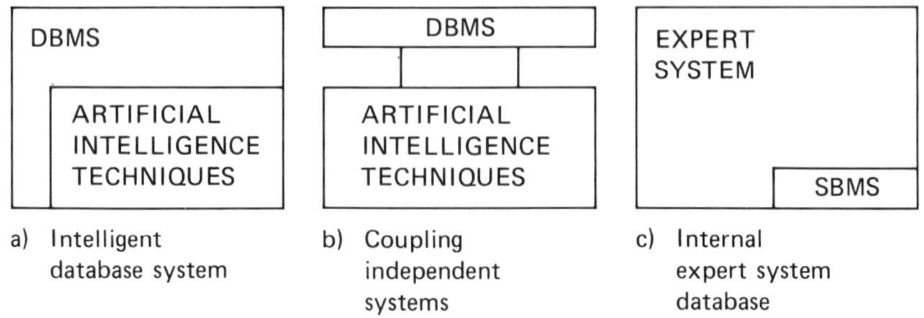

Fig. 1.

With the advent of high-level query languages, the issue of database query optimization has become a major factor in database management system performance, because an end-user could express queries that would be extremely costly to evaluate if performed in a straightforward brute-force manner.

Semantic query optimization is an approach to query optimization that uses knowledge of the semantics of the data to transform a query into another query that has the same answer (but which is quite different in its expression) and can be processed more efficiently, given the existing file structures and access methods.

The technique of semantic query optimization has been introduced by King (1984) and independently by Manner and Zdonik (1980).

In this chapter we are going to present, first of all, an overview of the system which carries out the semantic optimization of the queries. In this system three distinct parts are considered (Fig. 2). In the next section we present the way we can determine the query correctness. Later, we describe the kinds of information that can be expressed in the rule base, the language in which it is represented and a deduction mechanism for the optimization process. Lastly, we explain the third part of the system, which selects, among all the information obtained from the preceding operation, only that which permits the query transformation that is interesting, taking into consideration existing storage structures and access methods in the database.

2. OVERVIEW OF THE SYSTEM

In our approach the system which optimizes relational queries has several parts. Fig. 2 shows the different modules in its architecture.

In operational terms, the system starts with the query, expressed by a predicate calculus well-formed formula (wff) and determines whether it is a meaningful query or not (1). It then obtains all the information that can be derived from a rule and query base with a specific deduction mechanism; the

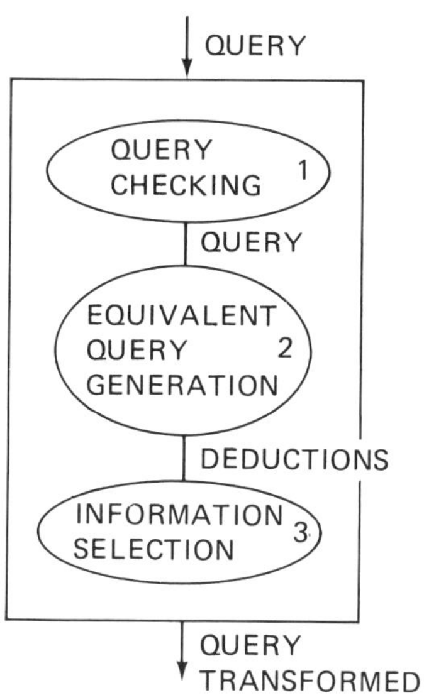

Fig. 2.

process terminates when no more information can be derived, or when one deduces that there is no answer for the query (2). Finally the system selects, among all the deduced information, that which permits the transformation of the query into some other one that can make a significant reduction in the cost of query processing (3).

3. MODULES OF THE SYSTEM

3.1 To determine the correctness of a query

Not all predicate calculus wff correspond to meaningful queries. For example the query: **−Father(x,a),** is not meaningful because it defines the complement of a set with respect to another one which is not specified in the query.

In order to avoid this problem, different authors have defined syntactically the wff classes which are known to be significant. These restrictions are generally more severe than is necessary, so we have chosen a method defined by Demolombe (1982) that works with a much wider class of wff: **'the evaluable formula'** (Fig. 3). We can easily test a formula to see if it is evaluable.

However, the definition of evaluable formula refers only to the syntactic form of the formula and does not involve the meaning of the predicates. For example, the query

Father(x,a) ∧ Mother(x,a)

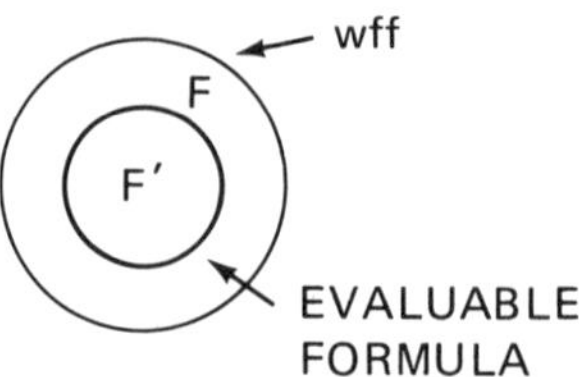

Fig. 3.

is correct syntactically but cannot have an answer because if we consider the following meaning of the predicates Father and Mother, we have the rules:

> if **x** is the father of **a** then **x** is a man
> if **x** is the mother of **a** then **x** is a woman

and knowing that **x** cannot be at the same time man and woman, we arrive at a contradiction.

For this reason Demolombe (1979) has also defined the semantic control of the evaluable formulae. With this method we can reject queries which have a defined sense but which, in the context of a clearly-determined application, cannot have an answer. These checks are very useful because the evaluation time for queries with an empty set as answer is often longer than for others.

3.2 To obtain equivalent queries

For the purposes of this part, we are going to use artificial-intelligence techniques. We have designed an inference mechanism in order to derive information from the rule and query base (Fig. 4).

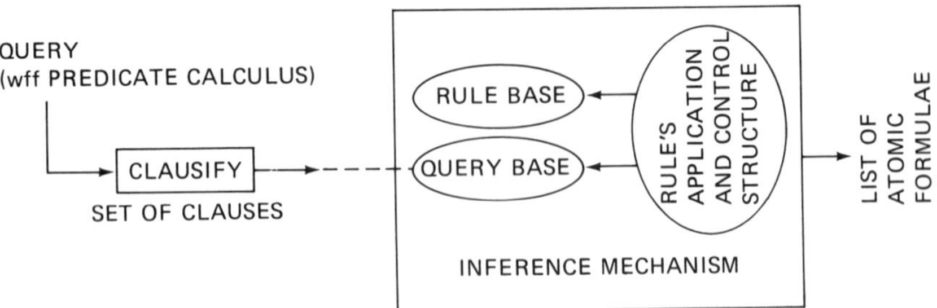

Fig. 4.

The **rule base** is defined in terms of a set of CLAUSES that express constraints on sets of objects in the database. The initial core of this collection will be constructed by the database administrator, and as time goes on, this initial base will be modified also by him, in order to reflect changes in the structure of the database.

The **query base** is defined in terms of a set of CLAUSES that are obtained from the query formulated by the user.

We use special **resolution strategy** (section 4) as a **deduction mechanism.** The resolution strategy is not complete but on the other hand, in our context, the target of the transformation process is not known (as opposed to a theorem whose proof is being sought), and we are interested in deducing from the rule base the information that has relation to the query and not all the deducible information. This objective permits us to work with an incomplete resolution strategy.

The deduction process is based on the following idea. Given a rule base KB, and a query Q(X), where X is the set of free variables of the query, we are looking for atomic formulae A(Y) which can be deduced from KB, and $Q(X_0)$, where X_0 is any tuple satifying Q, (in logic X_0 is a tuple of so-called Skolem constants). In this process we only work with a collection of declaratively-expressed facts about the application domain.

For the purposes of this part, we assume that among all the clauses that we can obtain in the deduction process, we select only those that are atomic formulae, the reasons for this being the problems that the general expression of a clause present in the later physical optimization and algorithm generation processes within our context.

For the successful application of the semantic knowlege to query processing, we consider (as King (1984) and Hammer and Zdonik (1980) do) crucial the control of the query-transformation process. For this reason we have chosen an approach defined by King (1984) in which the target selection is governed by a set of heuristics based on knowledge of query processing and file structures.

The main differences between our approach of semantic query optimization and the approaches introduced by King (1984) and Hammer and Zdonik (1980) are that we use a deduction method based on a resolution principle and we also admit all kinds of queries for possible semantic transformation, not only a subset of queries as the other approaches do. Minker *et al.* (1986) have also presented another approach of semantic query optimization, but our difference with their approach is that they are mainly interested in adding the exceptions in the query in order to transform it.

3.3 Analysis of implementation structures

Not all the atomic formulae that have been inferred from the preceding process will be interesting for making query transformations. That will depend on the existing storage structures and access methods in the specific state of the database.

In operational terms, this module starts with the first atomic formula A inferred and determines whether it is

(1) **a redundant atomic formula.** There is in the query an atomic formula B

which differs only from the atomic formula A in the name of the variables. That is, A is a variant of B.

(2) **a non-redundant atomic formula.** The atomic formula A is not in case 1.

In case 1 the module has to check whether the atomic formula B is really redundant. This will be done by running again the deduction process after removing B from the query base. If A is obtained again as a derived atomic formula, then the atomic formula B can be removed from the query, if it does not present any characteristics (e.g. index, etc.) that permit processing the query more efficiently. The atomic formula B can be eliminated without modification of the query semantics because in fact it is redundant.

Indeed if Q is of the form $Q(X)=Q_1(X_0) \wedge B(Y_0)$

and we have	$KB, Q_1(X_0) \vdash B(Y_0)$
then	$KB \vdash Q_1(X_0) \rightarrow B(Y_0)$
then	$KB \vdash Q_1(X_0) \wedge B(Y_0) = Q_1(X_0)$
then	$KB \vdash Q(X) = Q_1(X_0)$

In case 2 the atomic formula A will be added to the query if it presents some characteristics that permit the answer to be computed more efficiently.

From	$KB,Q(X_0) \vdash A(Y_0)$
we have	$KB \vdash Q(X_0) \rightarrow A(Y_0)$
then	$KB \vdash Q(X_0) = Q(X_0) \wedge A(Y_0)$

This module repeats the previous cycle until there are no more inferred clauses. All the clauses selected by this module will form the semantic optimization of the query.

4. AN ILLUSTRATION OF THE SYSTEM AT WORK

We now illustrate this abstract description of the system in terms of a concrete example. The example shows how the system analyses a query posed to the following database:

Set of relations:

TEACH(x,y):	Person x teaches the language y
SPEAK(x,y):	Person x speaks the language y
COUNTRY(x,y):	The country of the person x is y
CITIZEN(x,y):	The citizenship of x is y
LAN)(x):	x is a language.

A very simple knowledge base of general semantic rules accompanies the database in this example. It includes the following rules:

. **RULE R1.** If a person speaks **Euskara** then his country is **Euskalherria.**
SPEAK(x,Euskara)→COUNTRY(x,Euskalherria)

. **RULE R2.** If a person teaches a language and his country is **Euskalherria** then he speaks **Euskara**

LAN(y) ∧ TEACH(x,y) ∧ COUNTRY(x,Euskalherria) → SPEAK(x,Euskara)

. **RULE R3.** If a person teaches some language then he speaks that language.
LAN(y) ∧ TEACH(x,y) → SPEAK(x,y)

. **RULE R4.** If the citizenship of a person is **Spanish** then his country can not be **North_Euskadi.**
CITIZEN(x,Spanish) ∧ COUNTRY(x,North_Euskadi)

. **RULE R5.** If the country of a person is **Euskalherria** then the country can be **North_Euskadi** or **South_Euskadi.**
COUNTRY(x,Euskalherria) →
COUNTRY(x,North_Euskadi) ∨
COUNTRY(x,South_Euskadi).

. **RULE R6.** Euskara is a language.
LAN(Euskara)

The rules are represented as CLAUSES where the literals can be atomic formulae, or negation of atomic formulae. An atomic formula can be of the following two types:

−P(t_1, . . . ,t_m) **P** — Predicate symbol
t_1, . . . ,t_m variables or constants
−P)t_1, . . . ,t_m) (e) **P** — Predicate symbol
t_1, . . . ,t_m variables or constants
e subexpression between parentheses where the predicates
are only comparison operators and without quantifiers

The **knowledge base** is as follows (the boldface type is used to represent constants, the other type represents variables):

R1: **−SPEAK(x,Euskara) ∨ COUNTRY(x,Euskalherria)**
R2: **−LAN(y) ∨ −TEACH(x,y) ∨ −COUNTRY(x,Euskalherria) ∨ SPEAK(x,Euskara)**
R3: **−LAN(y) ∨ −TEACH(x,y) ∨ SPEAK(x,y)**
R4: **−CITIZEN(x,Spanish) ∨ −COUNTRY(x, North_Euskadi)**
R5: **−COUNTRY(x,Euskalherria) ∨ COUNTRY(x,North_Euskadi) ∨ COUNTRY(x,South_Euskadi)**
R6: **LAN(Euskara)**

We assume that all the variables that appear in the conclusion literal must appear in the some literal premise of the rule. This condition guarantees that the rules are meaningful formulae.

We now consider the **resolution process.** Let S_1,S_2 and S be three sets of clauses; we say that **S is the result of computing S_1 and S_2** iff: C{S is equivalent to 'C_1{S_1 and 'C_2{S_2 and C is a resolvent† of C_1 and C_2.

We consider two sets of clauses: A_0 that corresponds to the rule base and C_0 that corresponds to the query base. The strategy we use in order to derive the clauses that are interesting in our context is the following (Fig. 5):

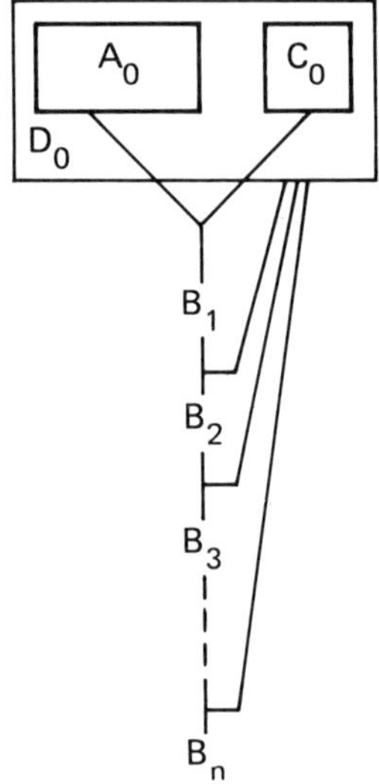

Fig. 5.

(1) B_1 is the result of computing A_0 and C_0.
(2) B_i is the result of computing D_0 and B_{i-1}, from $i=2, \ldots, n$ (where D_0 is the union of C_0 and A_0).
(3) The process stops for B_n if B_n is the empty clause or if it is the set that satisfies the following condition: the result of computing B_n and D_0 is the empty set: that is, no more information can be inferred from D_0 and B_n.
(4) If B_n is the empty clause then the result of the process, C, is the empty clause, else C={U B_i}. When the result of the process is the empty

† Given two clauses A and B, with no variables in common, a clause C is a **resolvent** of A and B if the following hold:

There is a subset $A'=\{A_1, \ldots, A_m\}$! A of literals all of the same sign, and a subset $B'=\{B_1, \ldots, B_n\}$! B of literals all of the opposite sign of the set A', such that s is a most general unifier of the set

$$|(A') \text{ U } (B')|$$

then we have

$$C=(A-A') \text{ s U } (B-B') \text{ s}$$

clause the answer of the query is empty whatever the content of the database is, so in that case it is not necessary to search for the answer in the database.

In order to make the resolution process more efficient we have introduced the **subsumption** concept of Chang and Lee (1973). A clause C subsumes a clause D if and only if there is a substitution s such that C_s!D. D is called a subsumed clause. For example let C=P(X) and D=P(a); Q(a). If s={a/x} then C_s=P(a). Since $C_{s'}$! D, C subsumes D.

With the following query we show what the system can deduce.

> *'List all the languages taught by the persons whose citizenship is Spanish and who teach Euskara'*
>
> Q(x,y)=LAN(y) ∧ TEACH(x,y) ∧ CITIZEN(x,Spanish) ∧ TEACH(x,Euskara)

First of all the CLAUSIFY module will translate the query to the clausal form.

QUERY BASE

C1- **LAN(y0)**
C2: **TEACH(x0,y0)** x_0,y_0 are Skolem constants.
C3: **CITIZEN(x0,Spanish)**
C4: **TEACH(x0,Euskara)**

We assume that the method defined by King (1984) has selected all the relations as target relations. Then the **resolution** process starts. (We do not present all the clauses that can be derived, just a subset of them in order to show what kind of information it is possible to deduce.)

B1:
F4 [R4,C3]: – **COUNTRY(x_0, North_Euskadi)**

. . . .

B2:
F7 [R5,F4]: – **COUNTRY(x_0,Euskalherria)** ∨ **COUNTRY(x_0,South_Euskadi)**

. . . .

B3:
F9 [R1,F7]: – **SPEAK(x_0,Euskara)** ∨ **COUNTRY(x_0,South_Euskadi)**

. . . .

B4:
F12 [R3,F9]: – **LAN(Euskara)** ∨ – **TEACH(x_0,Euskara)** ∨ **COUNTRY(x_0,South_Euskadi)**

B5:
F16 {C4,F12]: – **LAN(Euskara)** ∨ **COUNTRY(x_0,South_Euskadi)**

. . . .

B6:

F17 [R6,F16]: **COUNTRY(x_0,South_Euskadi)**

The process stops here. The result of the process is **COUNTRY(x_0,South_Euskadi).**

At this point, the system analyses whether the inferred clause is interesting to add to the query, taking into consideration the present implementation structures of the database.

It is interesting to remark that we do not work only with Horn clauses.

5. FURTHER REMARKS ON THE INFERENCE PROCESS

In section 3.2 we have assumed that the resolution strategy that we use is not complete, and we have explained that this is not a problem in our context. However, we are interested in having a decidable strategy in order to perfom the semantic optimization of the query in a finite time.

We have chosen the example presented by Bry and Manthey (1986) in order to illustrate this problem:

KNOWLEDGE BASE
R1. ¬ MAN(x) ∨ ¬ MARRIED(x,y) ∨ WOMAN(y)
R2. ¬ WOMAN(x) ∨ ¬ MARRIED(x,y) ∨ MAN(y)

QUERY BASE
C1. MAN(**Peter**)
C2. MARRIED(**Peter,**$\mathbf{y_0}$)

DERIVATION PROCESS
$\mathbf{B_1}$
F1. [C1,R1] ¬ MARRIED(**Peter,y**) ∨ WOMAN(y)
F2. [C2,R1) ¬ MAN(**Peter**) ∨ WOMAN($\mathbf{y_0}$)
F3. [C2,R2] ¬ WOMAN(**Peter**) ∨ MAN($\mathbf{y_0}$)

$\mathbf{B_2}$
F4. [F3,R1] ¬ MARRIED($\mathbf{y_0}$,y) ∨ ¬ WOMAN(**Peter**) ∨ WOMAN(y)
F5. [F3,R1] ¬ MAN(x) ∨ ¬ MARRIED(c,**Peter**) ∨ MAN($\mathbf{y_0}$)
F6. [F1,R2] ¬ MARRIED(y,z) ∨ ¬ MARRIED(**Peter**,y) ∨ MAN(z)
F7. [F2,R2] ¬ MARRIED($\mathbf{y_0}$,y) ∨ ¬ MAN(**Peter**) ∨ MAN(y)
F8. [F2,C1] WOMAN($\mathbf{y_0}$)
$\mathbf{B_3}$
F9. [F5,R1] ¬ MAN(x) ∨ ¬ MARRIED(x,**Peter**) ∨ ¬ MARRIED ($\mathbf{y_0}$,y) ∨ WOMAN(y)
F10. [F6,R1] ¬ MARRIED(z,x) ∨ ¬ MARRIED(**Peter**,y) ∨ ¬ MARRIED(y,z) ∨ WOMAN(x)
F11. [F7,R1] ¬ MARRIED(y,x) ∨ ¬ MAN(**Peter**) ∨ ¬ MARRIED ($\mathbf{y_0}$,y) ∨ WOMAN(x)
F12. [F4,R2] ¬ MARRIED(y,x) ∨ ¬ WOMAN(**Peter**) ∨ ¬ MARRIED($\mathbf{y_0}$,y) ∨ ¬ WOMAN(**Peter**) ∨ ¬ MARRIED($\mathbf{y_0}$,y) ∨ MAN(x)
F13. [F5,R2] ¬ WOMAN(y) ∨ ¬ MARRIED(y,x) ∨ ¬ MARRIED (x,**Peter**) ∨ MAN($\mathbf{y_0}$)

F14. [F7,C1] ¬ MARRIED(**y_0**,y) ∨ MAN(y)
F15. [F5,C1] ¬ MARRIED(**Peter,Peter**) ∨ MAN(**y_0**)

If we observe the derivation process, we can see that there are cycles in it. For example we find one cycle for the clauses F1, F6, F10:

— F6 is a binary resolvent of F1 and R2; WOMAN(y) and ¬ WOMAN(x) are the literals resolved upon.
— F10 is a binary resolvent of F6 and R1; MAN(z) and ¬ MAN(x) are the literals resolved upon.

In the clause F10 we find again WOMAN(x), so we can obtain a new clause F_i, where F_i would be a binary resolvent of F10 and R2, WOMAN(x) and – WOMAN(x) would be the literals resolved upon.

Continuing with the process, F_q could be obtained from F_i and R1, and so on. As we can see this process will be infinite, the reason for this being the existence of recursive rules (R1 and R2) in the knowledge base.

The general format of the clauses in the cycles will be:

¬ MARRIED(Peter,y_1) ∨ ¬ MARRIED(y_1,y_2) ∨ . . . ∨
¬ MARRIED(y_{n-1}, y_n) ∨ MAN(y_n) if n is even.
¬ MARRIED(Peter,y_1) ∨ ¬ MARRIED(y_1,y_2) ∨ . . . ∨
¬ MARRIED(y_{n-1}, y_n) ∨ WOMAN(y_n) if n is odd.

To solve this problem, that is to stop the process when there are recursive rules in the rule base, a number of solutions have been proposed (Lozinskii, 1986). One of these solutions (Minker and Nicolas, 1983) uses a subsumption concept in order to cut a cycle when an expression appears that is subsumed by one of its ancestors. This solution applies well to the class of singular recursive axioms.

We are interested in working with recursive definitions in general, and for this reason we have defined the following strategy:

For each new clause that the system infers with our resolution strategy, a check is made to see whether it is possible to reduce it to a clause with only one atomic formula. In order to check the condition we use a heuristic.

Heuristic: to apply resolution strategy only with the input clauses that permit the obtaining of new clauses with a length equal to or smaller than the length of the clause that we are checking. In this process we also use the subsumption concept. When this heuristic is applied it reduces again the strategy completeness.

Now, we illustrate this strategy on the previous example.

B_1
F1. [R1,C1] ¬ MARRIED(**Peter**,y) ∨ WOMAN(y)
F2. [R1,C2] ¬ MAN(**Peter**) ∨ WOMAN(**y_0**)
F3. [R2,C2] ¬ WOMAN(**Peter**) ∨ MAN(**y_0**)
B_2
F4. [F3,R1] ¬ MARRIED(**y_0**,y) ∨ ¬ WOMAN(**Peter**) ∨ WOMAN(y)
eliminated
F5. [F3,R1] ¬ MAN(x) ∨ ¬ MARRIED(**x,Peter**) ∨ MAN(**y_0**)

eliminated
F6. [F1,R2] ¬ MARRIED(y,z) ∨ ¬ MARRIED(**Peter,y**) ∨ MAN(z)
eliminated
F7. [F2,R2] ¬ MARRIED($\mathbf{y_0}$,y) ∨ ¬ MAN(**Peter**) ∨ MAN(y)
eliminated
F8. [F2,C1] WOMAN ($\mathbf{y_0}$)
$\mathbf{B_3}$
F9. [F8,R2] ¬ MARRIED($\mathbf{y_0}$,y) ∨ MAN(y) eliminated
The process will stop here. The clause inferred is **WOMAN($\mathbf{y_0}$)**

6. CONCLUSION

We present in this chapter a new solution to the problem of transforming a given query into another one which has the same meaning and a lower computational cost, by using artificial-intelligence techniques.

We have used a deduction strategy based on a resolution principle in order to obtain the information that can be used to achieve query transformations. Dealing with a resolution principle provides a well-known background in which it is easier to show that the deduction process stops in a finite time.

The main interest of our strategy is that it works with all kind of rules and queries, except for those containing function symbols in their clausal form.

On the other hand, our strategy is not complete but this is not a problem because we are not interested in all the formulae derivable from the rule base and query base. Instead since we just want to derive information which has some relation with the query and allows us to optimize the query evaluation.

The system is implemented in Prolog and POP11.

REFERENCES

Barrett, R., Ramsay, A. and Sloman, A. (1985)*POP-11: A practical language for Artificial Intelligence,* Ellis Horwood, Chichester.

Bry, F. and Manthey, R. (1986) Checking consistency of database constraints: a logical basis. *Proc. VLDB '88.*

Chang, C. L. and Lee, R. C. T. (1973) *Symbolic Logic and Mechanical Theorem Proving,* Academic Press.

Cholvy, L. and Demolombe, R. (1986) Querying a rule base. *First Conference on Expert Database Systems, Charleston, 1986.*

Date, C. J. (1983) *An Introduction to Database Systems,* Vol. I, fourth edition, Addison-Wesley.

Demolombe, R. (1979) Semantic checking of questions expressed in predicate calculus language. *Proc. VLDB '79.*

Demolombe, R. (1982) Syntactical characterisation of a sub-set of domain independent formulas. *Int. Rep. ONERA–CERT.*

Gallier, J. H. (1987) *Logic for Computer Science,* John Wiley & Sons Inc., New York.

Gardarin, G. and Gelenbe, E. (1984) *New Applications of Data Bases,* Academic Press.

Hammer, M. and Zdonik, S. (1980) Knowledge-based query processing. *Proc. VLDB 80.*

King, J. (1984) *Query Optimization by Semantic Reasoning,* UMI Research Press.

Lozinskii, E. (1986) A problem-oriented inferential database system. *Transactions on Database Systems,* **11** (3) (September).

Minker J. and Nicolas, J. M. (1983) On recursive axioms in deductive databases. *Inf. Syst.* **8**(1).

Minker, J., Grant, J. and Charkravarthy, U. S. (1986) *Workshop on Foundations of Deductive Databases and Logic Programming, USA, August 1986.*

Selinger, Griffiths, P. *et al.* (1979) Access path selection in a relational database management system. *Proc. ACM-SIGMOD Conference, May 1979.*

Ullman, J. (1982) *Principles of Database Systems,* Computer Science Press.

9

Integration of databases and expert systems through Prolog

P. M. D. Gray
University of Aberdeen, Department of Computing Science,
Kings College, Aberdeen AB9 2UB, Scotland

1. INTRODUCTION

The subject of expert systems started independently of databases in about 1976, when databases were seen to be largely about the keeping of integrated shared collections of commercial records. Since then, databases have been adapted to store much wider classes of data, and expert systems have begun to require access to data in databases. Thus the two subjects have become linked. One result of this was the First International Workshop on Expert Database Systems in 1984 (Kerschberg), and the International Conference two years later in Charleston (U.S.A.) which I reviewed recently (Gray, 1986).

A common topic of both subjects is making information more easily available to the everyday user. In the case of databases the information is mostly facts, held in tables. In the case of expert systems, the information is mostly in the form of rules and procedures, which have been gleaned from experts in a particular application domain. In both cases the aim is to capture information in a machine-readable form, so that it becomes available to a wide range of users, possibly over a computer network, instead of being locked away in someone's head, or in a filing cabinet.

Let me tell a story to illustrate the commercial potential of these ideas. A large firm had its own architect's department for designing and planning new buildings. The finance department, which was separate, handled the forms for tax rebates and grants towards buildings. One day, they decided that the rules had got so complicated, and since also their local expert was about to retire, they would try to put the rules into a computer as an expert system. The result was more successful then they had expected. The buildings department got access to the system and started to ask it questions, as a result of which they changed their ideas about some of their building activities, so as to get more grants and bigger tax rebates. When the information had been less easily available they had not made use of it. Now that it was more readily available, their firm could profit by it.

This story also illustrates one other crucial feature of a successful expert system. The rules that make up the program must be structured so that the program can answer queries that the programmer has not foreseen. Most of the older FORTRAN and COBOL programs, by contrast, are written to meet a precise specification of query types, and they use knowledge as procedures which are called in a particular sequence, largely foreseen by the programmer. The ideal expert system will have a large number of rules available which can be used in different ways. The system itself will decide how to use them by following a *search strategy*. These strategies are still fairly primitive, but it is the use of this kind of program architecture that provides the desired flexibility.

In what follows I shall start by giving a brief overview of expert systems, and explaining their architecture and the various search strategies. I shall then explain how in general this architecture extends to the use of databases. The chapter then focuses on the use of Prolog as an interface language, and discusses various examples to show how Prolog fits very nicely into this architecture, and is also beginning to perform very efficiently.

2. EXPERT SYSTEMS

An 'expert system' is a computer program or system that shows expert ability in some application area. The simplest examples are programs that provide conversational advice through a terminal. For example, MYCIN (Shortliffe, 1976) provides diagnostic advice on bacterial infections and their most probable source. The Drilling Adviser (Teknowledge) provides advice on how to recover an oil-well drill bit that has got stuck.

Another class of programs provide interpretation of data. For example, Prospector (Duda *et al.*, 1977) infers from geological data ('symptoms') the chances of mineral deposits. The Dipmeter Advisor (Smith, 1984) interprets oil-well logs of instrument measurements against depth so as to infer the presence of oil deposits. Yet another class of programs perform planning tasks. XCON, based on R1 (McDermott, 1982) is used by DEC to plan the configuration of modules and their wiring within cabinets so as to form a mainframe computer with specified peripheral interfaces. In all these cases the knowledge or expertise of a human at making judgements has been captured in a computer program. The program produces results on a terminal in the form of advice on an underlying cause, or on actions to take; possibly a detailed plan.

2.1 Rules, facts and searching

All expert systems have certain components. They need to store basic knowledge about the application area (*facts*) together with more generalized knowledge which is used in reasoning (*rules*). The combination of rules and facts is known as the *knowledge base*. To drive the system we need a piece of program which follows the rules according to a 'search strategy'. The kind of searching depends on the task of the expert system. Let us consider an example, with a collection of facts on family relationships:

Juan is Maria's father
Juan is Jose's father
Maria is Sue's mother
Juan is male

We may also have rules on how to recognize more complex relationships:

UNCLE(X,Y) if Brother(X,Z) and (Mother(Z,Y) or Father(Z,Y))
Brother(P,Q) if Male(P) and (Father(P,F) and Father(Q,F))
or (Mother(P,M) and Mother(Q,M))

2.2 Production rules

These rules are cast in the form of 'production rules'. The first one says that a person(X) is the uncle of a person(Y) if they are the brother of that person's mother or father. The mother or father is represented by the unknown variable Z. The second rule says that a person's brother must be male and must have the same parents. Note that the variables (P,Q) are just dummy variables, as in the definitions of Pascal or functions, and their values will be supplied or requested by the search mechanism. The variables (Z,F,M) on the right-hand side (the 'condition part' of the rule) act like local variables in a procedure.

Let us now consider some questions and ways of using these rules.

2.3 Search by backward chaining

We can ask whether Jose is Sue's uncle. One possible search strategy uses 'backward chaining'. This proceeds by matching the goal uncle (Jose, Sue) against the head of the rule, and then trying to see whether it can verify each of the goals in the body in turn left to right. These may in turn set off subgoals.

If we attempt these subgoals, as soon as we encounter them then we are searching 'depth first' as in the programming language Prolog. If, instead, we keep several lines of search open at once, visiting each subgoal in turn in a kind of round-robin fashion, then we are proceeding 'breadth first'. The depth-first proof proceeds by establishing that Jose is the brother of someone (Maria), who has the same father (Juan), and then that Maria is the mother of Sue. The advantage of the depth-first method is that it is easy to backtrack if a hypothesis fails, and that by printing out a trace of the final path we can justify the answer given by the system. This is very important. Thus, instead of just saying 'yes', we give the path followed by the proof, and the names of intermediate people involved.

2.4 Forward chaining

Another search strategy is to start from the facts and use them to deduce everything possible, until we hit the desired fact. Thus instead of working backward from the goal, we work forward from the facts to deduce new facts. For example, we can prove that Juan is Sue's grandfather, that Maria is female (because she is someone's mother), and so on. Each time we deduce new facts such as these we feed them back into any rule whose conditions are all satisfied and deduce a new specific instance of the head of the rule, i.e. that someone is someone's brother, or uncle, etc. This strategy is usually applied breadth first. Thus it cannot get stuck in an infinite loop, but it may run out of space instead, as ever more possibilities are added to the list to be explored. The search terminates when the goal Uncle(Jose,-Sue) is recognized. The forward-chaining strategy is used by the expert system language OPS5.

2.5 More general search

We may ask the system to find whether there exists a person who is Sue's uncle, and, if so, who that person is. Both backward and forward-chaining methods can be used. The backward-chaining method is adapted to pass back the name of the person X who turned out to be the brother of Z, who was found . . . . The forward-chaining method stops when it first generates a fact of the form Uncle(X,Sue), and reports the value of X.

We may ask the system to find the set of all uncles. Again, both methods can be adopted, but it is harder to decide when the forward-chaining system should stop. A still harder problem is to find how Sue is related to Fred, several generations back. In this case we gradually build up descriptions of Sue's ancestors and cousins (e.g. equal(Jose,brother(mother(Sue)))). This is sometimes known as a 'state-space search'. There may be several different paths between Fred and Sue, and we may want to use a technique that will find the most direct one.

Still more complicated problems are possible if we expand our example to provide birthdates. For example, we may have partial information about years of birth and about age differences between people, and limits on ages of mothers at conception, which may be used to deduce other facts. Such problems may be attacked by building up constraint information which is propagated until it becomes so restrictive that a unique solution is possible. This is well explained by Stefik *et al.* (1982), in an excellent review of expert systems.

3. DATABASES

We have used production rules (if . . . then rules) because they are a very general way of holding knowledge. In the MYCIN system, for example, the facts refer to symptoms (temperature,spots etc.) and the rule heads refer ultimately to particular causes of infection. The parameters are used to refine the cause more precisely.

Most expert systems to date have dealt with relatively small numbers of facts, which can all be held in memory while the system is running. They may be input directly from the terminal by a question-and-answer session, often driven by menus enumerating possible replies. They may also be typed in as a file of text in fairly free format, which is read into memory when the system starts up. The rules are written in a special language (e.g. Prolog or OPS5) and held on a separate text file.

More recently, people have found that the sheer number and complexity of rules and facts requires them to be organized in a database. This comes about for a number of reasons.

(I) *The facts are stored in an existing database*. For example, facts on oil wells, or birth and death certificates, may have built up over a long period. The database provides shared access to a number of users, together with forced integrity checks on update to keep the data consistent, and recovery mechanisms when hardware fails or the discs are damaged. By contrast, data which is entered into an expert system from a terminal is not shared, and is lost if the system crashes. Thus it is useful to treat the database as a kind of pretend person, whom the system can query. The query must be posed in a database query language, such as IBM's SQL, and sent over a communications network. Typically the expert system runs on an AI workstation or personal computer, whilst the database resides on a mainframe computer. This method is called *loose coupling* (Jarke and Vassiliou, 1984).

(II) *There are too many facts to store in the memory*. Although the facts need only be accessible from one computer, they may need to be held on secondary storage (disc). For efficiency they will need to be indexed by one of the standard methods used for databases (B-trees or hashing). The same facts may need to be indexed by different keys, e.g. by birth year and by name. They may need an ordered index, for example in order of year. The cost of building up these indexes is generally so great that it takes too long to construct them in the memory at the start of a session. The system will often use special indexes or access methods tailored to its requirements — e.g. for string matching. For quick response, it will access the database directly by low-level routines written in a systems programming language such as C. This is called *tight coupling*.

(III) *The rules need indexing and organizing*.The early expert-system shells assumed that merely by keeping rules in production-rule form, it would be easy to add new rules. However, as the number of rules grew, it was found that the builder might not realize where rules were inconsistent, or repeated the same information with slight variations. Also the time to search for relevant rules grew steadily. In reaction to this, people have developed *frame-based* systems, where rules become 'methods' attached to frames which represent objects, as in the Smalltalk system. The frames correspond to records containing information (facts) about the object, as held in a normal database. They also contain pointers to other frames, from which they can 'inherit' more general information about all members of the class to which the object belongs. The rules are, in effect, indexed via pointers from the frames to the corresponding methods.

Frames are used in systems such as KEE (Intellicorp). Currently the frame systems are built in memory, but it seems clear that they will eventually be maintained on disc in the fashion of a database.

4. USING PROLOG AS AN INTERFACE LANGUAGE

Early versions of Prolog appeared in the mid-1970s, but it was not until Warren's compiler for the DEC-10, and Clocksin and Mellish's book (1981), based on their PDP-11 implementation in 1979, that Prolog became a practical language. Since then it has taken off in a big way. Quintus Prolog now runs on workstations with many megabytes of main memory, and uses techniques of compilation and microcoding to achieve amazing speeds. For example, a sequential scan of tens of thousands of records can be achieved in a few seconds. This is much faster than conventional database systems working with kilobyte buffers.

One major firm that I know is seriously considering the use of large workstations with 4 or 8 megabytes, and loading the data into memory (or a virtual memory image). The cost of such workstations, as produced by Sun and Apple (Macintosh II,) is coming down to several thousand dollars, including an 80-megabyte hard disc. The ability to have information available at the fingertips of its key workers, with fast versatile retrieval through Prolog programs instead of waiting several hours for a batch-processing job on a conventional mainframe with an older DBMS, is what makes all the difference. Once again we return to the theme of rapid and convenient access to information that is otherwise lying dormant and unused.

4.1 Prolog clauses for fact and rule storage

Prolog is a tool for a professional programmer, with which one can quickly build interactive programs to satisfy the needs of an end-user. The end-user would probably be baffled by Prolog, but will be very pleased with the speed of construction of programs, and with their responsiveness.

Prolog programs have a similar architecture to expert systems, in that they are made up of facts and rules. Both are expressed as *clauses*. Facts are expressed as *unit clauses*, for example:

```
likes(juan, maria).
person(juan, male, 21).
```

Each unit clause starts with a *predicate* symbol (such as 'likes' or 'person') followed by a fixed number of parameter values which may be integers, atoms (such as 'juan', 'male') or some other constant. The predicates are asserted to be true when they are consulted (read in), so the above clauses stand for:

It is true that juan likes maria.
It is true that juan is a person who is male, aged 21.

Rules are expressed by clauses with *variables*, and usually include several predicates which are treated as goals to be satisfied, thus:

```
likes(maria,P) :- person(P, male, A), A > 20, A < 30.
```

Here P and A are variables standing for unknown values. We can read this rule: '*For any* P, maria likes P *if* P is a male person and *there is some number* A, such that A is the age of P, *and* A lies between twenty and thirty.'

Those familiar with the predicate calculus will recognise the italicised words as quantifiers and connectives in a formula of logic. The rule can be thought of as deducing facts. It stands for a large number of implicit facts which are implied by facts about persons such as juan. For example:

```
likes(maria, juan).
likes(maria, jose).
```

etc.

Thus we see that with Prolog it is very easy to implement *deductive databases* (Gallaire, 1983). For every record in a commercial file (or tuple in a relational database) we write down a corresponding unit clause. We then write down Prolog rules to deduce other data not explicitly present in the database.

4.2 Creating views of data

We can also write rules which present *views* by combining together data from several different files or tables in the database. They do not compute new or implied data; they just select it and regroup it. For example, suppose we wish to present a table of names of students who take computing together with the level of the class (1,2,3 or 4). We start with *tables* of facts which are represented by many unit clauses starting with the same predicate. Thus:

```
course(1277,'computing',1).  takes(pedro, 1277).  person(pedro, male,18).
course(2277,'computing',2).  takes(carlos,1246).  person(carlos, male,19).
course(1246,'maths',     1).  takes(pedro, 1246).  person(maria, fem, 19).
etc.                          takes(maria, 2277).     etc.
```

The rule (or Prolog procedure) which we use to produce the desired view can be written as:

```
aview(Pname, Age, Level( :- person(Pname, _, Age), takes(Pname, Cno),
                            course(Cno, 'computing', Level).
```

This would generate a sequence of facts forming a table thus:

```
aview(pedro, 18, 1).
aview(carlos, 19, 2).
aview(pedro, 18, 1).
aview(maria, 19, 2).
  etc.
```

Thus we have derived a new table from an existing table, extracting particular facts and relationships. This is a very common problem in commerce, where one wishes to produce a particular reports to fit columns laid down in a form. We should note here the remarkable feature of Prolog whereby it finds values to satisfy unknowns. Thus, instead of just enumerating the entire table implied by a view, we can treat it like just another goal;

we can supply values for some of the arguments, and get back values for others. Thus we can ask the Prolog query:

```
?- aview(carlos, 19, L), write(L), nl.
        and get the answer     2
```

or instead we can ask the inverse query

```
?- AVIEW(N, A, 2) write([N,A](, nl.
```

and get back successive answers:

```
[carlos,19]
[jose, 20]  etc.
```

Note that this is very different from a procedure call in a language such as Pascal, where some parameters must be given values and other parameters can only be used for output.

4.3 Comparison with SQL

It is interesting to compare the Prolog definition for 'aview' with the equivalent piece of SQL (the best-known of the database query languages).

```
DEFINE VIEW AVIEW(PNAME, AGE, LEVEL) AS
SELECT PERSON.PNAME, PERSON.AGE, COURSE.LEVEL
FROM COURSE, TAKES, PERSON
WHERE COURSE.SUBJ = 'computing'
AND   COURSE.CNO = TAKES.CNO
AND   TAKES.PNAME = PERSON.PNAME
```

The Prolog form of the query is more concise, and also more general, since Prolog is a full programming language. In particular Prolog is recursive, so one can write queries to find all the ancestors of a person to many generations, or list the complete bill of material for an assembly including parts for all its subassemblies. Likewise one can form lists of results and sum the items in the list, or work out other aggregate values. These are the so-called 'group-by' queries. More examples are given in suitable textbooks, e.g. (Gray, 1984).

4.4 Queries with default values

Let us now consider a slightly more complicated type of view, involving default values. Suppose that we have a number of facts giving the nationality of foreign students, of the form:

```
nation(pierre, french).
nation(jock,   scottish).
etc.
```

However, there are no facts for native students, whose nationality we shall take to be Spanish. Suppose we wish to add nationality to our view, to produce a new view 'nview'. We simply write:

```
nview(Pname,Age,Level,Nation :- aview(Pname,Age,
Level),nation(Pname,Nation),!.

nview(Pname,Age,Level,Nation) :- aview(Pname,Age,Level),
Nation='spanish'.
```

The first rule uses the rule for the view 'aview' to get the name, age and course level and then uses the nationality fact, if present, to get a value for the 'Nation' variable. The pseudo-predicate '!' (called 'cut') is used to stop the system using the second rule if the first one succeeds. If, however, we fail to find a name in the nationality facts, then we use the second rule, which just sets the Nation variable to its default value.

This seemingly simple task is surprisingly difficult to do in SQL, and is a good illustration of the generality of Prolog. The same technique can be used to deal with unknown values, where for example a measurement has not been made, by substituting a chosen atom such as 'unknown' in place of a numerical value. However, whilst this works for printing results, any rule which wants to use the measurement in an algebraic formula will have to test for it, thus:

```
val(X,R) :- X='unknown', !, R4='unknown'.
val(X,R) :- R is (2*X+5−3*X*X)/4.
```

Here val states the relationship between X and R through a numerical formula, which is not used if X is unknown.

4.5 Using Prolog rules to generate Prolog

A very important feature of Prolog is that, like LISP, it is its own *meta-language*. Thus it is possible to write rules which *generate* a query in the Prolog form. This is because Prolog rules can be used to build data structures and list structures of the same form as clauses. Thus, if a particular rule is not found to meet a given query, then a more general set of rules can be used to reason about the query and to transform it and to generate another query which will extract the required facts. This kind of technique is peculiar to AI languages and was pioneered in LISP, which deliberately uses list structures to express procedures, so that new procedures can be constructed during the execution of a program. By contrast, in conventional languages, all procedures must be declared beforehand and compiled.

As an example of this technique, consider the implementation of a very informal query language, where users are allowed to miss out phrases and the system attempts to fill them in. For example the user might type:

```
List age of person, cname = 'computing', level = 1.
```

They should have typed:

```
List Person.age where Person.pname = Takes.pname
    and Takes.cno = Course.cno and Course.cname = 'computing'
    and Course.level = 1.
```

The system first reads the query in as a list structure such as:

[List,age,of,person,',',cname,=,computing,',',level,=,1]

It then parses the list looking for operators e.g. *of* and = to produce a data structure such as:

list([of(person,age)],[equal(cname,'computing'),equal(level,1)]).

The rules for doing this parsing in Prolog are very straightforward. Next it searches the list for attribute names (such as *cname*) and assigns missing relation names (such as *course*). When it has the relation names it looks for the simplest way of joining the relations together, via a common attribute name, if present, and if not, via intermediate relations (such as *takes*). This technique was pioneered by Kaplan (1979). Finally it generates a data structure that represents a rule to find the query, and adds it to the rule base thus:

```
assert((answer(A) :- person(P,_,A),takes(P,C),course
(C,'computing',1)).
```

This is just an outline of a program that would take two or three pages of Prolog. Compared with ordinary programming languages its great advantage is in the ease with which it is possible to build and search list structures, and to fill in unknown values by the pattern matching process known as unification.

Another virtue is that Prolog programs can easily be *table driven*. For example, one can add a table of synonyms as facts:

```
syn(student,person).
syn(coursename,cname).
```

One can use this table to replace words in the informal query after reading it in. Such a table is then easily extended without changing the program.

4.6 Query optimization

Prolog has a very simple search strategy, encapsulated in the phase 'Depth first, left to right'. It treats the predicates in the right-hand side of a rule as goals to be achieved. It tries each in turn, and if any one fails it retries the preceding goal, to see whether it will then re-succeed with another value of a variable which will make the following goal succeed the second time. If not, it tries again, and so on. The effect is often to use the leftmost goal again and again to generate many values, which are tested by subsequent goals.

In the case of database queries, one must be careful to try goals in the right order, as pointed out by Warren (1981). Consider our Prolog definition for aview. As written, it is very inefficient.

```
aview(Pname, Age, Lev) :-
                person(Pname,_,Age),
                takes(Pname,Cno),
                course(Cno,'computing',Lev).
```

It will start by enumerating every person in the database, many of whom may not take any courses. Of those who do take courses, only a few will take *computing*. It is much more efficient to rewrite the clause in the other order, thus:

```
aview(Pname,Age,Lev) :-
                course(Cno,'computing',Lev),
                takes(Pname,Cno),
                person(Pname,_,Age).
```

In a compiled Prolog system, the clauses will often be indexed on their attribute values, so that the system will look up an index produced by the compiler to find just those clauses with the value *computing*. It then uses the value of *Cno* from those clauses to index clauses in *takes* with the same value of *Cno*. The same method is used to find clauses for *person* with the value for *Pname*. This corresponds to the way in which a database query optimizer works, although in this case the indexes will be maintained on disc.

It might appear that if Prolog has a fixed evaluation strategy, then one is condemned to have the query evaluated inefficiently. However, we can write rules in Prolog which inspect a query, treating it as a data structure, and rebuild the query in the re-ordered form so that it runs faster. This was done by Warren (1981) and is another example of the power of Prolog to be its own *meta-language*, as discussed earlier.

One of the big debates in expert database systems concerns 'who should do the optimizing?'. The standard approach is for the database management system (DBMS) to do the query optimization, since only it knows how the data is stored, which data is indexed, and how many facts there are of each kind. This is done in order to allow the database to be reorganized periodically, without changing the programs which access it. However, I think that a Prolog application program should be able to ask for the relevant optimization data from the DBMS, and then to do its own optimization, since it has good planning facilities and knows far more about the application and its access plan. This problem is discussed by Smith (1986).

4.7 Calling out from Prolog

Our examples so far have treated the facts as being held in a text file which is consulted at the start of a Prolog session and read into memory. However, Prolog predicates are implemented, ultimately, by calling pieces of code, and thus it is possible to call pieces of code not written in Prolog. A typical thing to do is to call routines written in Pascal or C which will access an existing database so that the original goal succeeds and returns in the same way that it would have done if the corresponding facts were in memory. Usually the facts are brought into buffers as they are required, since there is usually not time or space to bring the whole database into main memory. This technique has been implemented by several Prolog systems, including BIM-Prolog and SD-Prolog. Many more will follow!

The updating of data is more complicated than querying. It is possible to write routines which write newly asserted facts to disc, or delete facts which have been retracted in Prolog. However, this needs care when one is working with a shared database. It is also not clear whether the updates should just be done in main memory as a sort of *differential file* of changes, which is only committed at the end of a session when everything has been validated and the program has succeeded. Much more research is needed in this area.

4.8 Access to frame-based systems

Current databases mostly store facts as records in linked files, or else as tuples in relations. Thus the Prolog implementations mentioned above make use of relational databases. However, it is possible to store all the information about an abstract entity clustered together into a contiguous *object* on disc. One can also store with the object references to methods or procedures that are used to access its components, but which keep details of the internal storage representation of the object secret. These are *object-oriented databases* (Dittrich and Dayal, 1986), and they are very new. We have built one in Aberdeen which uses Prolog as its query language, and where the objects are treated very much like frames in the AI knowledge representation languages used inside large commercial AI knowledge-engineering systems, such as KEE and KnowledgeCraft. This is a new research area and it is only just beginning. It has been brought about by the inflexibility of relational databases when it comes to holding very large numbers of small relations, or many different types of facts, as found in AI applications. Thus queries may involve joining ten or more relations, which causes problems with query languages such as SQL. Also object-oriented databases need to be extensible, allowing new types of facts to be added dynamically, whereas conventional database systems require them to be declared in a pre-compiled schema.

5. CONCLUSION

We have seen how expert systems are based on a collection of rules and facts, forming the knowledge base. Increasingly, these rules and facts need to be organized and maintained on disc for shared access, and security. They also need special indexing facilities. Expert systems differ in the kind of use that they make of the data, and particularly in the search strategies that they adopt. Currently, much research goes into finding a good combination of the search strategy used by the expert system and the strategy used by the database query-language optimizer. Also, databases for storing information in a frame-based fashion, or as objects with attached methods, are very different from the databases in normal form used to hold relations, such as INGRES or DB2.

We have considered the problems of interfacing a knowledge-based system to a large database, and argued strongly in favour of using a subset of Prolog as an intermediate language. The main advantage is the ease with which Prolog can be used to provide 'customized views' of an existing database which suit the calling system. We have seen examples of this in the presentation of measurement data as columns containing special 'unknown' values for missing tuples.

Yet another advantage of Prolog is that it is very concise, and is its own meta-language. In consequence, one piece of Prolog can be used to construct a sequence of Prolog goals representing, for example, the standard 'select — from — where' query. This can then be exported as text to another process running on the same machine, or even over a network. Thus the method used can be hidden from the calling system, which does not need to know whether the database is on the same machine.

Furthermore, Prolog is a good language for query optimization. In particular, given the internal information normally used by a database query optimizer, it can make a good job of optimizing queries against a database on disc. Alternatively, the use of optimizing compilers for large numbers of clauses held in main memory makes this method very efficient, and as memories get larger this needs to be considered. This is an area of rapid development and improvement.

Finally, we have considered some of the newer types of database, including the use of object-oriented databases, which cluster data into objects and hide its internal representation, instead of presenting it as printable columns. These databases look suitable for use with frame structures as used in AI tools, and our Alvey project at Aberdeen (Gray *et al.*, 1987) has shown how Prolog can be used for this type of database also. Thus Prolog shows yet another aspect of its surprising adaptability and usefulness for the interfacing task.

REFERENCES

Clocksin, W. F. and Mellish, C. S. (1981) *Programming in Prolog*, Springer-Verlag.

Dittrich, K. and Dayal, U. (eds.) (1986) *International Workshop on Object-Oriented Database Systems*, IEEE Computer Society, Los Angeles.

Gallaire, H. (1983) Logic data bases vs. deductive data bases. In *Proc. Logic Programming Workshop 1983*, ed. L. M. Pereira.

Gray, P. M. D., (1984) *Logic, Algebras and Databases*, Ellis Horwood, Chichester.

Gray, P. M. D. (1986) Expert database systems. *AISB Quarterly* **59**, 22–23.

Gray, P. M. D., Moffatt, D. S. and Paton, N. (1987) A Prolog extension to the functional data model with modular commitment. *Computing Science Department Report*, University of Aberdeen.

Jarke, M. and Vassiliou, Y. (1984) Coupling expert systems and database management systems. In *Artificial Intelligence Applications for Business*, ed. W. Reitman, Ablex, pp. 65–86.

Kaplan, S. J. (1979) Cooperative responses from a portable natural language data base query system. *Ph.D. Thesis*, Moore School, University of Pennsylvania, also *Stanford Heuristic Programming Report HPP-79-19*.

McDermott, J. (1982) R1: a rule-based configurer of computer systems. *Artificial Intelligence* **19**, 39–88.

Shortliffe, E. H. (1976) *Computer-Based Medical Consultations: MYCIN*, Elsevier.

Smith, J. M. (1986) Expert database systems: a database perspective. In *First International Workshop on Expert Database Systems*, L. Kerschberg (ed.), Addison-Wesley.

Smith, R. (1984) On the development of commercial expert systems. In *AI Magazine,* Fall 1984, 61–73.

Stefik, M., Aikins, J., Balzer, R., Benoit, J., Birnbaum, L., Hayes-Roth, F. and Sacerdoti, E. (1982) The organisation of expert systems: a tutorial. *Artificial Intelligence* **18**, 135–173.

Warren, D. H. D. (1981) Efficient processing of interactive relational database queries expressed in logic. In Proc. 7th VLDB Conf., Cannes, pp. 272–281.

10

Modelling users' knowledge of a nursing records database, its structure and access

J. Thorpe and **J. Longstaff**
Leeds Polytechnic, Department of Computing Science, Beckett Park, Leeds LS6 3QS, UK

SUMMARY

With the growth of online databases and electronic mail, direct access to database information is becoming more and more commonplace. Increasing numbers of workplaces also have databases directly accessible. The computerization of nursing records is a good example. The major problem in direct database access is one of search: knowing what information is in the database, how this information correspond to your needs, and how to get to relevant information. We discuss methods of representing users' knowledge of the first problem — the information in the database — and the third — access to this information. An intelligent tutoring system incorporates these representations.

Advances in methods of modelling information for databases may hold some promise in improving general users' understanding of database structure. These methods were developed to aid the design of databases. There are a variety of methods, but all provide a formalism for representing knowledge about the domain of the database in a rigorous structure or schema which can then be used to generate the tables held in the database. The chapter investigates whether and how such schemes can be presented to users as a framework to aid their comprehension of the database.

Access for routing queries and updates can usefully be made by menus. More complex transactions are most efficiently made using a query language. Powerful query languages are rather difficult to learn for non-programmers. How users arrive at queries and the representation of queries is discussed; one representation has been selected as the basis for tutoring and guiding the user. The two representations, of database structure and of query formulation, are used in the expert module in a tutoring system. Methods of inferring individual user models are overlays of the expert data structure.

The pilot implementation is a front end to an Oracle database of nursing records, using binary semantic modelling methods and SQL. Nurses' experience with the system and directions for development are represented. The representation methods are transferable to other databases, using the same or other data modelling methods and query languages.

1. INTRODUCTION

This chapter describes the nursing process, its records and the system which we are developing to help users learn to use the computerized database system. The knowledge structures needed to understand and access the database are discussed, and the incorporation of these knowledge structures into expert module and user model.

2. THE NURSING PROCESS APPLICATION

Our application area is a nursing care information system, with special reference to the form of nursing process methodologies practised at St. James Hospital, Leeds, and taught to nursing degree students at Leeds Polytechnic. The aim of these methodologies is to help the nurses to give each patient individual care because they are patient-centred; they record patients' assessment, treatment and progress from the nursing viewpoint, which is wider than the purely medical viewpoint of doctors. At the start of the nursing process for each patient a nurse assesses the patient's symptoms and formulates a care plan for the patient. The care plan records the patients's problems and the actions to be taken in the treatment of each problem. An on-going record of the nursing care administrations to the patient is also recorded. At present more note taking is by handwriting entries on structured forms.

Our experimental computer system provides a menu of routine transactions to support the nursing process, including frequently programmed queries, and also a query language facility for nurses and nursing administrators to enter additional queries. The query language (QL) is a subset of the well-known database query language SQL.

Nurses show many of the characteristics ascribed to naive users. Often they hold the computer in some awe, while many dislike the idea of computers coming into the nursing process; indeed many entered nursing to get away from the mechanistic world associated with computing. On the other hand (and sometimes simultaneously) they can often see the possible benefits of computerized record-keeping. In many wards record-keeping is superficial and forms are completed with stock phrases conveying little information. Where the forms are filled in well they soon become bulky and often untidy and retrieval of information is time-consuming. Ideally, a nurse coming into the ward for the first time should be able to find out quickly and in detail the problems of each patient and the care he or she needs, and a nurse returning after a short break should have no difficulty in discovering from the records what changes and progress have occurred during the absence. The aim of our system is to smooth the nurses' path into and through the system by making it helpful, able to accommodate itself to user's knowledge and to explain itself to people who know a lot about their field but who often (but not always) know very little about computers.

A second aim is to allow nursing and administrative staff to utilise the vast amount of information that accumulates quickly in all kinds of hospital records systems but whose present use is confined to day-to-day patient care in the wards.

3. DATABASE STRUCTURE

3.1 Objects and their relationships

In designing a database, designers use modelling methods that start from the 'real world' objects. A popular method is entity relationship (ER) modelling (Chen, 1976). This data model allows the designer to define any relationships between objects as needed, so the semantic content of these links is unspecified. More recently, many data models have been influenced by semantic networks and use relationships such as classification, aggregation, generalization and association to specify more precisely the relationships between objects in the conceptual structure of schema of a database (Brodie, 1984).

The schema of a database can be used in help and explanation. The names of the real-world object types described in the database can be derived from the schema and presented to the user. A large database schema contains too many object types to give the user all at once. A semantic data model schema should have sufficient information in it to structure presentation of the objects in the schema to the user, but extra information has to be added to an ER schema of any size.

The system data model we use, the class link (CL) model, enables us to represent such information in ways corresponding to several different data models, for example the ER model and semantic hierarchy model (Brodie and Ridjanovic, 1984). This chapter does not focus on the CL model; for further details see Yeo *et al.* (1986) and Yeo (1986). Use of the CL model enables us to present to the user schemas which use a variety of different data models in terms of their respective data models and store the user's knowledge of these schemas. It also enables us to enhance the basic schema with more semantic information should that be necessary.

3.2 Presentation of database structure

Traditionally the user has been informed of the type of data in a database by text-based methods such as hierarchies of menus for naive users and query languages for experts. Menus appear to be well tolerated and used by naive users without much familiarity with the database. Systems that allow one to browse a database, such as RABBIT (Tou *et al.*, 1982) and KEE Connection, require a powerful workstation at present. Icons can effectively represent objects (Herot, 1980), but are less suitable for abstract objects or objects that are very similar. Other methods such as maps of hierarchical database structures have been used (Sutcliffe, 1986); interestingly, novices did not use these maps as intended, to direct navigation, but constructed a list of objects from the map and went down the list. The relational database management system we have available, ORACLE, has a utility for menu and form writing; we used this to write the interface that novices follow, after a brief initial description of schema and database structure. Experience with our users has shown that this is adequate.

Menus inform the user of the objects in the schema while serving primarily for access to data values. Query language will be discussed later; here we can note that to use most query languages to learn about objects in the database requires some knowledge of the database management system (DBMS) as well as the given query language.

3.3 The user's state of knowledge

At any given time a user will have several sources of information about the database: system explanation and help; DBMS answers to queries; other users; and independent knowledge of the domain. The system can record (to some extent) the user's knowledge of names and methods s/he has typed in, or has been told about by the system. In addition it may be possible to deduce that a user has some other knowledge as prerequisite to the knowledge exhibited. We have so far not addressed this problem.

4. ACCESS TO DATABASES

4.1 Access methods

As indicated above, menus are a popular way for users to get at data in a database. However, for more frequent users menus are slow and tedious, so these users tend to use a query language. Form-filling methods such as Query by Example (Zloof, 1978), which shows query templates modelled on the structure of relations, have proved successful; their disadvantage is that they can only show a few templates at a time, so the user has to know the database structure first. Similar problems beset systems where the user makes up a query by selecting from menus of attributes, logical operators etc. (Senko, 1977) and those systems where the user makes up a constrained natural language query by selecting from a list of English words (Tennant, 1984). Natural language interfaces that are not constrained in this way run well-known risks such as confusing the user by appearing more competent than they really are. Browsing methods allow data access as well as exploration of database structure, but do not lend themselves to gathering overall information about material stored in a database.

Our system builds on our experience with an earlier system, ERQ (Longstaff, 1982), which carried out a dialogue in restricted natural language, feeding back to the user paraphrases of the question in English and in query language. The present system allows the menu user to choose whether to see the paraphrases of the query; the user can then accept or reject the query formulated. In this way the user becomes familiar with the syntax and modes of use of the query language and can move over to query language with more confidence. Naturally, query-language users may also see paraphrases.

4.2 Query languages

A typical language is a high-level language used to write queries that retrieve data from the database. Several query languages also provide functions to manipulate the database and its structure; we shall not consider these functions here. Their limited purpose means that query languages are fairly small. We use the typical and widely used language SQL (Chamberlain *et al.*, 1976). An example question in our system, 'Find the actions taken for the ineffective breathing problem of patient John Smith', translates in SQL as:

```
SELECT    nursing_action
FROM      problem_table
WHERE     patient_name = 'John Smith'
AND       problem_description = 'ineffective breathing';
```

The keywords SELECT, FROM and WHERE turn up in most queries. The SELECT clause of the query has two parts: the first shows the attributes whose values are to be retrieved and displayed, the second, FROM, part shows from which relational table the data should be retrieved. The remaining lines of the query describe the restrictions on the search.

4.3 Conceptual models of query languages

How do users formulate queries? Little work has been done on this topic. Reisner (1977, 1981) suggests that users form a query template, e.g.

```
SELECT    --------------
FROM      --------------
WHERE     --------------
```

The users then translate or transform words in the English question into terms they know from the database and insert the terms into the template. From teaching experience this seems a sensible suggestion.

The FROM clause is an intruder in this picture. The corresponding word does not necessarily appear in the original question; the user is required to know the relational tables of the database; it prompts the user to a specific model of how SQL works, not required by the rest of the translation strategy. Reisner (1981, p. 25) suggests such a model as:

1. The computer first finds the table requested. In SQL this table is in the FROM clause.
2. Then it looks for the columns that have the information to be looked up. In SQL these data are in the left hand side of the WHERE clause.
3. Then it looks in this column for the information desired. This infor-

mation is on the right-hand side of the WHERE clause. It then pulls out the rows that have this information.

4. Then it looks in these rows for the answers required. These are the data in the column named in the SELECT clause.'

Other functions in SQL suggest and are more easily understood with such a procedural model of SQL's working, for example the GROUP BY function. A procedural model of SQL will influence the way a user writes queries, perhaps conflicting with a translation strategy. Welty and Stemple (1981) designed a language of equivalent functionality to SQL but overtly procedural; the forms of the language suggested to the user that the language carried out a series of operations on tables, transforming them into other temporary tables. Welty and Stemple's results indicate that their users found 'harder' queries (queries which include GROUP BY and other functions) easier to code in the procedural language than in SQL, while there was no significant difference in ease of use for easier queries. This suggests that procedural explanations would be helpful for some at least of the harder functions. The conceptual schema of a database can be used in help and explanation. The names of the real world object types described in the database can be derived from the schema and presented to the user. A large database schema contains too many object types to give the user all at once. A semantic data model schema should have sufficient information in it to structure presentation of the objects in the schema to the user, but extra information has to be added to an Entity-Relationship schema of any size. So far we have modelled mostly Entity-Relationship conceptual schemas, with supplementary information about relationships. Once this is done, the schema lends itself readily to formation of menus and outline explanations.

Our previous experience with query paraphrasing systems also shows that schemata and relational tables can be explained loosely but effectively in terms of entities and their relationships, and general users show that they have understood the schema by choosing the right tables from which to retrieve the data. When the users already have considerable experience of an explicit representation of the domain, explanation of structure can be minimal. When nursing students were told that the database held data from Nursing Records in tables but without further explanation of the database structure, nurses and students navigated quickly through the menus to access and add data in the same ways they would read and update the paper forms. The menu structure — together with their knowledge and experience of the forms — gave them sufficient information about the database structure.

In general, users of well-designed menu front-ends gain much information about the structure of a database from the context and meaning of data that they retrieve by following the menus. This then stands them in good stead when they have to use a database query language.

5. THE 'EXPERT'

Th expert modulc is also the teaching module. It uses the relational tables of the data model and nursing records schema to explain database structure. It also has a table of the syntactic parts of SQL, and uses the domain calculus representation to paraphrase queries, so it can find correct equivalents for many typical user errors. The system never passes on a 'corrected' query to the DBMS until the user has accepted it, unlike the proposal of Welty (1985).

For explanation the expert presents a translation strategy, with a procedural strategy backup. The system cannot parse natural language but engages in a dialogue with the user to clarify a query, in a manner similar to ERQ (Longstaff, 1982).

If a user wishes to ask 'List patients' names', and enters

```
SELECT NAMES;
```

the user an offer an SQL paraphrase

```
SELECT PATIENT_NAME FROM PATIENT_TABLE:
```

and a 'natural language' paraphrase,

```
SELECT NAMES OF PATIENTS
```

If the user's question is 'List names and ages of patients for whom all today's specified actions have been carried out' and the user enters

```
SELECT PATIENT_NAME, AGE FROM PATIENT_TABLE;
```

similar paraphrases to the above can be offered. If the user rejects this and requests help to complete the query, the system starts a clarifying dialogue, prompting for entities, qualifiers etc. The final paraphrase will be:

```
SELECT PATIENT_NAME, PATIENT_AGE
FROM PATIENT_TABLE
WHERE PATIENT_ID IN
    (SELECT PATIENT_ID)
     FROM PAT_PROB_ACT_TABLE
     GROUP BY PATIENT_ID
     HAVING SET (nursing_ACTION_ID) CONTAINS
       (SELECT NURSING_ACTION_ID
        WHERE ACTION_DATE=TODAY));                    (1)
```

```
SELECT NAMES AND AGES OF PATIENTS WHERE THE
PATIENT HAS HAD ALL NURSING ACTIONS WITH ACTION-
_DATE='TODAY'.                                        (2)
```

The SQL query (1) is a version of (2), but understanding of the details of the correction requires detailed knowledge of the database as relations and tables. To some extent the connection can be automated via macros, but not all the related computing questions are settled yet. One approach is to allow the user to attempt a query in SQL or a formalised SQLish English, and then to carry out an automated dialogue to refine the query (Longstaff, 1982; Luk and Koster, 1986). A satisfactory result can then be stored as a macro for later repeated use. However, such dialogues are often very lengthy.

6. MODELLING THE USER: WORK IN PROGRESS

For our present tutoring system (Armfield, 1988) the conceptual schema is itself represented by relations in Oracle. These can hold all the information in the conceptual schema including relationship and object types.

Also represented by relations are some of the essential concepts of the modelling method, such as entity and attribute, and elements of SQL syntax and semantics, based on the translation model of query-formation. As a result the system can sometimes suggest some simple queries that exploit the user's current knowledge of the database structure by working through from one type of relational table to another. It can also tentatively suggest ways of completing queries and correcting some simple syntax errors.

Relations, like predicates, are very powerful as a representation language but they face the same problems in structuring knowledge. At present the relation types to describe knowledge of the conceptual schema and the surface concepts of a modelling method such as Entity-Relationship modelling are fairly well structured.

Lacking at present are relation types to represent the many different kinds of underlying knowledge needed for good query-writing. The main direction in further research will be to investigate which of the underlying concepts in fields such as set theory, relational algebra and calculus are needed by SQL users at different levels of expertise. It seems certain that very different models will be needed by different SQL users. This will of course have considerable implications for knowledge-handling.

One minor advantage in using relations for representation is that they make it extremely easy to use as attribute values counters for valuations of different aspects of the user's exposure to and apparently successful use of the various entities and relationships.

There are a number of issues in the design of an intelligent tutoring system that are not addressed here, notably exploitation of a user model in adapting help and explanation to the user and the representation and use of pedagogical knowledge in modulating when and how the system should offer help, explanation and responses to user requests for help. For an overview of these and other issues, see Dede (1986); for an in-depth study, see Wenger (1987).

7. REFERENCES

Armfield, N. (1988) User modelling, Tutoring and adaption strategies for an SQL tutor. *Internal research report,* Dept. of Computing Science, Leeds Polytechnic.

Brodie, M. L. (1984) On the development of data models. In Brodie, M. L., Mylopoulos, J. and Schmidt, J. W. (eds.) *On Conceptual Modelling*, Springer-Verlag, NY, pp. 19–47.

Brodie, M. L. and Ridjanovic, D. (1984) On the design and specification of data models. In Brodie, M. L., Mylopoulos, J. and Schmidt, J. W. (eds.) *On Conceptual Modelling*, Springer-Verlag, NY, pp. 277–312.

Chamberlain, D. D., Astrahan, M. M., Eswaran, K. P., Griffiths, P. P., Lorie, R. A., Mehl, J. W., Reisner, P. and Wade, B. W. (1976) SEQUEL 2: a unified approach to data definition. *IBM J. Res. Dev.* **20**, 560–575.

Chen, P. P.-S. (1976) The entity relationship model: towards a unified view of data. *ACM Trans. on Database Systems* **1** (1).

Codd, E. F. (1971) A data base language founded on the relational calculus. *Proc. ACM SIGFIDET Workshop on Data Description, Access and Control*, pp. 35–68.

Dede, C. (1986) A review and synthesis of intelligent computer aided instruction. *Int. J. Man-Machine Studies,* **24,** 329–353.

Herot, C. F. (1980) Spatial management of data. *ACM Trans. on Database Systems* **5**(4), 493–514.

Longstaff, J. J. (1982) ERQ: controlled inference and instruction techniques for DBMS query languages. *Proc. Int. Conf. on Management of Data (SIGMOD 82)*, pp. 111–117.

Luk, W. S. and Koster, S. (1986) ELFS: English language from SQL. *ACM Trans. on Database Systems,* December 1986 issue.

Reisner, P. (1977) Use of psychological experimentation as an aid to development of a query language. *IEEE Trans. on Software and Engineering* **3**(3), 218–229.

Reisner, P. (1981) Human factors studies of database query languages a survey and assessment. *ACM Computing Surveys* **13**(1), 13–31.

Senko, M. E. (1977) DIAM-II with FORAL-LP: making pointed queries with light pen. *IEEE Computer* **16**(8), 57–68.

Sutcliffe, A. G. (1986) Database maps. In Oxborrow, E. A. (ed.) *Proc. Fifth Brit. Nat. Conf. on Databases (BNCOD5)*, Cambridge UP, pp. 155–165.

Tennant, H. R. (1984) Menu-based natural language understanding. *Proc. Nat. Comp. Conf., AFIPS*, pp. 629–635.

Tou, F. N., Williams, M. D., Fikes, R., Henderson, A. and Malone, T. (1982) RABBIT: an intelligent database assistant. *Proc. Nat. Conf. of Amer. Assoc. for AI*, pp. 314–318.

Welty, C. (1985) Correcting user errors in SQL. *Int. J. Man–Machine Studies*, **22**, 463–477.

Welty, C. and Stemple, D. W. (1981) Human factors comparison of a procedural and a nonprocedural query language. *ACM Trans. on Database Systems*, **6**(4), 626–649.

Wenger, E. (1987) *Artificial Intelligence and Tutoring Systems,* Morgan Kaufmann Inc., Los Altos, California.

Yeo, C. (1986) An architecture for an intelligent front end to a relational database system. *M. Phil. Thesis*, Leeds Polytechnic.

Yeo, C., Thorpe, J. and Longstaff, J. (1986) Knowledge base enhancements to relational databases. In Oxborrow, E. A. (ed.) *Proc. Fifth Brit. Nat. Conf. on Databases (BNCOD5)*, Cambridge UP, pp. 87–103.

Zloof, M. M. (1978) Design aspect of the Query by Example database query language. In Shneiderman, B. (ed.) *'Databases: Improving Usability and Responsiveness.*

11

A learning expert system for conceptual schema design

R. Yasdi and **W. Ziarko**
Department of Computer Science, University of Regina, Regina, Saskatchewan S4S 0A2, Canada

SUMMARY

The primary stage of the database design process is the design of conceptual schema. This process consists of creation of an abstract model of the part of the reality to be represented in the database. This involves specifications of entities, their attributes, relationships among entities, and integrity constraints. It is usually a complex task requiring good understanding of the semantics of the modelled reality and high level of expertise in database design. In what follows, we present the main ideas underlying the expert system EXIS which is intended to assist the designer of the database. The system contains a learning component capable of inducing schema-design rules from examples accumulated in the system. The conceptual schema is represented in the form of a database-oriented semantic network whose specific features are also described in the chapter.

1. INTRODUCTION

Since technology of databases has been developed remarkably in recent years, many researchers in various fields (literature, history, economics etc.) have the potential wish to construct databases for their studies by themselves. However, constructing a database is an extremely difficult task for such users owing to their lack of sufficient knowledge of computers or databases. As a result, they need an expert's help when they build their database. However, with the growing complexity of today's knowledge-based systems this task is becoming more difficult even for database designers themselves, particularly because of the lack of knowledge of the specific application. Consequently, it would be very desirable to have an expert system capable of advising the designer during the primary stages of database design. Potentially, providing suggestions concerning database schema integrity constraints would be most helpful to reduce the possibility of designing a database inconsistent with the reality. Such an expert system is not intended to replace the human expert by providing a black box of useful services but rather it is an open system which will enable the designer to acquire new knowledge and to transfer his expertise through the system to the end-user. Therefore, we argue that this kind of expert system needs to have a learning component to convert accumulated experience into a set of design rules to be used by a novice database designer. The system should be able to learn from example schemas and gradually improve its rules to reflect better the constraints of the reality. In what follows we describe fundamentals of such a system (referred to as EXIS) currently under development at the University of Regina (Yasdi and Ziarko, 1986).

Throughout this chapter we focus our investigation on the two main issues.

Firstly, developing a conceptual model which is intended to represent the full extent of the informational needs of the enterprise. This implies the determination of static and dynamic aspects of an application. A data model such as a semantic network represents the former, while an event model is developed for representing the latter aspects. Because of the space limitation here, we shall concentrate on static aspects only.

Secondly, research on learning is very important in the fields of artificial intelligence (AI) since it is one of the most fundamental mechanics of an intelligent system (Michalski, 1980). EXIS has been aimed to apply this technique to the generation of general rules based on the principle of inductive learning (learning and generalizing rules from examples).

Our approach is to use first-order predicate logic as a formalism for specification of the conceptual schema. This implies that the schema is to be represented by a set of axioms to constitute a theory (first order) which is interpreted according to the model theoretical approach. We present the main ideas of semantic networks in the context of database schema design methodology and illustrate them with an example. In addition, we discuss the learning method (algorithm PLA) of EXIS in the framework of the probabilistic rough set model (Wong and Ziarko, 1986c). The application of the PLA algorithm to generate rules is illustrated with a simple example.

2. SEMANTIC NETWORK REPRESENTATION OF CONCEPTUAL SCHEMA

The full extent of the informational needs of an enterprise is represented in a conceptual schema (or model). The role of conceptual schema in DB technology has much in common with that of knowledge representation in AI. By our definition it covers two aspects of an application, namely static and dynamic aspects. Data models such as semantic or relational represent the former, whereas concepts of event and transaction are used for representing the latter aspect. In the following sections we specify our conceptual schema (Yasdi, 1985) by adopting the pictorial syntax of semantic networks.

To capture the semantics of the real world with more precision and naturalness, many researchers have proposed several data models such as

SHM (Smith and Smith, 1977), SDM (Hammer and McLeod, 1981) and TAXIS (Mylopoulos *et al.*, 1980). The semantic network presented hereafter contains most of the concepts of semantic networks such as classification, generalization, aggregation. However, we emphasize here the precise definitition of schema integrity constraints and their formalization in the first order logic, which are extremely important for design of a conceptual schema.

A semantic network is a directed graph whose nodes represent individuals and whose arcs represent the relationships between individuals. It is defined as a triple

(NC, AC, IC)

where NC stands for the category of nodes, AC for the category of arcs and IC is the category of constraints. For each element of AC, there exists a function:

$$f = NC \times NC \rightarrow \{\text{true, false}\}$$

such that $f(n_i, n_j)$ is true if there exists an arc of class f between n_i and n_j, and false otherwise. The semantic network has the following beneficial features:

(1) Representation is very close to the natural language.
(2) It employs a number of abstract concepts which help to include more meaning about the observed objects.
(3) It can be used to obtain more efficient implementation.
(4) It can be extended so that it can have the same expressive power as predicate logic (Kowalski, 1979; Schubert, 1976; Sowa, 1986).

2.1 Concepts of the semantic network

Classification (entities or attributes)

Objects with similar qualities can be grouped into a class. For example, we can create the class of 'employee' for an entity-class (ec) and the class 'colour' for an attribute-class (ac). Elements of an entity-class are entities and elements of an attribute-class are values. For example e_5 is an instance of the employee-class and red is an instance of colour. A class is defined by a predicate; the predicate is satisfied by instances of its arguments (e.g. employee(x)=true).

Declaration

The arguments of attribute-class are associated with their types or with a domain by the predicate dec. For example, if we consider the predicate

person(P, Name : string, Age : ages, Address : address)

the arguments will be defined by

dec(ages, '[1.... 100]')

dec(address, '[Toronto, Frankfurt, London]')

The elements of different entity-classes are connected to each other by the following categories of arcs.

Association

This accounts for the binary relationship between two entity-classes. For example works-for (person, company), indicates that persons from class person work for companies from class company.

We use the notation $r(ec_1,ec_2)$ to specify the relationship between two classes and formalize it by:

$$\forall a \forall y[\text{works-for}(x,y) \rightarrow \text{person}(x) \wedge \text{company}(y)]$$

Note that relationships are recursive and linked bidirectionally; usually one direction is shown. Semantic networks offer an abstraction mechanism. This enables us to discuss an abstract class while temporarily deferring the details of its properties. We introduce some of the specific abstractions below.

Generalization

Generalization provides a concise way to express constraints that define some classes as 'more general' class of other ones. This relationship is also called the 'specialization',.when viewed the other way around, i.e. going from the more general to the more specific definition, e.g.

$$\forall x(\text{emp}(x) \vee \text{student}(x) \Leftrightarrow \text{person}(x))$$

The left-to-right implication states that the set of employees and the set of students are subclasses of the set of persons. The right-to-left implication states that all persons are either students or employees, or both. One can say that the later implication 'closes' the set of persons in that it prohibits an entity from being a person without also being an employee or student. Generalization is usually abbreviated by the keyword 'is-a' and represented by a 'g' arc whereas specialization is represented by an 's' arc.

Let $ec_1, \ldots, ec_n$ be the subclasses of ec and let e and e_i be respectively the elements of ec and ec_i: then $\cup e_i e$. The class ec is called a completely specialized class in this case; otherwise ec is called a partially specialized class.

Aggregation

Grouping classes into higher-level classes is called aggregation. It is a common-sense intersection of sets. In a mathematical sense aggregation corresponds to the Cartesian product. For example, the fact that author, publisher and title are components of the entity-class book is represented by an arc 'a' going from author, publisher and title to book. Thus,

$$\text{book(x)} \rightarrow \exists y \exists z \exists w(author(y) \wedge publ(z) \wedge title(w))$$

where the aggregation is defined downwards whereas the 'particularization' is defined upwards and shown by an arrow labelled with 'p'.

Equivalence

Equivalence specifies that two classes are equivalent. This is especially useful when it is important to see the same objects in different ways. Denotation $eq(ec_1,ec_2)$ specifies that two classes are equivalent. For example eq(student, sportsman) and eq(student, pupil) specify that student, sportsman and pupil are equivalent classes if we assume that all students practice one sport. More generally, $eq(x,y)$ is equivalent to the two following assertions: $g(x,y)$ and $g(y,x)$.

An example of a semantic network is portrayed in Fig. 1.

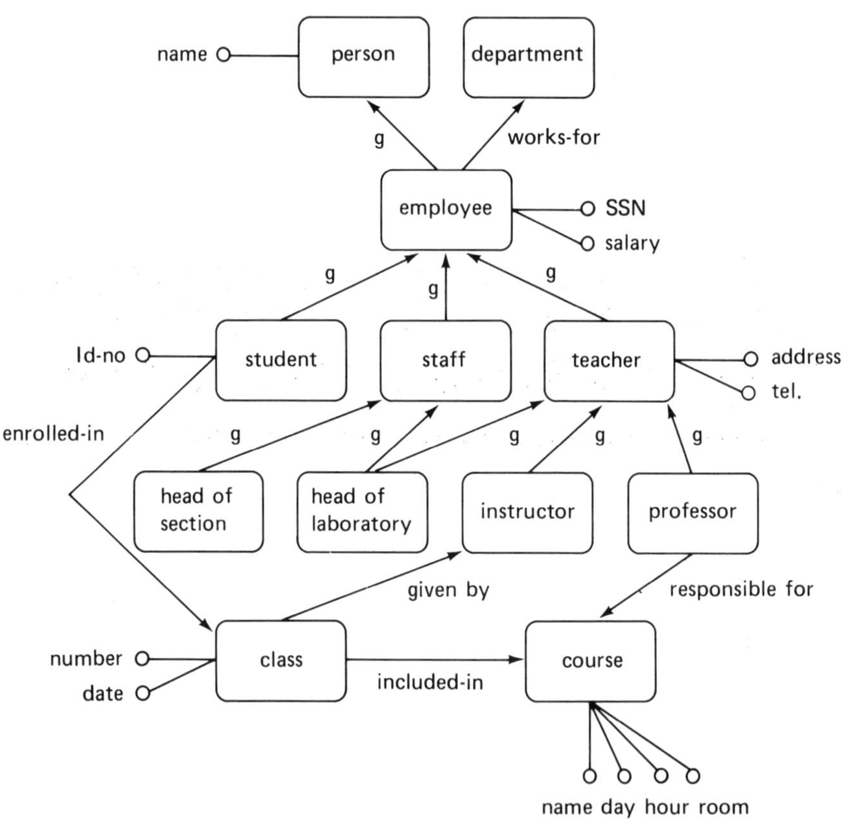

Fig. 1 — Example of the semantic model.

3. RULE GENERATION BY LEARNING FROM EXAMPLES

Our main objective in this section is to show how the concept of machine learning can be applied during design of an information system.

Particuarly, we are interested in the problem of acquisition of schema rules. Some of the schema rules, referred to as schema constraints, are known from database theory or can be learned explicitly by the database designer. In some situations, however, the lack of experience of the database designer leads to a conceptual schema which is inconsistent with the reality. This is due to the designer's failure to incorporate a sufficient number of correct constraints into the design process. To avoid this kind of problem, it is desired to have an expert system which would suggest, based on its internal knowledge and analysis of similar schemas, an appropriate set of constraints or relationships to be included in the schema being developed.

Because of well-known problems with knowledge acquisition in existing expert systems; we suggest the application of a new machine learning technique to acquire schema rules from example schemas.

There are a number of approaches to automatic learning or to the generation of decision rules by a machine (Michalski, 1983; Shortlifte and Davis, 1976; Forsyth, 1986). In particular, inductive learning, i.e. extraction and generalization of decision rules from examples of decisions, has attracted a great deal of interest in recent years (Dietterich and Michalski, 1979; Buchanan and Feigenbaum, 1978; Pawlak, 1984; Quinlan, 1983; Michalski; 1980; Wong and Ziarko, 1986d).

In any approach to inductive learning we encounter the following two major problems:

(1) How to represent the partial knowledge collected in the form of examples;
(2) How to generalize this knowledge in the form of decision rules so that they can be used in automated reasoning.

Both of these issues can be addressed in the framework of the theory of rough sets and of a formal model of the knowledge-representation system (KRS) introduced by Pawlak. In particular, the probabilistic learning algorithm (PLA) developed to induce decision rules from examples represented as feature vectors can be adopted here to generate decision rules. This enables us to incorporate the learning component into EXIS by making its inference rules dependent upon the contents of the example base. The example base consists of a number of schema design decisions represented by means of predicates. The PLA is used to produce generalized design rules which will be employed subsequently in advising the database designer. The system will be extendable and adaptive, i.e. correct or incorrect design decisions will be used by the system as new experience to increase the number or to improve the quality of decision rules.

In what follows we give an introduction to the main ideas underlying our approach to learning. We discuss the concept of the knowledge-representation system and explain the way we are going to apply it to represent the design knowledge. Also, we present basics of the idea of approximate classification which are necessary to describe the learning method of EXIS.

3.1 Knowledge-representation system

The basic component of a knowledge-representation system is a set of objects (entities), for instance, books or human beings. We assume that our knowledge about these objects is expressed through assignment of some features (attributes) and their values (attribute values) to the objects. For example, human beings can be described by sex and age.

The formal definition of a knowledge-representation system S (Orlowska and Pawlak, 1984) is given by:

$$S=\langle E, C, D, V, f\rangle$$

where:
— E is a set of objects,
— $At=C\cup D$ is a set of attributes, of which the two disjoint subsets of attributes C and D are referred to as condition and expert decision (conclusion) respectively,
— $V=\cup Va$, for $a\in At$
is a set of attribute values, where Va is the domain of attribute $a\in At$.
— $f{:}E\times At\rightarrow V$ is an information function such that

$$f(e,a) \in \forall a \text{ for every } e \in E \text{ and } a \in A$$

i.e., the function f assigns attribute values to each object e in E.

We extend the above representation by introducing predicates into the system to represent more complex situations. In particular this will allow us to deal effectively with the problem of representing schema-design decisions. In this extension the objects will be referred to as 'situations'. Each situation consists of a number of entity-classes and a number of predicates $p_1,p_2, \ldots, p_m$, corresponding to some relationships among selected elements. The predicates associated with situations fall into two disjoint categories referred to respectively as recognition predicates and attribute predicates. The recognition predicates are used to recognize that a given situation to be represented in the example base actually occurred. In other words, they all must be satisfied in order to include a representation of a particular situation in the table. The attribute predicates describe some properties of situations. Thus the condition and conclusion predicates of a rule will be constructed from the attribute predicates. They can be viewed as attributes of these situations with attribute values being true or false (T,F). Our knowledge about situations will be represented in KRS by truth values of these predicates.

As an example, let us consider the collection of situations $s=\{s_1,s_2,s_3,s_4,s_5\}$ given in Table 1. Each situation $s \in S$ is a vector $S=(X, Y, Z)$ characterized by the recognition predicates $c_1(X),c_2(Y),c_3(Z)$ and attribute predicates is-a(Y, X), is-a(Z, Y), is-a(Z, X).

Is-a(X, Y) is a generalization predicate which is satisfied whenever entity-class Y is more general than entity class X. The recognition predicates c_1,c_2,c_3 correspond to the domain of variables X, Y, Z respectively, that is, c_1={person, employee}, c_2={employee, teacher, staff}, c_3={teacher, staff, instructor, student, head-of-section}. The predicate is-a(X,Y) can be chosen as a conclusion predicate; all remaining predicates will be referred to as condition predicates.

Table 1

situation	X	Y	Z	is-a(Y,X)	is-a(Z,Y)	is-a(Z, X)
s_1	person	employee	teacher	T	T	T
s_2	person	employee	staff	T	T	T
s_3	person	teacher	instructor	F	F	F
s_4	person	employee	student	T	F	T
s_5	employee	staff	head-of-section	T	T	T

Our goal is to establish a set of decision rules which should enable us to predict whether the entity class X is a generalization of the class Z based solely on the information encoded in truth values of condition predicates.

3.2 Probabilistic approximate classification

Before we present the learning method adopted in our system some preliminary introduction to the idea of probabilistic approximate classification is needed. Because of space limitation it is rather sketchy. Readers interested in details should refer to Wong and Ziarko (1986a).

In general, our approach to learning is based on the probabilistic approach to modelling by rough sets. The basic assumption in this approach is that we do not know all possible situations. The set of situations contained in the KRS forms a sample which can be used to draw some conclusions. The conclusions, however, are bound to be uncertain. Therefore, we can look at the universe of all possible situations belonging to a certain homogeneous class characterized by specified recognition predicates from the probabilistic point of view as a space of elementary random events . Each conclusion and condition predicate becomes a random variable in this model. To explain the idea, assume for simplicity that there is only one conclusion predicate D representing an expert judgement (or concept) regarding the feasibility of decisions, and a number of condition predicates $b_1, b_2 \ldots, b_m$ reflecting the chosen properties of situations. It is known that a set of all possible values of a random variable or combination of them generates a partition of the space of random events into a family of equivalence classes $T_r = \{Z_1, Z_2, \ldots, Z_n\}$. The partition T_r of and the probability measure P on a -algebra of subsets of form a basis for a probabilistic approximation space (& T_r, P). In this approximation space we can find a probabilistic characterization of any unknown expert concept $Y \subseteq$. In other words, we can produce a set of probabilistic decision rules which will permit us to discriminate, with some uncertainty, between concept Y and its complement. Concept Y, for example, might be defined as satisfying the predicate 'entity-class X is a generalization of the entity-class Z'.

In the extended KRS model, each equivalence class Z_i of the partition T_r is associated with a unique specification Des(Z_i) in terms of the truth values of some condition predicates. This means that all situations in the class Z_i share the same values of some selected condition predicates. The specification assumes the form of a Boolean expression: $\mathrm{Des}(Z_i)=f(e,b_1)\wedge \ldots \wedge f(e,b_k)$ where $e \in Z_i$ and $b_i \in C$. For instance,

$$\text{is-a}(Y, X):=T\wedge\text{is-a}(Z, Y):=F$$

may form a plausible specification for a class in the example shown in Table 1.

Our objective is to characterize approximately each expert concept Y (in our case T or F) in terms of specifications $\mathrm{Des}(Z_i)$ of classes of T_r and conditional probabilities of Y with respect to Z_i. The concept Y represents the expert judgment expressed by assigning the same truth value of the predicate D to all situations in Y, so we would like to learn how to predict the expert judgment (i.e. value of D) based solely on the known values of condition predicates and estimated conditional probabilities. This can be achieved by associating the notion of probabilistic profile with each concept Y.

The profile of the concept of Y is the conditional probability distribution

$$P(Y|Z_i)=P(Y \cap Z_i)/P(Z_i)$$

for $i=1,2, \ldots, n$
Each value $P(Y|Z_i)$ can be interpreted as the probability that a situation satisfying the specification of the class X_i also satisfies the specification of the class Y. In this sense $P(Y|Z_i)$ is a measure of uncertainty when predicting the truth value of the predicate D based on the knowledge of truth values of condition predicates. In other words, each situation can be approximately classified into set Y with certainty $P(Y|Z_i)$. Whenever $0<P(Y|Z_i)<1$ for $Z_i \in T_r$, we say that Y is rough (in a probabilistic sense), i.e. the classification cannot be done with 100% accuracy. In this case, the probability distribution $P(Y|Z_i)$ may be used to define a set of probabilistic decision rules to predict the truth values of conclusion predicates, based on the values of condition ones. The central problem in this approach to learning is therefore the estimation and maximization of the probabilities $P(Y|Z_i)$ through generation of an appropriate partition T_r of the universe U.

However, all we know about the universe is included in our collection of example situations E. Consequently, the problem of generating a 'good' partition of the universe U reduces, because of our lack of knowledge, to the problem of finding a similar partition of the set of examples E. This is the primary task of a learning algorithm. Ideally, the learning algorithm should be able to produce an optimal partition, i.e. one which could be used to obtain a minimal set of highly generalized decision rules without giving away the accuracy of predictions.

Although finding an optimal partition turns out to be computationally infeasible, a reasonable degree of generalization of knowledge contained in examples can be achieved by employing simple heuristics in the learning process.

In order to describe the algorithm, we assume that our universe is the set of examples E. We have also to introduce the notions of lower and upper approximations of a set $Y=\{e \in E|f(e,D)=T\}$ in the approximation space (E, T_r, P) as follows.

(1) The lower approximation or positive region of Y is defined as

$$\mathrm{POS}(Y)=\{e \in E|e \in Z_i \text{ and } P(Y|Z_i)=1\}$$

(2) The upper approximation of Y is defined as

$$\overline{Y}=\{e \in E|e \in Z_i \text{ and } P(Y|Z_i)>0.5\}$$

In addition a boundary or doubtful region BN(Y) of the set Y can be defined as

(3) $\mathrm{BN}(Y)=\{e \in E| \in Z_i \text{ and } P(Y|Z_i)=0.5\}$

and the negative region NEG(Y) is given by

(4) $\mathrm{NEG}(Y)=E-(\overline{Y} \cup \mathrm{BN}(Y))$

The regions we defined have the following interpretations:

(1) Whenever a situation belongs to POS(Y) it can be determined with full certainty that this situation also belongs to Y.
(2) The same conclusion as in (1) can be made in this case. However, some statistical uncertainty will be connected with such a decision.
(3) No conclusion at all can be made if an object belongs to the boundary region of a set. Both choices are equally probable in this case.
(4) A decision with some degree of certainty can be made that a situation does not belong to Y if it belongs to NEG(Y).

Based on the above interpretations we can associate with each class Z_i a decision rule r_i according to the following criteria:

(1) $r_i :\mathrm{Des}(Z_i) \Rightarrow D$ if $Z_i \subseteq \mathrm{POS}(Y)$
(2) $r_i :\mathrm{Des}(Z_i) \overset{c}{\Rightarrow} D$ if $Z_i \subseteq \overline{Y}$

The parameter c is the certainty measure associated with this decision rule. The entropy function (Shannon, 1948) or simpler formula given below (which is equivalent to entropy in this case) can be used to compute c:

$$c=\mathrm{ABS}(P(Y|Z_i)-0.5)$$

(3) $r :\mathrm{Des}(Z_i) \Rightarrow$ "unknown" if $Z_i \subseteq \mathrm{BN}(Y)$
The certainty equals zero in this case.
(4) r $:\mathrm{Des}(Z_i) \overset{c}{\Rightarrow} -D$ if $Z_i \subseteq \mathrm{NEG}(Y)=(\mathrm{E}-\overline{Y})$
(5) r $:\mathrm{Des}(Z_i) \Rightarrow -D$ if $Z_i \subseteq \mathrm{POS}(E-Y)$

Rules defined by criteria (1) and (5) are referred to as deterministic decision rules. They can be used directly in the reasoning process using standard theorem-proving techniques. Rules (2) and (4) are nondeterministic. The reasoning process which employs these rules should be able to take into account the effect of combined uncertainty. Rules given by (3) are 'dead end' rules. The reasoning cannot proceed whenever this kind of rule is encountered.

3.3 Probabilistic learning algorithm (PLA)

To present the algorithm in precise terms let us denote by $Q(B)$ an equivalence relation defined on a set of sample situations E. The relation $Q(B)$ is defined by:

(1) B is a subset of condition predicates, i.e. $B \subseteq C$,
(2) $(e_i, e_j) \in Q(B)$ iff $f(e_i, b) = f(e_j, b)$, for all $b \in B$.

Since each such equivalence relation corresponds to a partition of E we can associate an approximation space, denoted here as $\langle E, Q(B), P \rangle$, with each subset of condition predicates B.

Additionally, we introduce the notion of a predicate discrimination factor of the collection of condition predicates B with respect to the concept Y. The discrimination factor $G(B, Y)$, given by

$$G(B,Y) = P(\mathrm{POS}(Y)) + P(\mathrm{POS}(E-Y))$$

measures the 'power' of the set of attributes B in distinguishing two concepts Y and $E-Y$ by combining the sum of probabilities of positive regions of Y and $E-Y$ in the approximation space $\langle E, Q(B), P \rangle$.

In the learning procedure we use $G(B,Y)$ in a similar way to ID3 (Quinlan, 1983) using the entropy function for this purpose. The core issue in learning is generation of the partition T_r of E which has the following features:

(1) The partition is not too fine; fine partition results in an excessive number of narrow decision rules whereas coarse partition corresponds to a low number of general decision rules
(2) The certainty of conclusions drawn from generalized decision rules is not affected by the generalization process.

The algorithm, which we present below, satisfies the objective (2) and attempts to satisfy (1) by applying the discriminationg factor $G(B, Y)$. Let

$$Y = \{e \in E | f(e, D) = T\}$$

Algorithm 1: Generation of the partition T_r on E.
Input: A knowledge-representation system.
Variables: F represents a set of samples, M or N represent a subset of predicates, T_r represents a family of subsets of E.
Procedure:
(1) Let $F \leftarrow E$; $M \leftarrow \emptyset$; $N \leftarrow C$; $T \leftarrow \emptyset$.
(2) Repeat until either $F = \emptyset$ or $M = C$:
  — let $N \leftarrow N - M$;
  — find a condition predicate p in N such that $G(M \cup \{p\}, Y)$ in the approximation space $\langle F, Q(M \cup \{p\}), P \rangle$ is maximised;
  — let $M \leftarrow M \cup \{p\}$;
  — compute $\mathrm{POS}(Y) \cup \mathrm{POS}(E-Y)$ in the approximation space $\langle F, Q(M) P \rangle$ by identifying those equivalence classes Z_i of $Q(M)$ such that
  $P(Y|Z_i) = 1$ or $P(E-Y|Z_i) = 1$; attach all these classes to T_r;

let $F \leftarrow F-(\text{POS}(Y) \cup \text{POS}(E-Y))$;
(3) If $F \neq \emptyset$, add all the equivalence classes of the relation $Q(M)$ on F to T_r.
Output: Partition T_r on E induced by the condition predicates.
The algorithm has been implemented in LISP in the form of a small decision tree generating program Infer (Wong and Ziarko, 1986b).

To illustrate the operations of the rule-learning system built according to this algorithm let us consider the collection of situations given in Table 1. The predicate is-a(Z, X) has been chosen as a decision predicate. Because the discriminating factor of the condition predicate is-a(Y, X) is maximum (i.e. equals 1) and is greater than the discrimination factor of is-a(Z, Y) we can conclude that is-a (Z, X) can be fully characterized by is-a(Z, Y). In other words the following decision rules would be extracted by Algorithm 1.

$$\text{is-a}(Y, X) := T \Rightarrow \text{is-a}(Z, X) := T \quad \text{and} \quad \text{is-a}(Y, X) := F \Rightarrow \text{is-a}(Z, X) := F$$

Consequently, one of the possible inference rules induced from Table 1 can be expressed as is-a(Z, X)$\leftarrow$is-a(Y, X) or in words, entity set X is a generalization of the entity set Z if the entity set X is a generalization of the entity set Y.

This rule (and eventually the other rules induced from the table) represent our current state of knowledge about relationships among predicate attributes. Future examples may invalidate this rule and some new rules may appear. In the longer run the system of rules will tend to stabilize to reflect real interrelationships existing among entity sets of sample situations.

4. SUMMARIZING REMARKS

In the preceding sections we presented the main ideas to be incorporated in the implementation of a learning expert system which is intended to help the end-user in designing an information system. We have initiated the project recently, so we cannot report from results, but from goals. Several of the techniques discussed here have been implemented elsewhere (Yasdi, 1985; Wong and Ziarko, 1986d). Most of the components are implemented but they are not integrated yet.

The main features of the system are summarized below:

- The conceptual schema and its associated rules are represented in predicate logic which can be adapted to any other application.
- the conceptual schema is based on the semantic model, which is close to natural language.
- Database design procedure starts with a naive description of an application and proceeds in the form of a dialogue between the system and the user.
- We adapt a learning mechanism by which the design knowledge can be acquired from example; either rules can be generated from examples or new design rules can be added explicitly to the existing ones.

ACKNOWLEDGEMENT

This research was partially supported by the Natural Sciences and Engineering Research Council of Canada.

REFERENCES

Buchanan, B. G. and Feigenbaum, E. A. (1978) Dendral and metadendral, their applications dimension. *Artif. Intell.,* **2**(11) 5–24.

Dietterich, T. G. and Michalski, R. S. (1979) Learning and generalization of characteristic descriptions: evaluation criteria and comparable review of selected methods. *Proceedings of the 6th IJCAI, 1979.*

Forsyth, R. (1986) *Machine Learning: Applications in Expert Systems and Information Retrieval,* John Wiley and Sons.

Hammer, N. and McLeod, D. (1981) Database description with sdm: a semantic data model. *ACM-TODS,* **6**(3) (September).

Kowalski, R. (1979) Logic and semantic networks. *CACM,* **22**(3) (March) 184–192.

Michalski, R. S. (1980) Learning by being told and learning from examples: an experimental comparison of the two methods of knowledge acquisition in the context of developing an expert system for soybean disease diagnosis. *Inter. J. Poly. Anal. and Infor. Sys.,* **4**(2) 125–161.

Michalski, R. (1983) *Machine Learning, An Artificial Intelligence Approach,* Springer Verlag, Berlin.

Mylopoulos, J. *et al.* (1980) A language facility for designing database intensive applications *ACM-TODS,* **15**(2).

Orlowska, E. and Pawlak, Z. (1984) Expressive power of knowledge representation systems. *Man–Machine Studies,* **1**(20) 485–500.

Pawlak, Z. (1984) Rough classification. *Man–Machine Studies,* **20** 469–493.

Quinlan, J. R. (1983) *Learning Efficient Classification Procedures and Their Application to Chess and Games,* Springer Verlag, Berlin.

Schubert, L. K. (1976) Extending the expressive power of semantic networks. *Artificial Intelligence,* **7** 163–198.

Shannon, C. E. (1948) A mathematical theory of communication. *Bell System Technical Journal,* **4** 379–423.

Shortliffe, E. H. and Davis, R. (1976) *Computer-Based Medical Consultations: MYCIN,* Elsevier, North-Holland, New York.

Smith, J. M. and Smith, D. C. P. (1977) Database abstractions, aggregation and generalization. *ACM-TODS,* (June).

Sowa, J. F. (1986) Semantic networks. *Encyclopedia of Artificial Intelligence.*

Wong, S. K. M. and Ziarko, W. (1986a) Algorithm for inductive learning. *Bulletin of Polish Academy of Science,* **34**(5–6) 271–276.

Wong, S. K. M. and Ziarko, W. (1986b) Comparison of the probabilistic approximate classification and the fuzzy set model. *International Journal for Fuzzy Sets and Systems.*

Wong, S. K. M. and Ziarko, W. (1986c) Infer — an adaptive decision support system. In *Proceedings of the 6th International Workshop on Expert Systems and Their Applications, Avignon, 1986.*

Wong, S. K. M. and Ziarko, W. (1986d) On learning and evaluation of decision rules in the context of rough sets. *Proceedings of ACM International Symposium on Methodologies For Intelligent Systems, Knoxville, 1986.*

Yasdi, R. (1985) A conceptual design aid environment for expert data base systems. *Data and Knowledge Engineering,* **1**(1) (March).

Yasdi, R. and Ziarko, W. (1986) An expert system for conceptual schema design: a machine learning approach. In *Technical Report CS-86-18,* University of Regina.

Part IV
Computer-aided instruction

12

CAPRA: an intelligent system to teach novice programmers

F. J. Garijo and **M. F. Verdejo**
Facultat d'Informàtica, UPC, Pau Gargallo 5, 08028 Barcelona, Spain
A. Diaz, I. Fernandez, K. Sarasola
Informatika Fakultatea, EHU-UPV, Aptdo 649, 20080 Donostia, Spain

1. INTRODUCTION

CAPRA is an ICAI system for teaching introductory programming concepts. The system is made up of the following modules: a tutor, an expert system to make programs, an interface for natural language dialogue, and a student model.

The EXPERT module builds a program to solve a problem, following a programming methodology. It is able to explain the reasoning process step by step, showing the knowledge used at every decision point.

The TUTOR guides and controls the interactive process by means of the DIALOGUE module. The emphasis is on the methodological aspects. Our tutor follows a Socratic style, combining explanations with skill verification. Instruction is tailored for each student. In particular, exercises are proposed, taking into account their degree of difficulty, and the student's previous performance.

The organization of this chapter is the following. Principles of programming methodology and domain knowledge are presented in section 2. The CAPRA knowledge base and its representation are described in section 3. Section 4 outlines the expert-system structure and functioning, while section 5 is devoted to describing a natural-language problem-acquisition module. Section 6 presents the tutor component and finally we conclude with a summary.

2. PROBLEM DOMAIN AND TEACHING METHODOLOGY

The idea of a scheme or plan for reasoning about program construction has been identified as a central issue by recent research both in programming methodology (Lucas *et al.* 1983) and in artificial intelligence (Soloway, 1986; Waters, 1982).

Our work (Garijo and Verdejo, 1984) follows this approach. Teaching becomes a process of transferring a mixture of schematic and heuristic knowledge where expertise is acquired by building up both plans and rules to choose and combine them.

The teaching process is carried through different stages. First of all the student learns to build algorithms from the formal specification of a problem and then he or she learns to obtain a program from the algorithm.

The first stage of learning is organized as a three-step cycle of progressive deepening: (1) understanding a problem (specifying data and objectives), (2) classifying a problem by means of the association of an initial scheme, and (3) building an algorithm by stepwise refinement. Fig. 1 shows the relationships among the different stages.

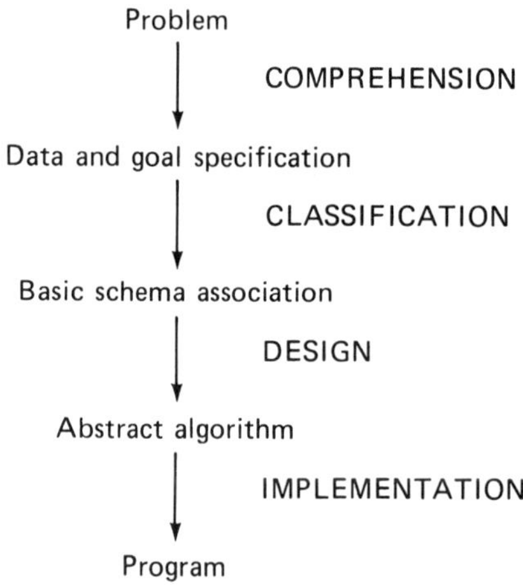

Fig. 1

The tutor can teach programming using two different domains (of different complexity). The first one (about 30 problems) is based on Karel the robot (Pattis, 1981). In Karel's world, a problem is a task to be performed by the robot. In this domain there are no data types, so the refinement strategy focuses on action decomposition.

The second domain is formed by a collection of 100 problems, to be solved with treatments of basic data types, sequences and sets. Some examples follow:

(1) Design an algorithm to read a number *N* and print all the natural numbers less than *N* having 3 or 5 as divisors.

(2) Given two words, design an algorithm to decide whether the first is contained in the second one.
(3) Let S be a sequence of integers and *M* an integer. Design an algorithm to write all the numbers of S ending with, and not being a multiple of, *M*.
(4) Given a character string, construct a program which produces as output a string formed from the input string, eliminating any blank character followed by another blank.

In the first stage (problem comprehension), a student is taught to accomplish:

— a clear distinction of data and goals
— a structured description of the goals (main and secondary ones).

In order to allow the user to specify a problem (using simple statements), high-level operators on sequences and sets are provided. For instance, the third problem is solved through the following steps. The first stage is specification:

```
Input: S sequence-of integers, M integer
Output: Write R sequence-of integers defined
        R sub-sequence-of S formed-by-all X of S such that
             (mod(X,M) ≠ 0 & mod(X,10)= M)
```

The second stage is classifying the problem: '*construction* of an output *sequence* by *selection over all* elements of an input *sequence*'. The scheme 'sequential machine with selector treatment' is proposed:

```
Initialise given-sequence
Initialise created-sequence
Foreach element in given-sequence do
        If Selection(element then Add(element, created-sequence))Endif
Endforeach
```

The third stage is the design. Linked to every scheme there is a set of criteria for focusing the refinement process. For the previous example, the next step is the study of the selector. In this case it can be written in terms of primitive functions taking as arguments the current element and the data *M*, so that there is no need for further decomposition.

Applying the scheme to our specification we obtain:

```
Initialvalue(M)
Initialise S
Initialise R
Foreach X in S do
        IfMod(X,M)≠0 & Mod(X,10)=M then Add(X,R) Endif
Endforeach
```

Successive refinement steps focus on sequential operations. S is an input sequence where all the elements have to be accessed and treated in the same way, so **Foreach** is refined in the **Read-sequence** scheme:

```
Initialvalue M
Initialise S
Initialise R
While-not-eos(S) do
Read(X)
     If mod(X,M) ≠ 0 & mod(X,10)=M then Add(X,R) Endif
Endwhile
```

and finally R is an output sequence, and so the **Add** operation is substituted by a **Write** statement, obtaining:

```
Initialvalue M
Initialise S
Initialise output
While-not-eos (S) do
Read(X)
     If mod(X,M) ≠ 0 & mod(X,10)=M then Write(X) Endif
Endwhile
```

3. KNOWLEDGE BASE AND REPRESENTATION FORMALISM

Knowledge used by the different components of the system is contained in a structured knowledge base. The following are the most relevant parts:

— Pedagogic knowledge:

- general: pedagogic plans to carry out teaching strategies
- domain: pedagogic structuring of the concepts to be taught
- student: model containing inferences about his or her learning history and communication style

— Domain knowledge:

- description of the domain concepts
- set of problems for every concept
- design and programming rules
- classification of misconceptions

— Natural language knowledge

- syntactic-semantic rules
- history of the dialogue
- speaker models

Domain knowledge used by the CAPRA system is represented using the RDES language (Garijo and Verdejo, 1984). The knowledge representation formalism is based on partitioned semantic networks in which two planes are distinguished: an abstract plane corresponding to the level of conceptual definition, and a concrete plane representing the instances of elements defined in the abstract plane which appear in the processing of each problem.

A concept is represented in the abstract plane by a basic unit called an elemental scheme, or by a composition of basic units forming a new unit called conceptual network.

There are two types of elemental schemes: descriptive, interpreted as units attached to the working domain, and structural (and, or, and ordered, equivalence, ...) having fixed semantics. The representation allows the description of hierarchically-organized objects, as well as concept definitions in terms of restrictions over concepts. The definition of rules and their association to form conceptual rules are also provided by the representation.

4. SINTALAB: AN EXPERT SYSTEM TO BUILD ABSTRACT ALGORITHMS

SINTALAB (Garijo *et al.*, 1986) is an expert system capable of building an abstract algorithm starting from the formal specification of a problem.

The input to the system is the specification of the problem to be constructed. The first task of SINTALAB consists of verifying the syntactic–semantic correction of this specification. At the same time, the knowledge expressed by the problem is studied and represented. After this knowledge acquisition–verification phase, the program construction is initiated by associating abstract schemas with the main goals. A concrete program is obtained by a refinement-step process over object and schema observations.

SINTALAB differs from other program-synthesis systems based on refinements (Barstow, 1979, Bartels *et al.*, 1981) in several ways:

— By its aim: SINTALAB is used to teach program construction by placing emphasis on the methodological aspects.
— SINTALAB provides a more complex process. For example PECOS constructs concrete implementations from abstract algorithms. SINTALAB starts from the formal specification of the problems.
— SINTALAB knowledge representation is based on RDES where the search space is well structured, facilitating the application of the rules.

The solution of goals by means of abstract schemas simplifies the refinement process, allowing a higher abstraction level and, therefore, the treatment of more complex problems. The inference mechanism is controlled by meta-rules which enable different strategies of program construction to be used in achieving a goal. In addition, changes in depth of a schema refinement as well as the solution of a specific goal can be formulated in a declarative way.

4.1 SINTALAB general structure

The system is formed from two modules:

— Knowledge acquisition to create and update the knowledge base (concepts and rules).
— A problem solver made up of: (a) a knowledge base containing concepts,

rules and meta-rules, (b) a working memory structured in a task space and a database, (c) an inference mechanism.

Fig. 2 shows the general architecture of SINTALAB.

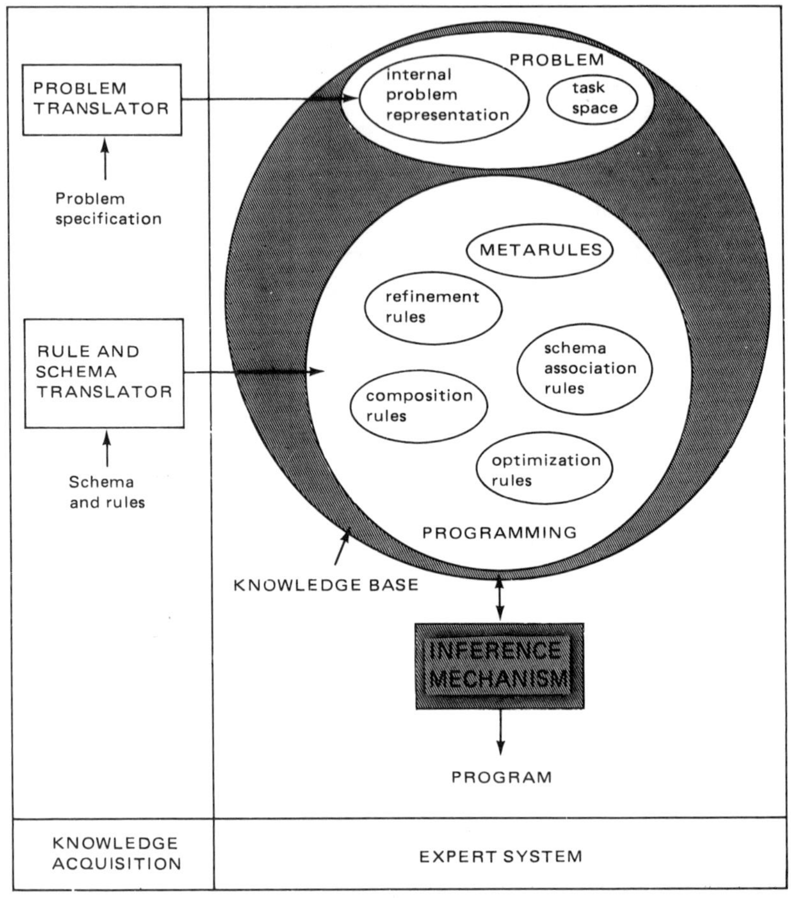

Fig. 2.

4.2 Expert system

The expert module is made up of:

— a rule and meta-rule knowledge base
— a working memory of database
— an inference mechanism

Knowledge base

The knowledge base contains permanent information relative to the application domain:

— Knowledge about basic programming concepts, i.e. data objects, schemas and rules.
— Program-construction strategies expressed in the form of meta rules.

Schemas

A schema is an abstract algorithm to achieve a type of goal. Instances of schemas are associated with each goal in the database (current problem) by inference rules.

Rules

Rules are stored in the knowledge base grouped in classes according to the task performed. Rule syntax follows the classic format:

If *condition* then *action*

where *condition* is a conjunction of conditions defining the hypothesis and *action* a sequence of actions to be performed in the case in which the hypotheses are satisfied. SINTALAB uses the following types of rules:

- Meta-rules

  Meta-rules express strategic knowledge about program construction. They drive the inference process. Their format is analogous to that of the rest of the rules, but the conditions as well as the actions are referred to the task space.

  Tasks are defined by three arguments:

  — Type of task: solve a problem, associate a schema with a goal, refine operation, composition of schema, optimize schema.
  — State of the task: active, wait, solved, failed.
  — Search space: a partitioned network containing the objects to the rules associated with the task.

  The relationship between tasks and rules is as follows:

TASKS	RULES
Solve a problem	Meta-rules
Associate a schema with a goal	Goal-schema association
Refine operation	Schema-refinement
Composition of schema	Composition-schema
Optimize schema	Algorithm-optimization

- Schema selection rules

  Schema selection rules express the relationship between goals and abstract schema. Their application produces an instance schema to solve the current goal.

  Goal characteristics are expressed in the rule-condition part. The action will consist of the generation of the corresponding instance schema.

  Example

  IF the goal selected by meta-rules is 'simple element'

THEN instantiate the schema
DECLARE (name, type, ELEMENT)
*CREATE (name, type, ELEMENT, property)

- Refinement rules
  Schemas are composed of refinable operation-sequences (denoted by *) upon which refinement rules apply. Each one of the refinable operations has an associated parameters list. These parameters carry all the information which is needed to transform the operation. Rule application produces a new operation-sequence with an equal or lesser abstraction level.

  Refinement rules have the following format:

  If the refinable operation selected by meta-rules is *operation(parameter-list) and
  condition-list over parameters hold
  THEN the operation *operation (parameter-list) is refined in Operation sequence.

  Refinement rules constitute a coherent body of knowledge about the programming process. They are grouped together according to the type of goals they solve.

- Composition rules
  The task of composition rules is to merge the schemas of two adjacent subgoals.

  The condition part takes into account the schema descriptions associated with the subgoals; the action part generates the new merged schema.

- Optimization rules
  Their aim is to improve the performance of the algorithm obtained by the system. This group of rules basically contains horizontal and vertical merge loop techniques.

Inference mechanism

The control module supervises the problem-solving process, consisting of the following cyclic sequence:

— Applying meta-rules (over the task space) with the purpose of breaking down a task into simpler ones.
— Applying specific inference rules (over the concrete plane of the problem) in order to solve the selected task.

5. CAPRATE: A NATURAL LANGUAGE ACQUISITION MODULE

The CAPRATE module (Sarasola and Verdejo, 1987) inteprets programming problems texts dealing with objects such as numbers, characters, sequences and sets, and generates their corresponding representation in CAPRA formal specification language. This module allows a collection of programs to be built and enriched in a simple way.

A set of 100 problems representative of a whole range has been collected to work with. Texts can be written indiscriminately in Spanish or in Basque, and therefore the translation system has to be designed to consider linguistic problems of both languages.

Translation is divided into two consecutive steps: the first one takes as input Spanish or Basque statements of programming problems and produces meaning representations for the objects appearing in the text. The second step is the creation of a specification after checking the correctness of the generated representation.

Domain knowledge is used extensively in the second step of translation to take into account global conditions of consistency. This process completes the definition of the objects and decides which ones will be part of the specification input and which ones of the output.

Similar kinds of applications in other domains are given by Burton (1976) and Mellish 1983). Our domain presents more ambiguity than the first one, and uses different input (Spanish and Basque) and formalisms (for parsing and representation) from the second one.

5.1 System components

The set of components designed can be classified as follows:

- General tools useful for any other application:
  - ATN interpreter
  - the RDES language of knowledge representation
  - knowledge related to the specific application
- Knowledge domain further divided into:
  - concept definitions in the abstract plane of RDES
  - inference rules expressing knowledge about the completeness of the final representation
- Linguistic+domain knowledge:
  - Dictionary with syntactic and semantic information
  - Lexical parser
  - Syntactic–semantic ATNs for Spanish and Basque.

5.2 ATN interpreter

Our ATN interpreter is based upon the standard ATN of Bates (1978). The strategy followed by the interpreter explores all possible parses, trying to eliminate incorrect choices as soon as possible by means of semantic information. Semantic expectations are created by a nucleus of meaning units (verbs in sentences, nouns in noun phrases, ...) about their complements. A filtering process will select for each expectation among waiting candidates. In order to achieve this work three new actions and one test must be available in the ATNs, as follows:

- WAITSEM <compl> <role>. This action will be used when a complement appears in the text before the expected nucleus. This causes the complement to be saved in a waiting list with the role it plays in the phrase or sentence.

- POSSEM <lex-unit>. This action activates all the possible uses of a lexical unit as nucleus of a phrase or sentence, examines the correctness of the complements waiting for it and builds for each success a new state of parsing.
- FILTER <compl> <role>. This action examines whether the complement is compatible with any expectation created by the previously activated nucleus. If it is compatible then it creates a new state of parsing, else no new state is created (so that the parse is discarded).
- USECOMPLETE. This test is to be used at POP arcs. If all the complements requested by the nucleus have been completed and no other complement remains, the associated semantic actions will be executed. The actions create the representation in RDES for the completed parsed meaning unit. Ellipsis and possible references will be treated by searching appropriate objects among the previously-represented ones.

The structure of sentences in Spanish and Basque is completely different. In Basque, analysis is mainly performed in terms of waitsem and possem combinations, because complements appear before nouns and verbs. On the other hand possem and filter are the usual constructions in the Spanish ATN.

5.3 Knowledge domain concept definitions in the abstract plane of RDES

'Specification', 'simple-element', 'sequence', 'set', 'objective', 'condition', 'expression' are examples of conceptual networks used by both the expert and the translator.

In addition to this common knowledge base, our translation module needs other generic concepts such as 'object' and 'object-collection'.

Instances of 'object' and 'object-collection' are partial descriptions. They are refined continuously and completely classified at the end of the whole text parsing.

The following five functions will help to manipulate objects in RDES:

- ADDOBJECT <object>. This function will be used to add a new object to the current object collection. The object representation will be defined with its type, name and properties.
- ADDESCRIPTION <object> <description>. This function adds a description to the object representation. The object can be expressed as a direct reference or as the result of a search function over the current object collection. The description is a specification of the type, name or a new property.
- GETDESCRIPTION <object> <description-path>. This function takes the value corresponding to the description-path of the object. The description-path specifies the type, name, property wanted or one of their components.
- GETOBJECT <object-collection> <description-pattern>. The result is another <object-collection> with the objects from the object-collec-

tion matching the description-pattern. This function will be used to solve references.

- CHECK-DESCRIPTION <object> <description-pattern>. This predicate checks whether the object matches the description-pattern.

5.4 Inference rules expressing knowledge about the completeness of the final representation

After the whole structure has been parsed, an object-collection is obtained. Then every object will be examined to verify its correct and complete definition and to separate input objects from output objects.

Some examples of rules follow:

— An object has a unique value. If there is more than one description, those must be compatible.
— Objects explicitly defined as input data or results in the structure will be put in the input or in the output respectively.
— Definite objects with no specification about their value will be considered as belonging to the input.

6. DESIGN OF AN INTELLIGENT TUTOR

Control modelling is an important factor to consider in designing an intelligent tutor. The question is how to generate observable behaviour in real human tutoring. Our approach presents a framework based on dynamic planning. Different aspects of the tutoring task are separated in specialist components. Behaviour is modelled as a cooperative process among diverse knowledge sources to accomplish a goal. As in other systems (Clancey, 1983; Woolf, 1984), teaching strategies are independent of domain knowledge; furthermore, in our system control structure is expressed in a declarative way by means of plans and conflict-resolution rules.

Work on protocol analysis suggested to us a classification of instructional activities, leading to the definition of a number of components, each one ecapsulating a type of task. At the highest level of abstraction, we consider a 'pedagogic decision' module where a general teaching approach is planned. In particular two kinds of actions are considered:

— Choosing a combination of strategies to attain a pedagogic objective.
— Developing the strategies established.

The refinement of a pedagogic objective in terms of specific subject matter is carried out by the 'thematic decision' component. Explaining and controlling the acquisition are the main tasks performed by the 'teaching component'. Communication is managed through the 'dialogue module'. The 'supervisor' focuses on conflict resolution among tutor and student's objectives, informing 'pedagogic decision' if strategic changes are needed. Fig. 3 shows the dynamic relationships among the described modules.

Control is shared by the different components, following a blackboard architecture (Fernandez *et al.*, 1987). Each component encapsulates a

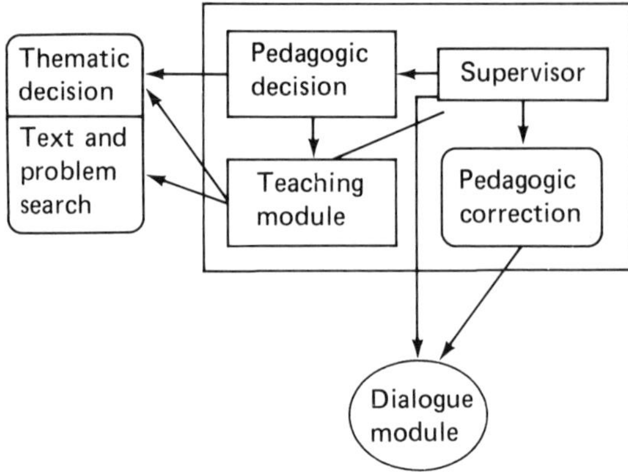

Fig. 3.

source of knowledge to solve a type of goal. The representation scheme is the same for all of them. Components are modelled as a knowledge base of plans and rules. A plan is composed of a set of actions and subgoals.

6.1 Pedagogic decision module

Different strategies (obtained from the study of teaching experiences) have been classified into general and local ones. Among the first, we have the following: to introduce the student into the system, to remember briefly, to revise any conflicting points, to introduce new concepts, to finish a session, etc. Among the second we have the following: to check a concept, to resolve a doubt about a problem statement and to give an example.

A **session** can be seen as a result of the application of a set of strategies. A typical example would consist of 'a general review, an introduction of new concepts, a review of conflicting points'; others would be 'introduction of new concepts', or 'a brief review of the last session and an introduction of new concepts'.

An **objective** (OB) has different plans associated with it. Depending on the strategy, one plan will be selected in order to achieve the objective. A **plan** is expressed as a composition of objectives and actions.

Actions can be of two types: elementary actions (EA) and starting actions (SA). The first ones can be described in declarative form (by rules) or procedural form. The second ones establish subobjectives that will be resolved in other levels.

Therefore, the knowledge base of the pedagogic decision module is composed by:

(a) a structured description of the pedagogic objectives, the pedagogic strategies and the associated plans;
(b) a set of rules for determing a pedagogic goal and for selecting strategies;

(c) a set of rules to choose a plan to carry out a goal with a given strategy.

A sequence of strategies is selected in terms of parameters, for example time between sessions and different information about the student. Rules for **plan selection** consider the current objective, the point of the session and the established strategy. Their general form is the following:

If *objective description* and
strategy description and
state of the session
Then apply plan X

One of the rules for the above example says:

If the objective is 'start the session' and the strategy is 'general review'
Then apply Plan 7

For instance the objective (P-OB5) 'start the session' can be resolved by different plans:

Plan 5: (P-SA1) select (initial concept C, explanation detail ED)
(P-SA2) introduce concept C with explanation detail ED

Plan 6: (P-SA1) select (revision concept C, explanation detail ED)
(P-SA3) remember concept C with explanation detail ED
(P-OB7) decide to check concept C

Plan 7: (P-SA1) select (list of concepts CL)
(P-SA3) remember the list of concepts CL
(P-OB7) decide to check the list of concepts CL

In cases where the previous rule could be applied, Plan 7 would be selected. It is composed of the starting action (P-SA1) 'select the concept list' (goal for the thematic decision module) and (P-SA3) 'remember the concept list' (goal for teaching module) and finally the pedagogic objective (P-OB7), in order to decide whether checking is necessary or not.

6.2 Thematic decision module

Once the pedagogic decision module has established the associated plan for a strategy, it is necessary to refine it for the conceptual domain.

Thematic decision chooses the specific concepts that are going to be taught or reviewed, or the problems that must be proposed to the student so that he or she learns a particular concept. To perform this task the pedagogic meta-level is consulted. It consists of a hierarchy organizing domain concepts in levels, in terms of their difficulty and prerequisites.

When a concept has been selected, the search for a suitable text and problems with adequate profundity and/or difficulty level is also performed.

6.3 Teaching module

The structure of the teaching module is similar to that of the pedagogic decision one, in the sense that there are teaching objectives which are reached through plans composed of objectives and/or actions. In this module no strategy is determined since it is previously defined by the pedagogic decision module.

For instance, the objective (T-OB1) 'The student has acquired concept X' has the following associated plans:

Plan 1: (T-OB2) the student has acquired the X prerequisites
(T-OB1) the student has acquired concept X

Plan 2: (T-OB3) teach the concept X
(T-OB4) the student knows how to use concept X with a degree of certainty Y

Plan 3: (T-OB5) the student has acquired the X subconcepts

Plan 4: (T-OB3) teach concept X
(T-OB5) the student has acquired the X subconcepts

The association of plans to objectives is carried out by rules belonging to the general scheme

If *objective description* and
list of concepts conditions and
state of the session
Then apply Plan X

For the previous objective, one of the rules says:

If the objective is 'the student has acquired concept X'
and ((There are no prerequisites for X) or (the student knows the X prerequisites))
and X is an active node
and X has no subconcepts
Then apply Plan 2

The execution of a teaching-module plan involves selecting texts for explanations and problems for verification. In addition, student's interactions have to be handled. The search of texts and problems is done by the texts and problem search module. The starting actions whose effect is to maintain the interaction with the student activate objectives of the supervisor module.

6.4 Supervisor

The supervisor module detects and solves conflicts arising between the strategy followed by the TUTOR and the student's objectives.

To accomplish it, the supervisor compares the tutor's objectives (current and waiting) with the student's objectives (established by the dialogue module). Conflicts are resolved by including local strategies or restating the general strategies. In any case the application of a strategy is a task belonging to the pedagogic decision module.

The structure of the supervisor module also fits the model of objectives, plans, actions, and rules of selection which has already been discussed. The rules for plan selection have the following general scheme

If *objective description* and
description of student's objectives and
state of the season
Then apply plan X

For example the following type of supervisor goal (S-OB3) 'respond to the student's objective' has the associated plans:

Plan 3: (S-SA2) detect errors
(S-EA1) count the number of answers
(S-EA2) detect conflicts
(S-EA3) If CONFLICT Then decide whether to follow the general strategy or to insert a local strategy
Else decide a correction strategy
(S-SA3) apply a strategy
Plan 4: (S-SA2) detect errors
(S-EA3) If CONFLICT Then decide whether to follow the general strategy or to insert a local strategy
Else decide a correction strategy
(S-EA4) TYPE-MESSAGE(Problem) = 'NOT ACTIVE'
(S-SA3) apply a strategy

One of the rules to select a current plan is the following:
If the objective is 'respond the student's objective' and
the student's objective is 'evaluable-answer' and
the number of answers is less than LIMIT
Then apply plan 3.

6.5 Dialogue module

The human–computer interaction module carries out two types of tasks:

— sending messages from the tutor to the student
— understanding student's answers which are expressed in natural language (Spanish) and reporting them to the tutor.

Decisions relevant to discourse management such as 'focus on topic' or 'explanation detail' are made by the tutor before activation of the dialogue module.

Conversely, the interpretation of student's answers is a task performed by the dialogue component. This includes recognizing student's intentions. A categorization of objectives has been established; some of them are 'question about proposed exercise', 'more explanation about concept', 'evaluable answer', 'confirmation of proposed solution' etc.

6.6 Pedagogic correction module

This module is invoked to correct the student's solution to a proposed problem, once the error-detection module has diagnosed the incorrect concepts from the error types produced.

As for the other components, it consists of a set of error-correction plans and a set of selection rules. Misconceptions of the student's answer and the correction strategy selected by the supervisor are included in the preconditions of the selection rules. In this way the most suitable correction form is selected, from the indication of the most important error to the exhaustive correction of every error.

Now we are carrying out, to the full extent, a study of protocols to build a complete knowledge base containing all correction forms and selection rules.

7. SUMMARY

In this chapter we have described the structure and working of an ICAI system for teaching introductory programming concepts. The CAPRA system is made up of the following modules: a tutor, an expert system to build programs, an interface for natural language dialogue, and a student model. The tutor and expert modules have been studied in detail.

The main contributions can be grouped in two categories:

- *Methodological aspects*. Problem solving is performed in four stages: characterization of goals, selection of initial schema through classification, design by stepwise refinement, and implementation. Emphasis is set on learning of programming as the progressive acquisition of two types of knowledge: abstract algorithm schemas and rules to choose schemas and to combine them.
- *Design issues*. Previously-developed approaches have relied upon static planning (Peachey and McCalla, 1986). The CAPRA tutor's activity is formalized as a dynamic planning process. This improves efficiency because replanning is avoided. In addition teaching strategies are independent of the teaching domain and are expressed in a declarative way.

Further development will involve (1) error treatment and student model and (2) implementing a prototype to integrate the modules described.

ACKNOWLEDGEMENTS

The CAPRA project is partly financed by the Spanish Advisory Commission of Scientific and Technical Research (Comisión Asesora de Investigación Científica y Técnica) under contract number 1381–82.

REFERENCES

Barstow, D. (1979) *Knowledge-based Program Construction*, Noth-Holland.

Bartels, U., Olthoff, W. and Ranfels, P. (1981) APE: an expert system form automatic programming from abstract specifications and data types and algorithms. *IJCAI, 24–48 August 1981.*

Bates, M. (1978) The theory and practice of augmented transition network grammars. In: Bolc, L. (ed.), *Natural Language Communication with Computers*, Berlin.

Burton, B. (1976) Semantic grammar: an engineering technique for constructing natural language understanding systems. *Report 3422*, Bolt Beranek and Newman Inc, Cambridge, Mass.

Clancey, W. (1982) Methodology for building an intelligent tutoring system. *Heuristic Programming Project, Report HPP-81-81*, Department of Computer Science, Stanford University.

Clancey, W. (1983) Tutoring rules for guiding a case method dialogue. In Sleeman, D. and Brown, J. (eds.), *Intelligent Tutoring Systems*, Academic Press, pp. 201–225.

Clancey, W. and Letsinger, R. (1981) NEOMYCIN: reconfiguring a rule-based expert system for application to teaching. *Proceedings of the 7th IJCAI*, pp. 829–836.

Dede, C. (1986) A review and synthesis of recent research in intelligent computer-assisted instruction. *International Journal of Man-Machine Studies* **24**, 329–353.

Fernandez, M. I., Diaz, A. and Verdejo, M. F. (1987) Diseño de un tutor mediante planificación dinámica. Submitted to *IBERAMIA 87.*

Garijo, F. and Verdejo, F. (1984a) CAPRA: an intelligent system for teaching programming concepts. *FISS-I-5.1-IT/P-84.*

Garijo, F. and Verdejo, F. (1984b) Knowledge representation for teaching programming in an ICAI environment. *First IEEE Conference on Artificial Intelligence Applications, Denver, Colorado.*

Farijo, F., Inchausti, C., Hernandez, L. and Verdejo, F. (1986) Sintalab: an expert system for the synthesis of abstract algorithms. *Proceedings of the 6 Int. Workshop on Expert Systems and their Application.* Avignon, 1986, pp. 1497–1499.

Lucas, M., Peyrin, J. P. and Scholl, P. C. (1983) *Algorithmique et Representation des Données*, Editorial Masson.

Mellish, C. (1983) Incremental semantic interpretation in a modular parsing system. In Sparck Jones, K. and Wilks, Y. (eds.) *Automatic Natural Language Parsing*, Ellis Horwood, pp. 148–155.

Pattis, R. (1981) *Karel the Robot. A Gentle Introduction to the Art of programming*, Wiley.

Peachey, D. and McCalla, G. (1986) Using planning techniques in intelligent tutoring systems. *International Journal of Man–Machine Studies* **24**, 77–98.

Sarasola, K. and Verdejo, M. F. (1987) CAPRATE un sistema de adquisicion de problemas en lenguaje natural. *Tercera Reunion Anual de la Sociedad Española para el Procesamiento del Lenguaje Natural, Barcelona, 1987.*

Soloway, E. (1986) Learning to program=learning to construct mechanisms and explanations. *Communications of the ACM* **29**(9) (September), 850–858.

Waters, R. (1982) The programmer's apprentice: knowledge based program editing. *IEEE Trans. on Software Engineering* **8**(1) (January), 1–12.

Woolf, B. (1984) Context-dependent planning in a machine tutor. *COINS Technical Report 84–21*, Department of Computer and Information Science, University of Massachusetts.

Woolf, B. and McDonald, D. (1984) Building a computer tutor: design issues. *Computer IEEE* (September), 61–73.

13

Differences between expert systems and domain components of intelligent tutoring systems

Paul Kamsteeg and **Dick Blerman**
University of Amsterdam, Psychology Department, Psychonomy section, Weesperplein 8, 1018 XA Amsterdam, The Netherlands

1. INTRODUCTION

An intelligent tutoring system (ITS) needs knowledge about the domain it is tutoring about. The most elegant architecture (by way of general accesibility, maintenance and conceptual clarity) is to represent this knowledge in a separate component, the domain-knowledge component, to which the other parts of the total ITS can refer. Often an existing expert sytem is used for such a domain-knowledge component. Most authors agree that this can only be done if the **factual** and **procedural** knowledge† of the expert system are represented explicitly, i.e. if it is a 'glass box' expert system (e.g. Sleeman and Brown, 1982).

Experiences with such a 'glass box' expert system — MYCIN — in a tutoring context‡, lead Clancey (1983, 1986) to the conclusion that, apart from this, a domain-knowledge component must also have explicitly-represented **strategic** (when to apply procedures), **structural** (classification of knowledge) and **supportive** (why knowledge is valid) knowledge.

The demands or constraints stated above are put in rather general terms. It is not immediately clear what their implications are for the architecture of a specific expert system. Moreover, it is questionable whether these constraints are all that should be imposed. In our own experiences in trying to build an ITS around an existing 'glass box' expert system (in our case one for

† To avoid confusion between the *content* of knowledge and the *implementation* thereof, we shall use the following notation throughout this chapter. With regard to content of knowledge, we shall speak of *factual* and *procedural* knowledge (and of strategic, structural and supportive knowledge). With regard to the implementation, we shall speak of *declaratively* vs. *functionally* represented knowledge. In AI literature, often the words 'procedural' and 'declarative' are used both with regard to content and implementation. That is, both declarative and procedural knowledge may be implemented declaratively or procedurally.

‡ Clancey claims that his remarks pertain to all kinds of expert systems. However, in his classification of problem types (Clancey, 1985) he does not include physics transformation problems.

solving thermodynamics problems, called PDP), we have also come across several difficulties rooted in the expert-system design. This has led us to state additional demands to be placed upon a domain-knowledge component of an ITS. Some of them would make the program virtually unusable as a expert system. We shall discuss them further on, but first we shall give some examples of different kinds of knowledge (drawn from the domain of thermodynamics), argue why it is difficult but necessary to distinguish between them, and describe what in our opinion an ICAI system for this domain must do, specifically concerning the diagnosis of pupil actions.

1.1 Examples of knowledge in the thermodynamics domain

Strategic knowledge might be: 'To do a problem, first make an informal sketch of the problem, then formalize this sketch, only then start to solve the problem', *or* 'If a problem has only one state, don't look for difference-values'.

Procedural knowledge is for instance: 'If the value V1 of a variable is given in units U1, and the standard unit for this variable is U2, and a mapping function U2=f(U1) exists, then perform this function on V1 to get the normalized value V2 of the variable in standard units U2'.

Factual knowledge consists of physical and common-sense definitions, e.g. 'Volume, also named vol or V, is a state-variable with standard unit m^3 and actual unit one of litre, dm^3, m^3', relations, e.g. 'X m^3=1000*X litre' (a mapping function), and possibly other facts.

Structural knowledge consists of structural relations between items of procedural and factual knowledge. These structures permit manipulations to be represented in a more general, more concise way. Structural knowledge is exemplified by type-hierarchies, e.g. 'Volume is a kind of state-variable', but also by more special relations, e.g. the observation that 'Poisson's laws are stronger than Boyle's laws' (in that they can derive unknowns using fewer knowns). These are instances of structural knowledge pertaining to factual knowledge. Another kind of structural knowledge pertains to procedural knowledge. It is used to index different procedural knowledge items as belonging to a certain kind of problem solving 'act' (such as making a drawing, finding formulae, etc.), e.g. 'Finding out what kind of container there is belongs to making a drawing'.

Support knowledge is not directly used by the expert system in the problem-solving process, so it may be represented informally, e.g. in natural language 'scripts'†. Examples of such knowledge: 'The pressures on two sides of a free-moving partition are the same, **because** otherwise the partition would move in the direction of the least pressure until the pressures are the same' or 'Frictionless does not imply free-moving, **because** the frictionless object might be held at its place'.

1.2 What is in a knowledge type?

What exactly constitutes and distinguishes the abovementioned types of knowledge is not clear. There is no inherent criterion by which to index

† In that case, as a consequence, this knowledge itself would not be further explainable.

knowledge as factual, procedural or strategic. The indexing choice is dependent upon the way one wants to **use** the knowledge. For instance, there is the well-known 'procedural–declarative' controversy', but in the same vein one can also discern a 'strategic–procedural controversy'. That is, the choice whether to implement a certain piece of knowledge as declarative, procedural or strategic is to an extent arbitrary. At the lowest level the distinction even ceases to exist: all knowledge is coded in equivalent computer-language structures.

Still, especially in a domain-knowledge component of a tutoring system, the indexing choice is very important, since it will directly affect the diagnosis of pupil actions and the resulting tutoring interactions. For example, if the pupil thinks 'isolation' means 'temperature is constant' this can be treated as a wrong procedure (malrule) or as a confusion between two concepts ('temperature' and 'heat'), yielding different remediations.

The way one wants to use knowledge in an ITS is different from the use in an expert system, if only because an expert system does not have to account for all kinds of cognitive 'bugs'. Therefore, knowledge must be differently indexed in an ITS vs. an expert system. In essence, this is what Clancey (1983) is arguing.

It is important that, the indexing choice being made, this choice is adhered to consistently. For example, if a class of knowledge items is taken to be strategical, every knowledge item in this class should only manipulate (the order of) procedures. Wielinga and Breuker (1986) have given criteria to make such a consistent choice. The main reason to demand consistency is that, in order to limit the search space, we want to distinguish between **what objects** (facts) a pupil is manipulating, **how** (procedure) and **when–why** (strategy) — see the following section.

In the following, we shall discuss factual, procedural and strategic knowledge in separate sections. We shall not devote a separate section to Clancey's (1983) concept of structural knowledge. We do not think it is a separate knowledge-type; rather, it permeates all other knowledge. We can only say that the number of different structural-link types must be as small as possible, to allow for reasonably general search mechanisms.

Neither shall we discuss Clancey's 'support knowledge' in depth, since it can either be represented as extra factual, procedural and strategical knowledge (being subject to the same constraints), or have the form of fixed explanation 'scripts', linked to the relevant knowledge (in which case there are no real constraints).

1.3 Tasks of a tutoring system for transformation problems

More specific demands upon a domain knowledge component arise when the tutoring task is specified. In this chapter we focus on a tutoring task with which we have experience: that of teaching pupils how to solve **physics transformation problems** (more specifically thermodynamics problems) in an effective way. This is done by monitoring a pupil, **only** interfering when necessary. Thus the tutoring system does not normally ask the pupil to perform certain tasks: the monitoring is dependent upon spontaneous notes and drawings the pupil jots down on a 'graphic scratchpad' (Bierman and Anjewierden, 1986). These notes contain statements about the problem, which as such represent results of inferences. Thus, we view the execution part of the problem-solving process as a progressive extension of the knowledge about the problem situation, brought about by a series of consecutive operations on specific objects.

For each note the pupil makes, the tutoring system must recognize what the pupil is trying to do, that is infer the type of pupil action and the object(s) on which this action is performed. Furthermore it must diagnose this action. This can be conceptualized as a cycle of generalizing the actual note to a **type** of result, linking this result-type to a generic inference, and specifying the generic inference to a normative inference, yielding a normative result (see Fig. 1). This generalize–link–specify cycle is equivalent to the one Clancey

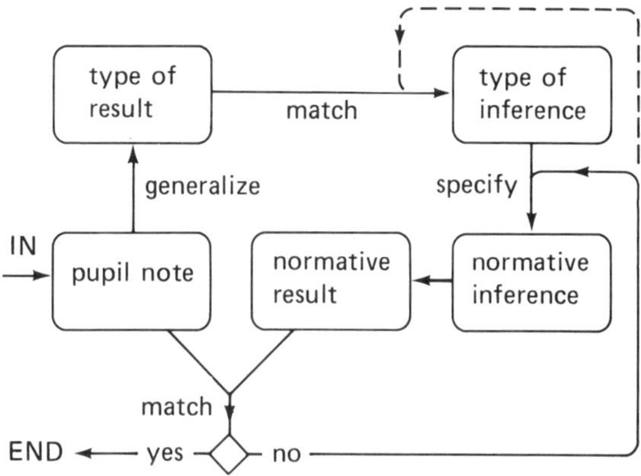

Fig. 1 — Diagnostic cycle of a tutoring system.

(1985, p. 5–8) describes for diagnostic problem-solving. The normative result can be matched to the original note; a mismatch implies that another specification of the inference type should be made, or perhaps even that another generic inference should be hypothesized. The recognized (=reconstructed) pupil solving action may be correct, illegal, useless, incorrectly executed or performed on wrong objects. Note that this diagnostic scheme will only work if knowledge types are consistent, as stated in the previous section.

Having recognized the pupil step in this way, the tutoring system will have to fit this step into an evolving pupil problem-solving plan, and infer the deeper reason(s) for possible deviations from a correct problem-solving process (e.g. misconceptions, bad strategy etc.). Consecutively, one or more tutor action(s) must be executed.

2. ARCHITECTURE

To recognize a pupil action in the way described in section 1.3, it must be possible to execute a (set of) procedural knowledge item(s) at every desired moment. Furthermore, to try out different instantiations† of a procedural knowledge item, the results of previous tries have to be undone.

Principle 1: 'Partial executability'

Procedural knowledge items must be independent of the interpreter mechanism to the extent that it is possible to execute them at will. Peculiarities of the programming language or the inference machne must not influence the problem-solving knowledge.

Principle 2: 'Retractable instantiations'

The additions to the problem-specific factual knowledge which are made by an instantiated piece of procedural knowledge must be filed, and these additions must be selectively retractable.

For the problem-solving knowledge to be manipulable, at least two more constraints upon the architecture of the expert system must be fulfilled:

Principle 3: 'Specific to generic links'

The instantiated problem-solving knowledge (e.g. elements of a trace) has to be linked to the corresponding generic knowledge, so as to try out different instantiations with variants of the generic knowledge. More specifically, for each problem-solving action there must be an indication of the generic procedural knowledge used.

Principle 4: 'Trivial interpreter mechanism'

Decisions about the sequence of actions should be represented in (strategical) knowledge items, not in the procedural shell of the expert program. The (functional) interpreter mechanism should be as small and as simple as possible.

In a relatively simple domain, the relevant knowledge may be restricted to procedures, algorithms to follow for obtaining a solution. Moreover, in such a simple domain it is often possible to represent exhaustively **all** ways in which each procedure might be wrong ('malrules'). The diagnosis then boils down to mapping each wrong pupil action onto a (combination of) malrule(s), as is the case in BUGGY, the ITS for arithmetic problems.

In a more complex domain, however, although possible in principle, this approach does not work. The number of (mal)rules to account for all possibilities would be very large owing to the combinatorial explosion, and the rules themselves would be very complicated and very specific. One has to generalize by distinguishing factual, procedural and strategic knowledge (correct or buggy) and building the actual solve actions by combining these. However, then we have to be sure about what type each item belongs to, and about which combinations are valid. Even if criteria for categorization of knowledge are arbitrary, the categorization must be consistent.

Principle 5: 'Consistent knowledge types'

† The term 'instantiation' relates to a specific instance of a generic concept. For example, the generic concept 'chair' can be instantiated as 'this chair (on which I am sitting now)'.

> Knowledge items must be unambiguously typed, and must have consistent interactions with other knowledge types. That is, procedural knowledge items must always transform factual knowledge to other factual knowledge (often subject to some condition), strategical knowledge must always (and only) guide the sequence of procedural knowledge, etcetera.

This principle also implies that one knowledge item should not contain different types of knowledge. A procedural knowledge item should contain no strategic information, etc.

Preferably, the knowledge items should be identifiable by type: the coaching system should be able to 'see' what kind of information a specific piece of knowledge contains. This identifying information is a kind of 'meta-structural knowledge'. It is not meant to be conveyed to the pupil and is therefore better implemented outside of the normal knowledge types.

3. FACTUAL KNOWLEDGE

Clancey (1986, p.18) distinguishes two types of factual knowledge: facts which are generally valid in the domain ('general model'), and facts which are true about the problem at hand ('situation-specific model'). Wielinga and Breuker (1986, p.4) also discern a 'generic domain model' (they call it the 'domain level' of knowledge), but no 'situation-specific model'. Instead they posit an 'inference level' of knowledge, containing both **general** problem-related knowledge (such as 'a variable is a quantity') and inference rules.

It would be very convenient for a tutoring system to be able to distinguish between general facts about the domain and about problems, but the separation of generic and situation-specific knowledge is essential. These two types must be kept separate, since the instructional program needs to know which facts are always true, and which are only true in the current problem. Note, however, that since the problem-specific knowledge is inferred from the generic knowledge, there should be connections between them, as stated in principle 1.

> **Principle 6: 'Separation of generic and specific knowledge'**
> General domain knowledge must be kept separate from specific problem knowledge.

In the thermodynamics expert system PDP generic concepts (structured in a class hierarchy) can be **instantiated** to separate, but related, specific instances which inherit all properties of the generic concepts.

Sometimes it may be convenient, or even necessary, to represent generic domain knowledge in different ways. However, as this knowledge is instantiated, there must be no confusion as to which interpretation is used: either one interpretation must be used in instantiation consistently, or all interpretations must be instantiated.

> **Principle 7: 'Consistent instantiations of factual knowledge'**

A problem-specific factual knowledge item must always be represented the same way.

This principle will become more clear by an example: in PDP, the fact 'a container is closed' can be represented in two ways. An instantiated 'container'-concept can have a 'property'-role 'closed'; or an instantiated 'close'-concept can have a 'object'-role 'container#'. The choice between these two representations is not consistent. This makes a general way of checking pupil actions impossible.

To know that a concept is absent is different from not knowing whether it is present, and both are different from knowing it to be irrelevant for the problem at hand. These three types of 'negative knowledge' should be distinguishable.

Principle 8: 'Discrimination of different types of absent knowledge'

There must be different representations for negative, unknown and irrelevant factual knowledge items.

In physical transformation problems, usually some sketch of the problem situation (e.g. a drawing) is made. To account for this, the problem-specific knowledge must contain some qualitative description of the problem, in which objects play well-defined roles and are related both in space and in time. The qualitative problem representation of PDP, for instance, is difficult to map on a pupil drawing because in PDP the qualitative objects are not related and there is no time scale.

Principle 9: 'Qualitative representation'

The problem-specific knowledge must contain a qualitative description of the problem, consisting of an interrelated structure rather than loose qualitative aspects.

4. PROCEDURAL KNOWLEDGE

As stated before, in diagnosis the solve actions of the expert system have to be compared with those a pupil performs. Therefore the procedural knowledge items have to be represented (e.g. as rules) on a suitable level, i.e. one action of the expert system† should map onto one action of the student, not onto several. Furthermore, there should be no 'administrative' rules that perform no cognitive problem-solving task but only serve to keep things in order in the expert system; these tasks should be performed on a lower, not explicit, level. Since the span of one cognitive action gets greater as the pupil becomes more experienced, we cannot demand that one cognitive action be not divided among several rules. However, such rules should still not be smaller (i.e. on a more detailed level) than the basic cognitive actions posited by the (cognitive or educational) theory. There may only be a set of

† To avoid confusion betwen actions of the expert system and actions of a pupil we shall denote the former by the words 'rules' or 'rule sets'. Note, however, that we do not mean to imply that the expert-system actions should be represented as production rules.

rules to account for one cognitive action if the conditions of the rules within the set are mutually exclusive, i.e. as long as only one rule in the set can fire.

> **Principle 10: 'Cognitive validity of procedural knowledge items'**
> A procedural knowledge item must be equivalent to a cognitive action, and must not perform more than one cognitive action. A procedural knowledge item must not perform cognitively irrelevant tasks.

We have already argued why procedural knowledge items must contain information about generic input and output, besides the generic condition and action statements.

> **Principal 11: 'Aspects of procedural knowledge items'**
> Each procedural rule of the expert system should consist of: type(s) of input data, condition for use, action to be performed (the transformation *per se*), and type(s) of output data.

As noted above, in executing a rule, the interpreting mechanism should note the rule being used together with the specific input and output of this rule. The output type of a rule is used to match a pupil action to an expert-system rule, even when the pupil action might not be correct: since we can only monitor a pupil action by its output, we need a corresponding output typing in the expert rule. The other three elements of a rule are necessary to differentiate between possible types of errors the pupil might make: performing an illegal action (condition), performing an action on wrong data=performing a useless or meaningless action (input data), and performing an action in a wrong way (action).

Tying a type of output data to a procedural knowledge-item sometimes can be a problem, because it is not always exactly definable **which** procedure produces an item of factual knowledge. This is because strictly speaking there are several processes involved in producing a problem-specific fact (e.g. 'V1=2 litres is given') in this domain:

(a) Recognizing a concept as **relevant** in the problem (e.g. in certain problems, the volume of the gas might not matter; its colour never does matter in this domain). This is equivalent to instantiating the concept; it might mean instantiating several objects (e.g. 'V1=V2' implies an equality-instance and two volume-instances).
(b) Recognizing the **role** the instantiated concept plays in the problem (e.g. an instantiated volume might be given, or asked, or part of a relation).
(c) (if appropriate) Attaching **properties** (e.g. a value) to the instantiated concept. More than one property might be in order (e.g. a variable might have a given value and a standardized value).

These processes might be divided among several procedural items. Indeed, sometimes this even *ought* to be the case, since different cognitive actions are involved (e.g. attaching a given value vs. a normalized value to a variable). If one had to choose then the second of these should be the action taken to imply the production of the problem-specific knowledge-item.

The condition and action parts of a procedural rule should be simple, i.e. they should contain as few conditional and branching constructs as possible, preferably none. Of course looping constructs are also out, since they would imply that more than one cognitive action is taken in the rule. Conditional branchings should be provided for by different rules with the conditions in the conditional parts; or, better still, the underlying reason for the branching should be abstracted and explicated as a strategic rule.

In a set of rules, a later one should not depend upon performance at a previous one. More specifically, a rule should not make implicit use of a test or an action done in a previous rule, and it should not be implicitly dependent on failure of previous rules (this is the reason why rule-conditions within a rule set must be mutually exclusive). Simply stated:

Principle 12: 'Independence of rules'

Procedural rules should be independent of each other and of the context in which they are executed.

If a construct such as 'first try rule a and if it fails try rule b, is needed, this information should be expressed in a strategic rule if it can be abstracted to strategic information. Otherwise the two procedural rules should be made independent by making their conditions mutually exclusive. This amounts to specifying in more detail when rule a and rule b are valid. Care must be taken to ensure that this does not mean 'secretively' adding control knowledge!

In physics problems, usually there are defaults. That is, the problem solver has to assume values for certain variables in the absence of pertinent information about them. However, defaults do not always apply. For instance, a gas may be considered ideal, but only if it is fairly light and the pressure is not every high.

Apart from the generic factual knowledge that a concept can have a default value, there must be explicit procedural knowledge about when to apply this default.

Principle 13: 'Explicit representation of default use'

There must be procedural rules for assuming default values, the same as other inference rules. Their conditions must state when they may be applied.

5. STRATEGIC KNOWLEDGE

Strategic knowledge is used to plan the problem solving process: to choose among alternative problem solving routes (goal A can be satisfied by doing subgoal a or subgoal b), to expand goals (goal A can be satisfied by doing both subgoals a and b), and to order goals in a conjunction (to satisfy goals a and b, first do goal a then b). Furthermore, in executing some strategy, strategic knowledge is used to monitor this execution, doing some replanning if necessary.

Each strategic knowledge-item can use several components: **first,** knowledge of the goal it tries to satisfy; **second,** knowledge of the set of alternative (combinations of) subgoals which can satisfy the supergoal; **third,** some kind of cost-benefit criterion to order these (combinations of) subgoals by 'attractiveness'; **fourth,** a success criterion for each subgoal; **fifth,** a precondition for each subgoal by which to order combinations of subgoals into sequences and/or conjunctions.

Thus, we can distinguish 'procedural' and 'factual' strategic knowledge.

In expert systems there often is no strategic knowledge. And if there is, it usually has the form of a fixed strategy (Wielinga and Breuker, 1986). For instance, in PDP, there is a goal hierarchy representing a problem decomposition. One would say this constitutes a strategy to solve the type of problems PDP can handle. yet nowhere are explicit **choices** made. Choices are not relevant anymore since the planning has been done beforehand, as it were, by the programmer. Clancey (1983, p.239) makes use of a similar structure in which 'meta-rules are organized hierarchically (. . .) into tasks'.

When it comes to teaching a pupil how to go about solving certain problems, such a fixed strategy is not flexible enough. There are usually alternative strategies possible, some of which may be equally effective. A tutoring system must be able to model and evaluate deviating strategies which a pupil may be using. These deviations can range from irrelevant sequencing differences to serious strategic errors. In between are deviations which may lead to a correct solution but are not optimal (because they introduce useles inferences or pose unnecessary problems).

Principle 14: 'Multiple strategies'

The strategic knowledge must at least allow for legal deviations, and contain some measure of seriousness of these deviations.

A tutoring system such as the one we describe in section 1.3 only has results of pupil actions to work with. The pupil's problem-solving strategy has to be inferred bottom-up from those results. For this, a two-way linking between supergoals and subgoals is necessary.

Principle 15: 'Goal-hierarchic backpointers'

Besides knowledge to expand goals into subgoals, there must be backpointers linking subgoals to the supergoals to which they may belong.

If the focus of the tutoring system is on teaching problem-solving **strategies,** extra knowledge is needed to talk about and explain strategic matters to the pupil. The necessary amount and structure of this knowledge depends on the depth of intended tutoring. In many cases support knowledge in the form of precooked scripts may suffice.

6. CONCLUSION

The abovementioned constraints follow from three central demands, which in turn are derived from our view of diagnosis as a data-driven construction process, separating **what objects** (facts) a pupil is manipulating, **how** (procedure) and **when–why** (strategy), and working bottom-up from intermediate results through a (sequence of) procedure(s) to a solving plan. These three central demands are:

(a) Knowledge items must be indexed unambiguously as factual, procedural or strategical; within each category each knowledge-item must have the same syntax and semantics (this is also directly a constraint).
(b) More specific (or instantiated) knowledge must be back-traceable to more general (or generic) knowledge.
(c) The domain knowledge must be partially, repeatedly and flexibly executable, trying out different sequences of different combinations of correct and buggy knowledge.

Although the abovementioned demands and the constraints derived from them look fairly trivial from an ITS point of view, our experience is that even the expert system PDP, which has been designed to be as explicit as possible, fails in all these respects. This is no shortcoming of the expert system as such. The way knowledge is best represented is dependent on the use we want to make of it. In an ITS system, we essentially want to **reconstruct** a problem solving process in a data-driven way. An expert system is meant to **execute** problem solving, working in a more or less goal-driven way. This means that, to use an expert system as domain-knowledge component of an ITS system, not only would we have to add knowledge (e.g. incorrect knowledge, more levels of detail), but we would have to change its representation in order to make it more explicit. Because of this, and directly because of the reconstruction task instead of the execution task, the architecture would have to be changed. We would, as it were, have to cut the expert system to pieces and to hang it upside down. This of course amounts to writing a new 'expert system', specifically designed for use as a domain knowledge component of an ITS. This new 'expert system' however would hardly be able to function as a real stand-alone expert system.

ACKNOWLEDGEMENTS

This research was funded in part by the Foundation for Educational Research (SVO). We would like to thank our colleagues on the 'knowledge acquisition in formal domains' projects, especially Joost Breuker, Wouter Jansweijer, Maarten van Someren and Bob Wielinga, for their useful comments on earlier drafts.

REFERENCES

Bierman, D. J. and Anjewierden, A. A. (1986) The use of a graphic scratch pad for students in 'Intelligent Computer Assisted Instruction'. *Proc. 27th ADCIS Conference, New Orleans.*

Clancey, W. J. (1983) The epistemology of a rule-based expert system — a framework for explanation. *Artificial Intelligence* **20,** 215–255.

Clancey, W. J. (1985) Heuristic classification. *Working paper KSL-85-5,* Palo Alto, Stanford University. To appear in *Artificial Intelligence.*

Clancey, W. J. (1986) Qualitative student models. *Annual Review of*

Computer Science **1,** 381–450.

Sleeman, D. and Brown, J. S. (eds.) (1982) *Intelligent Tutoring Systems,* Academic Press, London.

Wielinga, B. and Breuker, J. (1986) Models of expertise. *Proc. European Conference on Artificial Intelligence, ECAI '86, Brighton.*

Index